NO FLEAS ON US
ANIMAL SHELTER TALES

BY

LINDA C. GREENBERG

PublishAmerica
Baltimore

First printing

ISBN: 1-4241-8135-6
PUBLISHED BY PUBLISHAMERICA, LLLP
www.publishamerica.com
Baltimore

Printed in the United States of America

Contents

DEDICATION

I would like to dedicate this book to Friends of Marblehead's Abandoned Animals. It is a no-kill animal shelter located in the animal control office in the town of Marblehead, Massachusetts. It is a tiny shelter and not very fancy. The shelter is very special because life-saving miracles happen there daily. Approximately two hundred orphaned, stray, abandoned, abused animals are saved yearly and placed into forever homes. There are not enough adjectives to express the enormous amount of decency, generosity, kindness, love, and so much good which takes place in that modest little structure. You have to be there to experience it, and I have been there for almost sixteen years. I consider the shelter hallowed ground.

I would also like to dedicate this book to the volunteers past and present, who have cared for the animals in the shelter twenty-four/seven. They are the most dedicated, devoted, and selfless human beings you will ever encounter. The volunteers make sure the animals are clean, fed, comfortable, and medicated, if necessary. They go beyond the call of duty to see to the animals' needs. I am proud to be their colleague and have the highest respect for them. They are very special people. I would hate to think what would happen to those poor animals, if the shelter and the loyal volunteers were not there for them.

Of course, I have to include my family in this dedication. They have put up with my animal escapades for many years! My family is so very understanding and patient with me because they know my passion for animals. My husband, children, and grandchildren are well aware of my enormous desire to help animals, and my loyalty to the shelter. I am truly blessed to have such a close and wonderful family.

WE
ARE A
LITTLE
SHELTER
BUT
WE
DO
BIG THINGS!

INTRODUCTION

When I was a little girl, the public was ignorant of the importance of spaying and neutering their pets. My father was a bread baker and worked nights. A lot of cats lived in the bakery because they kept the work place clean of pests. One of the cats in the bakery had a litter of kittens. When the kittens were weaned from their mother, my dad surprised me and brought home one of the kittens. The kitten he surprised me with was an adorable female brown tiger tabby. My dad knew I loved tiger cats. We named her Sandy.

Sandy grew up to be a beautiful wonderful family pet. I loved her very much. She was my best friend and playmate. She was never spayed and had litters of kittens. I adored playing with the kittens. Sandy was a nurturing mom and did a wonderful job caring for her babies. There was one particular litter of kittens I will never forget.

This may surprise some of you, but at one time there was no such thing as a television set. When television first came on the market, my parents purchased one. The television had a ten-inch screen and attached to the screen was a magnifying glass to make the picture larger. At the time it was really something to behold. We had the first television set in the neighborhood and all the neighbors and their kids came over to watch. The popular children shows at the time were *Kuckla, Fran, and Ollie*, *Big Brother Bob Emery*, and *Fudini*. Not long afterwards the most popular kids show aired on TV—*Howdy Doody*. I was mesmerized with television and ran home

11

every day from school to watch it. Our living room was used only when we had company until we got the TV set. Now our living room was the most popular room in the house.

Like so many days, I would rush home from school to watch TV, but on this particular day an extra special event was going to take place that I was totally unaware of. I went into the living room, put on the TV, sat on the floor with a foot stool between my legs, eating a snack, and was glued to whatever was on the screen at that time. Sandy, my cat, who was pregnant, came over to me and affectionately started rubbing against me. It was with her body language she was telling me she loved me. I responded by affectionately petting her back. I was so immersed in the program that was on at the time I never noticed Sandy had left my side.

When the program I was watching was over, I wanted to quickly get another snack before the next show came on. Just as I turned to get up; I saw Sandy in the corner of my mother's reddish raspberry silk Victorian sofa cleaning four newly born infant kittens. There I was only arm's length away from the sofa. Sandy didn't make a sound during delivery because I would have heard. I missed the whole thing. The show I was watching couldn't compare with one of nature's miracles, and I missed it! It was so beautiful to see Sandy with her little kittens.

Suddenly, the light bulb came on! My mother was going to be furious with me for allowing Sandy to give birth on her precious sofa. I quickly transferred Sandy and the babies to a big box we had ready for her. When I went back to survey any damage to the sofa, there were a couple of blood stains. I worked tirelessly to remove those blood stains before my mother came home, but with little success. The good thing was the stains blended in with the reddish raspberry color of the sofa.

My mother came home and just as I suspected she was very angry and scolded me. That living room was strictly used for company only. My mom still hadn't accepted the fact that with the invention of television the living room had become the focal point in the house. My mom liked animals, but didn't love them as much as my dad and me. She just went along with it. She quickly calmed down after she looked in the box where Sandy and her babies were nursing and snuggled together peacefully. It was an exhausting day for Sandy and she needed to rest.

When the kittens were weaned from their mom, we would find good homes for them. Almost everyone in those days had cats because they were on pest patrol at all times and kept homes clean of little rodents.

For the first time, we were having a hard time placing a litter of four of Sandy's adorable kittens. This was a first. It seemed liked everybody we knew already had cats. We tried and tried to find them a home with little success. The kittens were growing and running all over the house. We were living in a four-room apartment in a six-family house. My mother was losing patience with the whole situation. She knew how attached I was to the kittens and didn't want to upset me. She finally suggested I take the kittens to the Animal Rescue, which was only three blocks away from my house. Mom told me that people go there to adopt animals and not to worry. I didn't want to take those little darlings there, but was up against it.

The next day I put the kittens in a corrugated box and walked three blocks to the Animal Rescue with my girlfriend. I was so very sad. When we reached the rescue, it was nothing like the rescues we have now. This was an old, unkempt house with a garage at the end of a long driveway. I knocked on the front door, and a woman answered. For the life of me I can't remember what that woman looked like. I completely blocked her out of my mind. I asked her if she could take the kittens and find good homes for them. The woman did not respond to my question. She told us to follow her to the garage. We figured that was where all the animals were housed. I was a trusting eleven-year-old child at the time. She took the box with the kittens and told us to leave. It broke my heart leaving those kittens with her. My friend and I slowly walked away from the garage down the long driveway. I turned to have one more look and couldn't immediately grasp what I thought I saw. It was horrible! The woman was putting those four little kittens into a black box that was next to the garage. The horror was the box had no air holes. She was going to suffocate my babies. I ran back to the woman and begged her to give me back my kittens. She wouldn't give me back my kittens. I cried and fought with her, but she wouldn't give back the kittens. The only thing left for me to do was run home for help. I ran and ran and ran and couldn't get home fast enough. My friend couldn't keep up with me. My mother wasn't home when I got there, but my dad was. He was sleeping because he worked nights. I woke him crying and screaming and completely overwrought with emotion. I told him the story. He dressed quickly, grabbed my hand, and took me back for my kittens. It was too late; they were dead.

It was so hard for me to comprehend why this awful thing had happened. It was so hard to understand. I was young and felt so guilty. My mother never would have sent me there if she thought the kittens were in harm's way. For weeks and months I had terrible nightmares and woke up crying. I couldn't help thinking about it all the time. I blamed myself for killing those poor little babies. Time is a great healer, but the memory of that disturbing incident will never entirely go away. To this day something may come up that will jog my memory about that horrible experience. My body will tense up all over. On one occasion I told my husband the story, but was too ashamed to ever tell the story to anyone else. For well over fifteen years as adoption coordinator at the shelter, and finding wonderful forever homes for hundreds of animals, you would think I could vindicate myself. Nothing will ever make up for that black day in my young life.

Without question that incident had a great impact on me. I learned at an early age just how much animals rely on us humans. Their destiny is in our hands. Like children, animals have to be lucky to get into a good responsible home. Great numbers of animals are being put down every day because of human irresponsibility, ignorance, cruelty, and abuse. This is why our shelter is so special and necessary. We, the volunteers, witness ignorance, cruelty, and abuse all the time. These unfortunate creatures come to our little shelter and get quality care until they are placed in a loving forever home. There is no fear of them being needlessly put down. All the animals that are lucky enough to come into our shelter enter a no-kill, true-to-life sanctuary.

HOW I GOT INVOLVED

Chapter 1

The little seaside community of Swampscott, Massachusetts, where I live is north of Boston, set right on the Atlantic Ocean with a perfect view of the Boston skyline. I was born and brought up in the city of Lynn, which is just over the line. I have lived my whole life in this area of New England.

In the 1870s Swampscott was a community of summer estates for the very wealthy. Calvin Coolidge, our thirtieth president, and his spouse Grace summered in an estate called White Court. It was located on Littles Point. What a beautiful spot it is. The estate is still there; however, it is now a coed college called Marion Court.

There was also a magnificent hotel called The New Ocean House. During the summer the rich and famous from all over used to summer there. The hotel was something to behold. It was old world with a grand ballroom reminiscent of the Great Gatsby era. I once had the opportunity to go into this grand and elegant structure before it completely burned to the ground. Something that special can never be replaced.

Swampscott has changed considerably since the era of summer estates. It is now one of the densest communities in Massachusetts, however because the town is situated on the ocean, it gives the illusion of wide open spaces. It is a beautiful part of the country.

My husband, Harvey, loved this area as much as I did. We decided to settle here and purchased a modest cape style home a block away from the ocean. That was forty-six years ago. We have three wonderful daughters, approximately a year apart. I was a pretty busy person in those days. Frankly, when I think back, I do not know how I did it. I loved my job as a wife, mother, and homemaker.

All three girls Tami, Toby and Terri went through the Swampscott school system and graduated from the University of Massachusetts in Amherst. They married and I have wonderful sons-in-law. They all settled in and around Swampscott. Each of the girls has a boy and a girl. Who would have bet on that? It is an advantage to have your family close by and watch your grandchildren grow up.

The grandchildren call me Bubbe and my husband Zayde. They are Yiddish words. Zayde means grandfather and Bubbe means grandmother. To me they are words of endearment. We adore those beautiful children. I promised the kids I would mention them in my book. Harry, my oldest grandchild, then Haley, Jake, Rachel, Fredi, and Jared, the youngest. Bubbe keeps her promises. I love you all so much!

Now I would like to tell you about the rest of my family, whom I love dearly, too. There is Mighty Moses, my eight-year-old Bernese mountain dog. He is magnificent, handsome, and definitely the king of the house. I am mad about the breed. There is Annie Missouri, my five-year-old red bloodhound. She was a gift, and came all the way from Missouri. She has that comical, but at the same time regal appearance. I love her. They say bloodhound brains are in their noses; if they get any kind of an attractive scent—good-bye. Bloodhounds have the most sensitive noses of any canine. I inherited my youngest daughter's twelve-year-old golden retriever, Wellington. Her circumstances changed and she could not give him the proper care. I am not finished. There are my four cats; Stinky Poo Poo, sixteen; Spooky Dee, eleven; Prissy Velvet, ten; and Grayson, eight—he is a handsome dude.

Their companionship, loyalty, and love mean so much to me. My home is full of life and that's the way I like it.

Growing up my dad taught me many things and there are certain things I will forever be grateful for. He taught me to appreciate good music. There is not a day in my life when I do not go to my radio or CD player and listen to beautiful music. Depending on the mood I am in, the music transfers me to a ballet, a symphony, a Broadway show, the movies, and much more. He also taught me to love nature. My blood curdles when I read about the deforestation of the rainforests. We are losing plants that could possibly cure disease and animals are becoming extinct because of it. My father respected and was so gentle with animals. Thousands of homeless animals are being destroyed every day. I cannot bear to think of it. Through his understanding of nature and animals I developed a passion for them both since I was a little girl.

In my kitchen on a wall hangs a needlework sampler. On one-half of the sampler there is a chipmunk climbing a tree going after berries. On the other half of the sampler it says, "THE EARTH HAS MUSIC FOR THOSE WHO LISTEN." That little saying means a great deal to me. Because I am so in tune with my surroundings, those words express my inner feelings.

I consider myself a very fortunate person. Life has been good to me, and it certainly has not been dull. What I did not know was that a wonderful adventure was in store for me at the age of fifty-three. By an accident of fate, destiny brought me to the Marblehead Animal Shelter and enriched my life beyond my wildest dreams. I am compelled to tell the story.

Approximately sixteen years ago, summer was over and we were coming into the fall season. The trees had not started to turn, but the air was clean and crisp. It was a wonderful New England day, my favorite time of the year. I received a call from my middle daughter Toby's friend, Robin. She was in a bit of a panic. Before she even said anything, I knew her call was animal related just by her tone.

People call me all the time with questions about animals. Certainly, I am no expert on the subject; however, I have been vocal about animal issues at our town meetings and in our local newspaper. I was a volunteer docent at the Stone Zoo in Stoneham, Massachusetts. My husband, Harvey, and I have been walking our dogs in town for the past forty years. When you live in a small town, your neighbors know who's involved in what. Why wouldn't people call to pick my brain?

Robin and I said our hellos and now, the purpose of her call. Here it comes. I was right. She found a mother cat and four infant kittens in her cellar window well outdoors on the side of her house. "What should I do? What should I do? Can you help me?"

I really dread getting calls like this, because I get so emotional when it comes to animals. Now I am instantly involved. When it comes to an animal in distress, in this case it is an orphaned family in trouble, I could never say no. My mind immediately went into action and at the same time I was trying to put Robin at ease.

There is a lot to think about in order to make a rescue like this successful. You cannot just walk up to the mother and her kittens and expect to put them in a box and take them away. It's not that easy. First we must consider if the mother cat is feral.

Feral means: wild, reverting to the wild state, as from domestication. That is the dictionary definition. In short, feral cats are born in the wild and rear their offspring in the wild. There is no interaction with humans. Humans are the enemy. However, they socialize very well with other cats. Sadly, their lives are hard and short. Feral animals have to constantly search for food—of which there is very little. They live outdoors and must find shelter in all kinds of weather. They must protect themselves from predators such as dogs, raccoons, coyotes, humans, and the biggest predator of all small animals—the automobile. There are millions of feral animals out there, and it is very sad. Let's hope our little mother is not feral, so we will not have to use a have-a-heart trap. A have-a-heart trap is a trap that will not hurt the animal you are trapping. They come in all sizes depending on the animal you are trapping.

The second obstacle we must face is where do we bring the mother and her infant kittens after we capture them? Unfortunately, in most cases, it is possible there might not be an answer to that question.

This whole situation is very frustrating. I cannot take in this feline family. My house is full of animals; it just is not the right environment, besides my husband will divorce me if I bring any more pets into the house. Robin cannot take the family in because her children are allergic to cats. Off hand I do not know anybody else who would take them. I now feel responsible for this pathetic little family that I have not even seen yet.

The next step is to consider an animal shelter. We do not have one in Swampscott, but there are two in the city of Salem and one in the town of Marblehead. They both border my community. Every shelter has a different philosophy, so we want them to get proper care, and we absolutely do not want them to be put down. When I use the expression to put down, it means to put to sleep—to put to death. People who work with animals professionally use the term *put down*.

Some animal shelters advocate they are a no-kill shelter; that means they do not put down any animals. Then there are animal shelters who claim they are no-kill; however, they take the poor unfortunate animal elsewhere to be put down. This way their conscience is clear to say, "We are a no-kill shelter." I hate that kind of dishonesty. Lastly, there is the shelter that has to pick and choose which animals are adoptable and which animals have to be put down.

I do not like it, but at least they are honest and you know what you are dealing with. One thing I do know is 99% of animal shelters will not deal with feral cats. They will turn them away and not accept them, or they will accept them and then put them down.

When a feral cat is captured and put into a cage, it is difficult to care for it. They do not want to be touched because of their fear of humans. They will huddle as far back in their cages as they can. They are unpredictable and may attack. If you're smart, you use specially made extra heavy gloves to manage the cage. I suggest an experienced person handle these types of cats.

There are few shelters who will deal with feral cats. They are rare and hard to come by. The work is time consuming, tedious and frustrating. These dedicated people try to rehabilitate and domesticate the feral cats. In rare cases it works. The younger they are, the better the chances they will come around. Most feral cats are miserable and would rather die than be in a cage. They want to be free! It is so heartbreaking. If the animals only understood we are trying to help them.

My personal philosophy about feral cats when they are captured is to spay or neuter them depending on their sex, so they cannot reproduce. When they recover release them where they were found. Their life is a struggle, but it is the only life they know. They want to live just as much as we do. Every community, with the help of their animal control officer, should consider having a spay/neuter and release program. Little, by little, the feral cat population will decrease.

I know a lot about feral cats. You see I captured one seventeen years ago at the back of one of our local restaurants in town. I thought it was an abandoned kitten about three months old. When I took it to the veterinarian's office for shots, he told me she was about seven months old. He could tell by her teeth. She was so small because of malnutrition. I named her Spooky because she was so spooked and skittish. I hoped in time she would come around. Seventeen years have passed and she still will not let me touch her and runs away if I get anywhere near her. Spooky is not vicious; she is timid and frightened. Strange as it may seem, I feel she has had a good life, even though she never goes outside. There are two very large bedrooms and a bathroom upstairs in my home that has been vacant for many years. My three daughters used to occupy those rooms. Now Spooky and my other three cats hang out there. They call this space their own.

Very often, when my grandchildren sleep over, Spooky hides. At night she comes downstairs when everyone is asleep. I love my little Spooky and understand her. With her own little body language, I know she loves me too.

I'm still on the phone with Robin; while she was talking, my mind was still racing. It is time for the process of elimination. I have decided not to bring our little feline family to either shelter in Salem. I have lived in this area my whole life. Whenever we wanted to adopt a pet, we went to one of the shelters in Salem. We knew we were going to save a life. Unfortunately, at one of those shelters, if some animals were not placed after a certain period of time, they would be put down. That particular shelter gets hundreds and hundreds of animals because of animal overpopulation. They eventually have no choice but to put them down. I will not chance that happening to our little family.

The other shelter in Salem has a reputation of being particular. I already know they will not take the mom and her babies at this time. They would want the kittens after they are weaned from their mom. Kittens are easy to place and the mother might not pass their standards. If she is feral, forget it. I need help now!

My mind is made up; we must take a chance on the shelter in Marblehead. I have heard they are a true no-kill shelter and are doing wonderful work. The shelter is right on the main road going into Marblehead. I have been by it a million times, but could not bring myself to go in. My heart breaks for those homeless animals.

I interrupted Robin and told her, "I am going to call the animal control officer, explain the situation, and ask her to meet us at your house with a have-a-heart trap. Let us keep our fingers crossed and hope this will all work out."

Robin's house was only two blocks away from my house. I called the animal control officer. She agreed to meet us. I grabbed a can of cat food and ran out of the house.

Just like clockwork we all converged at Robin's house. My heart was beating so fast with anxiety. I wanted this rescue to be successful. The animal control officer arrived in the town's animal control truck with the have-a-heart trap. Robin came out of the house to show us where our subjects were hiding. I introduced Robin to the ACO (animal control officer). Ever so quietly the three of us walked over to the cellar window well where the mother cat was hiding with her kittens. We got there, looked down, and to our amazement they were gone.

It was obvious the mother cat knew Robin spotted her and her kittens. Intuitively she had to find new shelter and get her babies out of possible danger as soon as she could. Mother cats will go to great lengths to save their young, even at the risk of their own lives. When people say animals are dumb, I cannot help but thinking those same people are the real dummies.

We were all standing there flabbergasted and disappointed our little feline family was gone. All I could think about was winter is coming, and if they do survive, they too would reproduce more kittens, and the beat goes on. We missed our opportunity.

Suddenly, while we were busy talking about our missed opportunity, Robin spotted the mother cat. She was all black with a white spot on her chin. The ACO and I immediately started to follow her in hope she would lead us to the kittens. We followed her through Robin's neighbors' back yards. If anybody was watching us, they would have thought we were nuts, and called the authorities to pick us up. Finally, we came to an opened garage, and at the same time the mother cat stopped and hid behind a bush. We sensed the kittens were close by. While I continued to watch the mother cat, The ACO went into the garage to search for the kittens. After about ten minutes, I heard the ACO call out, "I found them!" Luck was with us! We are back in business! I ran to the truck for a pet carrier for the kittens; meanwhile, the mother was still behind the bush watching intensely. I brought the pet carrier into the garage and saw four adorable infant kittens. Their eyes were still closed. They were tucked away in a pile of rags on all sorts of junk. Two of the kittens were all black and two were black and white.

The mother cat was all out of joint; you could see it in her face. She was so concerned for her babies. My heart was breaking for her. How would you like it if somebody took your babies? It was so pitiful how she kept watching and following us as we took the kittens to the truck.

Only half of the rescue has been accomplished. We must capture the mother cat, so she can provide nourishment, comfort, cleanliness, and love for the kittens to survive. When you deal with animals, you must have lots of patience because they are unpredictable. Observing the behavior of the mother cat, I was positive she was feral. She runs away when we approach her, and she does not come anywhere near us even though we have her babies. This makes our rescue a little more difficult, but we are determined.

Back in Robin's driveway from a distance the mom cat is still watching for the kittens. We got a have-a-heart trap from the truck and set it right next to the cellar window well, where she previously hid her kittens. I opened the can of cat food I brought with me and put it in the trap. Everything was all set. We ran and hid behind the truck and made sure we had a clear view of the trap.

As soon as we left the mother cat went over to the trap and sniffed all around it. I am sure she was really hungry and could use a good meal. The food was enticing, but not enticing enough for her to go into the trap. We waited about thirty minutes and nothing was happening. This cat was a smart cookie. We had to come up with another plan, but what? The ACO could not stay here all day; she had other calls to make. Things were getting desperate.

I stood there like a dope, so frustrated, when all of a sudden the light bulb came on! I yelled out, "Let's put one of the infant kittens in the trap."

We took one of the kittens from the carrier. The little thing was whimpering for its mother. As we approached the trap the mother ran off and kept her distance. I took the food out of the trap and put the kitten in as far back in the trap as I could. I did not want the kitten to be in any danger when the trap sprung. I also knew this was going to be a test for the mother cat. If she goes into the trap, she will be putting her life in great danger for the love of her baby. There is a great possibility she will not enter the trap.

This is our last chance. The defining moment has come. The kitten is crying, the trap is set, I am biting my nails, and we took off and hid behind the truck again. The mother cat slowly approached the trap. She walked all around it sniffing and sniffing. She did not know what to do. She was bewildered, and she kept walking around it. We were all getting antsy. Finally, her maternal instincts were stronger than her fear for her own life. Into the trap she went for her baby. Thank God! What a wonderful mom! She deserves every chance to have a life as well as her babies. We were all so happy, including the mother cat. At least she had one of her babies back. What a relief, even though it is temporary. We have one more obstacle to overcome. Will the Marblehead Animal Shelter accept our little feline family?

The mother cat is feral; we must respect that, and handle her very carefully. We kept her and the kitten in the trap and put them right beside the kittens in the carrier. They were all safe now in the animal control truck. The animal control officer took off and I followed her in my car. Our destination is the animal shelter in Marblehead. It will take us less than ten minutes to get there. While driving, I was praying for my homeless family.

I thought it would be a good idea to have the ACO accompany me to the shelter. The Marblehead animal control officer and our officer know each other very well. They are in the same field of work and fill in for each other on occasion. I needed all the influence I could get, or should I say our feline family needed all the help they could get.

We arrived at the shelter, parked our vehicles, got out, but left the mother and her kittens in the truck. Remember, I have never been in the shelter, so I followed my ACO to this large garage door with a small door built into it. Attached to the left of the garage was a small building. To the right of the garage was a driveway and to the right of the driveway was the Marblehead Police Station. We knocked on the small door, opened it, and walked in. I saw a very large garage converted into an animal shelter. There were several cages for dogs and some were occupied. There were cat cages on top of the dog cages and elsewhere. Most of those were occupied. There was a washer and dryer in an area full of folded towels, sheets, and blankets. There was another area with a little sink and all kinds of pet supplies. The rest of the place was filled with junk. It was obvious this was an under-funded shelter. Dogs were barking and cats were meowing. I will never forget that sight as long as I live.

In the middle of it all stood the Marblehead animal control officer, wearing her official uniform. She was a strong-looking woman in her forties, approximately five feet, seven inches tall, with bleached red hair. She was not heavy and not thin. Instantly, you knew she was the one in charge just by her demeanor. There were volunteers working in there too. Some were cleaning cat cages and some were going to walk dogs. There was a lot going on. It was so nice to see those people giving their time to care for the animals.

I was introduced to the Marblehead ACO; her name was Linda. Coincidentally, we had the same first name. I do not know why, I told her I was a volunteer at the Stone Zoo. I guess I thought that might influence her decision. After the introductions, I proceeded to tell her about the orphaned family in the truck, and how desperate I was to find them shelter. I did not want the mother and her kittens to keep reproducing more and more feral cats. This way we could place the kittens, spay the mother, and just possibly the mom will come around, and get placed too.

Linda looked very stern and the two ACO's went to the corner of the garage for a private discussion. Suddenly, I got a very sick feeling. It was apparent there were some issues those two had to straighten out. Instead of standing there looking sick, I walked around looking into the cages. I was getting nervous. Maybe I should have come alone? Do I need this aggravation? On the other hand, I felt confident about Linda accepting the cat family. Little, by little, she built this shelter up on her own. I felt that she was a person with tremendous compassion for animals, which is why she will not let our abandoned family down. Let's see if I am right about her.

Finally, the two ended their discussion and came walking toward me. It was apparent Linda had cleared the air and appeared satisfied. As they approached me, I hoped my feelings about Linda were right. We were face to face and Linda said, "I will take the family in." Those words were music to my ears. My whole body started to unwind. Linda instructed one of the volunteers to prepare a cage for the feline family. We went out to the truck and brought the mother and the kittens into the shelter. I thanked our animal officer for all her help and she left.

I watched a volunteer prepare the cage. She put in a litter box, clean towels, fresh water, dry cat food, and a whole can of wet cat food. Wet cat food is canned cat food. A hungry nursing mother needs lots of protein to keep her strength up to care for her babies.

When the cage was ready Linda very gently put in the three infant kittens in the cage, which were in the carrier. The volunteer and Linda lifted the have-a-heart trap with the mother cat and the fourth kitten to the opening of the cage and opened the trap. It did not take much prodding to get the mother out of the trap. She was impatient to get to her other babies; their safety was her only concern. Lastly, but carefully, Linda took the fourth infant out of the trap and put it into the cage with its siblings. The family has been reunited and is safe.

I watched with relief as the mother cat checked each kitten individually to see if they were okay. She smelled all around the cage, and proceeded to have a good meal. I am sure all that food must have been quite a feast. Who knows if she ever had a decent meal? I was very satisfied with the outcome of this rescue.

Now that our little family is all settled in, Linda was interested in the work I do at the zoo. She told me her dream was to be a zookeeper at a zoo in California. She liked the warm climate, had no family, there was nothing to keep her here, and one day she was going to take off for California.

I told her, since I was a little girl, my dream was to go on a safari in Africa. My dream came true. For my thirtieth anniversary my husband, Harvey, arranged a three-week safari in Kenya. Without a doubt it ranks very high as one of the most wonderful experiences of my life. The country was so vast and majestic. Our encounters with those magnificent animals will stay in our memories forever. We also went on a hot air balloon safari, and after we landed on the savanna there was a champagne breakfast waiting for us. I felt I belonged there. I was so close to nature. The trip was even better than I had dreamed.

When I came back from the trip, I wanted to do something to educate people about the importance of respecting nature and the animals. The land and the animals must be preserved, so our grandchildren and their children can witness the majestic beauty that I witnessed.

One day my husband and I were in the car, when a commercial came on the radio. The commercial said they needed volunteers at the Stone Zoo. It sounded like that was right up my alley. I called the zoo and made an appointment for an interview. Next thing you know, I was taking a ten-week crash course in zoology. It was fascinating, and I learned so much. I became a docent at Stone Zoo. A docent is a teacher. My job was to take different groups of people through the zoo and provide them with all kinds of information about the animals that were on exhibit.

For example: The biggest attraction at the zoo was Major the polar bear. His habitat is the cold arctic tundra like the North Pole, Alaska, Russia, Greenland, and Canada. Major was captured in Siberia. He is a carnivore, which means he is a meat-eater. Polar bears look white, their skin is black, and their hair has no color at all. Each hair is really a hollow tube that you can see right through. The sunlight makes the polar bear look white. His fur is waterproof, so when he comes out of the cold arctic water, he dries quickly. His huge feet act as snowshoes to prevent sinking in deep snow. He can stay submerged two minutes under water and is an excellent swimmer. His sight and hearing are poor, but his smell is so acute it is claimed a polar bear can smell the scent of a whale's carcass twenty miles away. He is a predator, powerful, and a very dangerous animal.

Not only did I tell my groups about the animals, I had specimens of animal fur, feathers from different birds, antlers that shed and grow back, and reptile skins that were shed too. It was a rare opportunity for the visitors to be able to touch and feel these specimens of exotic animals. Everybody's favorite was a lion's canine tooth that had to be extracted. It was very large and everybody compared it to their own teeth.

In addition to all that, I would give my group interesting facts about the wonders of nature. (1.) A giraffe has the same number of vertebra in his neck as a human—seven. (2.) Are zebras white with black stripes, or black with white stripes? When baby zebras are born they are brown and white and their white stripes are not all connected yet. It appears that zebras are black with white stripes. (3.) Birds have hollow bones that make their bodies lighter, so they can fly. There are hundreds and hundreds of facts like this about animals. I enjoyed sharing them with my groups and in turn they would have fun learning. This was a sample of my job as a docent.

I helped educate school children, brownie troops, summer camp groups, birthday parties, garden clubs, elderly groups, retarded children, hearing-impaired with interpreters, and many more. It was extremely rewarding.

On Wednesdays I was volunteer captain. That means I would instruct the other volunteers where they would be stationed on that day. There was the ticket booth, refreshment stand, gift shop, clean-up duty, and demonstrating animals for the visitors at the zoo. My favorite demonstration animal was a boa constrictor, which used to curl around my body, named Leroy. I loved being at the zoo. I was like a kid in Disney World, and it was an honor to be in the company of all those exotic animals.

I commended Linda on the work she was doing at the shelter. She and her volunteers were saving lives that otherwise would be put down. She interrupted me and asked if I would like to see the rest of the shelter. I said, "The rest of the shelter? I thought the garage was it!" I followed her out of the garage to the little building on the left. She opened the door, we were greeted by a strong odor, and I followed her inside. I was astonished, overwhelmed, and speechless. I could not believe my eyes.

There was a room about fifteen feet by fifteen feet. In the rear of the room was a large desk for the animal control officer. The rest of the room was filled with cats in cages and other cats were running loose. One cage was on top of the other, at least three high. There had to be, without exaggeration, fifty or more cats. There were cats of all ages, sizes, colors, and all were abandoned for one reason or another. The reputation this shelter has was true. This was definitely a no-kill shelter! They were not kidding! Why, there were more animals here than we had at the zoo.

I had a million questions, but my biggest concern was who takes care of all these animals? Linda explained that there were teams of volunteers who come in every day to feed the cats and clean the cages. Today's team has not come in yet; that is why the strong litter box odor.

My mind was racing again. First I felt a little guilty giving her five more mouths to feed. Knowing how much I love animals, this is another opportunity to help animals. How can I leave this place and not offer my services? I do have the time. I do not work. My children are out of the house. It will not conflict with my work at the zoo. Before I knew it the words came out, "I would like to volunteer."

Linda said, "Great, there is an opening on Tuesday night, so come next Tuesday at six." It just so happened, Tuesday nights work out good for me. At the time my husband was a salesman, and he was on the road Tuesday through Thursday. I told Linda I would be there.

It was time for me to leave. I could not thank her enough for all her help. I did want to check the mother cat and her kittens before I left. I went back into the garage and over to the cage where our little family resided. The mother was lying there cleaning her babies. The kittens were nestled into her tummy suckling mother's milk. They were well fed, content, and alive. We all had quite a day. Everything was so quiet and serene, and felt I was in a holy place.

On my way home I could not help thinking about the events of the day. I felt good about myself and looked forward to beginning a new adventure at the shelter. As I was driving along, the words on my needlepoint sampler came to mind, "The Earth Has Music for Those Who Listen." Today my life was filled with music.

There is a post script to this story. The mother cat was named Garbo and was adopted by Laura, who was a volunteer at the shelter. Laura eventually became the assistant animal control officer. Garbo could not have received a better home. All four kittens were placed in good homes too.

MY BEST SHOT

Chapter 2

It is an absolutely beautiful Tuesday evening just before six o'clock, and I am on my way to the animal shelter in Marblehead.

The town of Marblehead is a community steeped in history. General John Glover of Marblehead commanded a regiment called Glover's Marbleheaders in the Revolutionary War. Glover's Marbleheaders crossed the Delaware River during a Christmas Eve blizzard with General George Washington. In 1789 George Washington stopped by to visit the town to thank Marbleheaders for their war efforts. The original painting, "The Spirit of '76," is a well-known tribute to the town's role in the American Revolution and is housed in Abbot Hall, which is a historic building and presently, Marblehead's town hall.

Within Marblehead there is an area called Old Town. Old Town is very quaint and charming. Like out of the past it has narrow, winding streets with old homes and buildings. As you drive through this area, you will notice plaques on these old structures with dates indicating when they were built. Some go back to the 1600s. There are many little shops of all kinds. There is Marblehead Harbor, one of the most beautiful harbors in the world. In season the harbor is filled with so many kinds of boats, it appears you could jump from one boat to the other and get to the other side of the harbor. Tourists from all over the world come to visit these sites.

As I get closer to the shelter, it occurred to me, I signed up to be a volunteer on Tuesday evenings, but I never asked what it involved. It was an emotional day when I signed up. I rescued the little cat family and I saw all those needy homeless animals at the shelter. It broke my heart. Sometimes I am impulsive and do not think about what I am getting myself into.

I should have asked about their no-kill policy. I do not want to start taking care of cats, get to know them, and find one day they are not there anymore because they were put down. Emotionally, I cannot handle that kind of atmosphere. If an animal is sick, or suffering, and cannot be helped, putting them down is the humane thing to do. When an animal is no longer at the shelter because it was placed in a good home that is what it is all about. I am also anxious to know if my new partner and I will be compatible. I was in my fifties, and hoped physically I would be able to do the work. There were more than fifty cats and that is a lot of feeding and cleaning.

Anytime you start something new, it is natural to be a little skeptical. Well, it is too late for me to have any doubts. I have arrived at the shelter, and I am going to give it my best shot.

I parked my car, got out, walked over to the garage, knocked, and went inside. Linda, the animal control officer, was standing there. I acknowledged her and immediately walked over to the cage where my rescued cat family was residing. I looked in the cage and saw a contented family. The kittens were well fed and growing. Garbo, the mom cat, was still skittish, but that was to be expected. They were in good hands now.

Linda presented me with a key to the shelter. Every volunteer gets one because she is not always there to let us in. She also presented me with a pile of clean towels to bring over to the little building where most of the cats were. I followed her outside like a little puppy dog with the big pile of towels into the little building. The cats knew why we were there. They were going to get fed, petted, clean linens, and clean litter. They were meowing, rubbing against their cages, showing all kinds of body language because they were excited to see us.

If you recall in the previous chapter the room in the shelter was about fifteen feet long and fifteen feet wide with cages three high. There was a large desk in the rear corner and the area where you get from one end of the room to the other was very narrow. It was like a maze. There could only be two or three people cleaning at a time. I did not notice on my first visit, in the back of the main room was a very narrow area that held supplies for the cats as well as cleaning supplies. Off that area was a door and behind that door was a teeny tiny bathroom with a small sink and toilet. You could hardly fit in there. I think you have the picture.

Standing there holding the towels not knowing what to do, I watched Linda open one cage after another so the cats could come out for exercise. I stood there frozen with my eyes popping out of my head. There was not enough room in the place when the cats were in their cages. Where do they go when they're out of their cages? Cats were everywhere and I mean everywhere. They were jumping on cages, running after each other, climbing on shelves, and relaxing on the desk. It was like a three-ring circus. I did not know where to look first. My grandchildren would say, "This is awesome!" It is absolutely amazing how animals adapt to their environment. For a person such as me, who loves animals, it was like being in animal wonderland. I loved it. I knew immediately I was going to enjoy volunteering here. Of course, not every cat could come out of its cage. There are cats that do not get along with other cats. There are cats that are stressed out just by being there— the poor things. Some cats are shy, timid, and some are a little fresh and frisky. Their cages are their sanctuaries. Cats have different personalities just like humans. I am sure I will get to know the animals, after working there for a while.

I was going to ask about my partner, when I heard a key in the door latch. It was my partner. Linda introduced us, told her I was her new partner and left. Her name was Joanne and she was a lot younger than I. My guess is she was in her middle thirties and had beautiful eyes. Just by looking at her, somehow, I knew we would work well together.

Joanne welcomed me and welcomed the help. It was too much work for one person. There was a lot to do so we got started immediately. She told me there was a protocol we had to follow. I would take one side of the room and she would take the other side of the room. On the outside of every cage was a card with the cat's name, age, any special needs, and a description of its diet. Not all the cats have the same diet. Some cats need special food. Hooked on the inside of every cage were a dish with dry cat food in it and a dish of water. We gave all the cats clean water and freshened up their dry food. Joanne taught me what to do with the dirty linens. She showed me how to take care of the dirty litter boxes. She pointed out the cats you should handle with caution. There were some cats only Linda could handle because they were feisty. While all this was happening, the cats were running around having a ball. Every once in a while there would be a skirmish, but it did not amount to much. When all the cages were prepared, it was time for the wet food. Wet food is canned cat food. Most cats love wet food. Dry cat food is the meat and potatoes and good for healthy teeth. Wet cat food is the dessert and important for their diet. As we opened the cans, the cats knew they were going to get their dessert and jumped into their cages. Of course, there were some cats we physically had to pick up and put into their cage. There were about six feral cats, which were always loose in the shelter. We left food for them and cleaned their litter boxes. The dirty linens and the bag of dirty litter were placed outside. We needed room to sweep the floor, wash the dirty dishes, tidy up the place, and lastly, wash the floor.

Before we left Joanne pointed out the shelter log book. That is how the volunteers communicate with each other. For example: If we are low on food, write it in the log. Whoever is responsible for picking up the cat food reads the log and replenishes the supply. If a cat is showing signs of unusual behavior such as sneezing or vomiting, write it in the log, and the medical team goes into action. If there is an emergency you call Linda immediately. Whatever has to be said about shelter business is put in the log, good or bad. Believe me occasionally, there were some pretty nasty things written in there, but for the most part it was very useful.

It took us over three hours to finish the work. The work is not glamorous, but a labor of love. Joanne was a terrific instructor, and I looked forward to working with her next Tuesday. While we worked we talked. I learned Joanne is single and owns her own home in Marblehead. She works full time in Boston. She put in a full day at work, went home to change her clothes, and put in another three hours of work at the shelter. She has been doing this every Tuesday for the past couple of years. I understand there are several volunteers at the shelter just like her. The one thing all the volunteers have in common is that we are committed to help the animals.

As we were leaving, we could not help noticing that the animals were peaceful and content. A moment ago, it was a madhouse in there and now everything was still. They were back in clean cages, they were exercised, and they were well fed. It was good. We shut the lights and locked the door. Outside Joanne picked up the bag of dirty litter and threw it in the trash barrel. I picked up the pile of dirty linens and brought them into the garage, where the washing machine was located. I wondered who cleaned the cages in the garage. Joanne told me Linda and some other girls.

Joanne had to go home and eat her dinner, and I had to go home and walk my dogs. We said good-bye and drove off. What a wonderful experience. I cannot wait to tell my family all about it. It was hard work, but I loved every minute of it and looked forward to the next time.

Every Tuesday evening Joanne and I worked together as a team at the shelter. I was very lucky to have her as my partner. She was dependable, and we were definitely compatible. The area we work in is so small that it is vital we get along.

During the next few months, little by little, I learned more about the shelter. I always called it the Marblehead Animal Shelter. The official name is Friends of Marblehead's Abandoned Animals (F.O.M.A.A.). The buildings have two purposes. The first is for the animal control officer and the second is for the shelter. We are not entirely free to do what we want. We must answer to the town of Marblehead and operate under its guidelines. The town has been very considerate to us and we are grateful that they allow us to care for the animals. There are people in town who do not like the idea of having a shelter there because they think the town is paying for the animals' food, supplies, and medical care. This is not true. We are using the building rent free, and providing a great service to the town, but we are not funded by the town.

Friends of Marblehead's Abandoned Animals is a non-profit organization established by volunteers. It was formed in 1993 for the sole purpose of raising funds to provide food, shelter, medical care, and good homes to dozens of animals abandoned each year. All money raised and goods donated are used for this purpose. This is an all volunteer organization with no paid staff positions. Donations of equipment and miscellaneous useful items are also welcomed. We always have a wish list of items needed from pads of paper, pens, towels, cleaning supplies, and food.

We are always in need of additional volunteers to help us. Tasks to be done include: walking the dogs, cleaning cat cages, feeding the cats, cleaning dog cages, medicating sick animals, laundry, general cleaning of the shelter, assisting with administrative tasks, working with the media, helping out with fund-raisers, petting and loving the animals. Volunteers can sign up for an hour, a week, a day a week, sporadic visits, or whatever fits into the volunteer's schedule.

Most important of all, we are truly a NO-KILL SHELTER! We are saving lots of animals that would otherwise have to be put down. I am sorry I didn't get involved sooner. I am loving it.

The shelter was getting low on funds, which was not unusual. We needed to do a fund-raiser. There was a meeting and I was able to meet a lot of the other volunteers. It was decided we would do an auction. An auction is a big undertaking. To do it properly you need a lot of help; however, the volunteers were willing. Along with the other volunteers, I worked very hard to make the auction a successful fund-raiser. I took on some extra responsibilities because most of the volunteers worked for a living, and I did not. I am a good organizer. With three daughters I've had a lot of experience organizing. I have done family holiday dinners, parties, three bat mitzvahs, three weddings, dog shows, and many other events. The most important thing for me is establishing myself as a dedicated and effective volunteer to the cause.

The auction went off like a charm, and it was a huge success. We made about five thousand dollars. Never before did the shelter make that much money. The money will pay our outstanding bills. Our money problems are temporarily over, so we can relax for a short while.

For well over eight months now I have volunteered at the shelter on Tuesday evenings and at the zoo on Wednesdays. Homeless animals continue to come into the shelter. We do everything we can to make their stay as pleasant as possible. On this particular Wednesday a stray dog wandered into the zoo. As long as I have been at the zoo, I have never seen a dog wander in. Cats come in from time to time. People sneak in small animals they no longer want and leave them where the zoo keepers can find them. There have been pet birds set free in the aviary. The dog was approximately two years old, a male, and a brown and white border collie mix. The poor thing was very tired and hungry. He appeared to have been wandering for a long time. Naturally, the dog could not wander through the zoo, so the zookeepers went into action to capture the dog. The capture was less than exciting. The dog was well behaved, not dangerous, and at the first sight of food he walked right over to the keepers. The zookeepers put the dog into a pen right next to my office. They fed him, gave him water, and he rested. Someone called animal control in Stoneham. Nobody had called for a dog with that description. One of the zookeepers was going to take the dog to the pound at the end of the day. The pound was a veterinary hospital in the city of Stoneham.

I was in and out of that office fifty times a day. Every time I went in and came out, I passed the dog. I looked into his eyes, and worried about his future. I felt so bad for the dog. It was not a good day for me at the zoo because I was very concerned about that dog. I knew his future looked very bleak.

That night I did not sleep well. The dog was on my mind. I felt so helpless. The next morning I decided to call my friend who volunteered with me at the zoo. She was familiar with the law when a stray animal is picked up. I called her and did not like what she told me. Legally, a dog has to be kept for ten days at the pound. An ad is put in the newspapers describing the lost animal. If the dog is not claimed in ten days, he will be put down. I was sick! The dog's eyes were fixed in my brain. I felt compelled to do something to help him, but what? My friend suggested, if nobody claims him, to bring him to the shelter in Marblehead. What a great idea! The thought never even occurred to me. I would have to get up enough courage to ask Linda for another favor. I had to take that chance; after all, the dog's life was in jeopardy.

Before I spoke to Linda, I decided to call the pound to get all the facts. I explained I volunteered at the zoo and was present when the dog was captured. I wanted to know what was going to happen to him. Essentially, they told me everything my friend at the zoo told me, except for one thing. The dog was so nice they were going to keep him two extra weeks and try to place him. Wow, that takes some pressure off. That extra two weeks will give the dog a chance to get placed, and give me a little more time before I have to speak to Linda. A lot can happen in two weeks. With luck the dog will be claimed or adopted.

I explained to the people at the pound that I volunteered at a no-kill shelter in Marblehead, and I might be able to transfer the dog there before his time is up. They were willing to work with me. We would be in close touch, so I provided them with my telephone number in case the dog was claimed. I implored them not to put the dog down, without speaking to me first. How do I get myself in these in these predicaments?

The clock was ticking. Six days had passed since the dog was taken to the pound. I could not wait to call the pound to see what was happening. I called and nobody had claimed the dog. I reminded them again, and again, not to put the dog down. I did not want them to inadvertently make a mistake. Horrible things like that have happened. They reassured me that nothing was going to happen to the dog.

The tenth day had come, and I called the pound. There was nothing to report. What a sick feeling I had; nevertheless, there was still hope. He would go up for adoption for two more weeks. The clock had started to tick again. Another week had gone by. The dog had not been placed. The people at the pound told me there were some families interested in the dog, but they ended up taking another dog.

I had not slept well since this whole incident started. Somehow the responsibility of this dog's life was put in my hands. My husband, Harvey, knew how these things bother me and he did not like me to worry. I kept my ordeal with the zoo dog from him.

Two days into the dog's last week, I received a call from the pound. They told me there was a family interested in the dog; however, they want to take a couple of days to think about it. Of course I was delighted to hear that, but I was not going to get too excited. I kept my fingers crossed. After two days, I received another call from the pound. They said the family decided not to take the dog. I was disappointed and sad for the dog, but realized everything happens for a reason.

Time was running out, and I had to act. If I did not act now, unless a miracle happened, the dog would die. I was going to have to speak to Linda. Here I was, a grown woman, a grandmother, yet I was so nervous about asking her for another favor. I was not in the habit of taking advantage of people, but this was a matter of life and death. I got up my nerve and drove to the shelter. As usual, Linda was there. I went in, held my breath, and told her the story. She was not exactly jumping for joy. She asked me one question, "Is the dog adoptable?" I described the dog and replied quickly, "Yes." She gave me the okay to bring him in, if he was not placed. Instantly, the clock in my head stopped ticking, and the heavy burden I was carrying disappeared. The dog was going to live and there was still a chance the dog could be placed. He had less than a week at the pound.

The dog was not placed, so my next step was to arrange to pick the dog up on Wednesday after work at the zoo. While volunteering at the shelter on Tuesday night, I borrowed a large dog crate and put it in my Jeep. The next day I went to the zoo and left early to go to the pound for the dog. The people at the pound were so nice. They gave the dog all his shots and had him neutered. All that work saved the shelter a lot of money. I thanked them and took off with the dog to Marblehead. The dog did not know it, but somebody up there was looking out for him. It was exactly four weeks to the day the dog wandered into the zoo. If I did not intercede for the dog, today would have been his last day on earth. What a horrible thought.

It took about one hour to drive back to Marblehead. Linda helped me take the dog out of the Jeep. She looked the dog over and liked what she saw. She named him Alex. This was his temporary new home and he was put into one of the dog pens. Well, am I glad this ordeal is over, what a relief! Tonight I will sleep like a baby.

The best part of the story is Alex was not at the shelter three weeks when he was placed. A very good-looking dentist, who volunteered at the shelter as a dog walker, fell in love with Alex and adopted him. I never knew the dentist's name, but he lives right in Marblehead. Alex and the dentist bonded and became inseparable. On occasion driving through town, I would see Alex and his master walking together. My eyes would well up with tears of happiness. Alex was alive and so happy.

Just recently, while food shopping, I ran into a shelter volunteer, Karen. She knew Alex's owner very well. We started reminiscing about the shelter. She told me Alex was doing great and has the cleanest teeth of any dog on earth. His master is a dentist and not only does he clean his teeth, he scales his teeth too. The funny part about it was Alex enjoys it. We had a good chuckle about that. Karen also told me Alex and his master moved to California. I would have liked to have seen him one more time.

This whole incident with the dog had a tremendous impact on me. The fact that I was instrumental in saving the dog's life was awesome. I cannot explain how wonderful I felt. The personal fulfillment I received was incredible. You know when you are feeling really happy you have a spring in your step. Well, I was walking three feet off the ground. Call it destiny, fate, or whatever, but something is stirring me in the direction to save animals. It is almost like a calling. Even though volunteering at the shelter every Tuesday night is an extremely important part of the puzzle, I yearn to do more. For me saving animals has become addictive, I experienced a wonderful high, and I have a need to do more.

I started thinking how I can do more hands-on work saving animals, and then I got the notion to look into adoptions at the shelter. Dealing with the public was a huge part of my job at the zoo, and I was good at it. Working at the shelter every Tuesday night, I know all the cats as if they were my own. I have not a clue what adoptions involved, so I decided to investigate

Adoption hours were on Friday and Saturday afternoon, so on Friday I went to the shelter to see what I could learn. There was a sign on the lawn in front of the building that said, "Open for Adoptions." I went inside and the place was in tiptop shape. The cleaning crew must have come in early on Friday and Saturday to get the place ready for the visiting public. Karen, a very pretty woman and the same person who knew Alex's master, was in charge of adoptions. She lives in Marblehead and is a flight attendant. We worked together on the auction fund-raiser. I told her, "I was riding by and dropped in for a visit." I wanted to get the lay of the land; however, I was very careful. I did not want to step on anybody's toes.

While in the shelter, I played with the cats, and Karen went about her business. People started coming in to look at the cats. Some looked and left and some stayed. Those who stayed appeared to be interested in a cat. Karen approached the interested people, when she sensed they needed some questions answered. As much as she wanted to place a cat in a good home, she was not overly anxious. She was cool as a cucumber. You have to understand, we at the shelter are not trying to get rid of our cats. We want to place them in the best situation possible. The requirements for adopting one of our cats are strict.

The interested people wanted to know the history of the cat. In most cases the animal control officer picks up strays and abandoned cats, which have no history. Owners move away in many cases and leave their pets behind. People think cats are independent and can fend for themselves. That is not true. Domestic cats need food and shelter; otherwise, they starve to death or get sick and die. As I explained in the previous chapter, feral cats can fend for themselves; however, their life is hard and short. Cats are surrendered by their owners for a host of reasons. The most common are: people have allergies, people go into nursing homes, people die, people move where they do not allow pets, and people no longer want the responsibility. Thank God we are there for these unfortunate animals. The alternative is devastating. Karen tells the interested couple everything she knows about the history of the cat. There is no reason not to.

Usually, the next questions from every perspective adopter are always in this order. What is the age of the cat? What is the temperament of the cat? What is the health of the cat? The age of the cats are on the little cards attached to the cage. The veterinarian can tell the approximate age of the cats from their teeth. Karen, who is in charge of adoptions, has to know the temperament of every cat, so that she can place them in homes that suit their personalities. We don't want the adopters to have any surprises after they get home with an animal. If a cat has any issues, we will tell them the truth, because we do not want the cat to be returned to the shelter. To the best of our ability we want you to be completely informed about the animal you are adopting. The health of the animals is a major concern. When an animal comes into the shelter, it is brought to the vet for a complete examination. We make sure all the animals get a rabies and distemper shot. The cats are tested for FeLV (feline leukemia) and feline FIV (feline immune deficiency). All the animals six months or older are checked for fleas, ear mites, worms, and any other ailments. Most important we have all our animals spayed or neutered before they are placed. That is a strict policy of the shelter. If an animal is under six months old, they are too young to be altered, so we provide the adopters with information for a low-cost spay or neuter from an organization called the Friends of Animals. We also call the adopter to remind them that it is time to alter their pet. It is so important the animals are altered, because there are too many unwanted animals in the world, and thousands are being put down every day. It is truly the only way to prevent over-population and unnecessary deaths.

Continuing to mind my own business while petting the cats, I observed and listened intently to Karen while she was talking to the prospective adopters. I wanted to learn as much as possible. The couple was asking all sorts of questions. Karen was asking questions as well. They were general questions to get some background and a feel for the potential adopter. The couple did not realize they were being screened.

The talk is over. The couple wants the cat. Now they must fill out an adoption application, so they will be screened even further. You can really evaluate adopters from the application. Aside from the usual name, address, and phone number, we want to be sure that the cat will be safe in this home and compatible with these people. We are the advocates for the cat. We have to know if there are children living in the home. Some cats are not good with children. We have to know if anyone in the family has allergies. We have to know if the adopters own or rent. If they rent, they have to bring in a written consent from their landlord that animals are allowed. We would like to know if there are any other pets in the home. Some cats do not get along with other animals. We would give them information on the proper way to introduce a new animal into a home with other pets. Some cats want to live alone and will not adjust to other pets. If the adopters had pets in the past, it is good to know what happened to them. It is extremely important to know if they spayed or neutered their pets. We need to know their veterinarian, in case we have to call for a recommendation. All that information will have to be answered on the application.

The most important question on the whole application has yet to be answered. The million dollar question is, "Do you let your cats go outside?" If the answer is yes, a cat from our shelter will not be placed with them. Linda is adamant about that. Every cat at the shelter has suffered some kind of trauma. They come into the shelter starving, sickly, diseased, wounded, mutilated, and some are bewildered because they do not understand why they were surrendered to us. Just being in the shelter is stressful enough for these poor creatures. They are confused. Some adapt quicker than others. The volunteers work and care for these animals with their heart and soul. Linda is sick when she picks up one of our cats out of the gutter dead after it has been hit by a car. I do not blame her for being furious. This is why there is such a strong resolve in not placing our cats in homes where they are going to be let outside. There are also deadly diseases cats could get like FeLV and FIV by being outdoors. Let's not forget that cats are coyotes' favorite meal. Since the coyotes' habitats are being encroached upon, they have infiltrated our cities and towns and have adapted their hunting and eating habits accordingly.

Long before I joined the volunteers at Friends of Marblehead's Abandoned Animals, the organization adopted this policy. I personally let my own cats go outside because they are seventeen years old and cannot change their lifestyle. Besides, they hardly go out that much anymore. Whenever I get another cat, it will be an indoor cat. I understand where the shelter is coming from because since I have been volunteering, I've been educated to the dangers of having outdoor cats. Lots of potential adopters come into the shelter and only want an indoor cat. Some people come into the shelter and swear they will keep the cat indoors, but have no intention of doing so. Many people come into the shelter and are angry because they cannot understand the indoor cat policy. They ask, "Is it better for the cat to rot in a cage, than have a good home and go outdoors?" It is a catch twenty-two. Maybe we are playing God. I do not have the answers. That is why the million dollar question on the shelter application is, "Do you let your cat go outside?"

The second extremely important question is, "Do you declaw?" Again, the policy at our shelter is not to place cats to a home where they are going to be declawed. It is a very painful procedure, and we feel it is not humane. Many veterinarians refuse to do this kind of surgery.

The couple finished filling out the adoption application and gave it to Karen. Without a doubt, Karen took a peek at the two most important questions first. I knew immediately the adopters wanted an indoor cat, otherwise, Karen would have instantly explained that she was unable to place the cat with them. She went behind the desk and studied the rest of the application. I was getting excited because I sensed I might witness my first cat adoption. At this point Karen must have a good idea of what this couple is all about. It is time for Karen's good judgment and gut feeling to make a decision. Will this be a good placement for the cat? If she still has doubts, she will tell the adopters the animal control officer has to look at the application, and they will be called. This will give Karen time to investigate further and clear up any doubts she may have. Maybe she will call the adopter's veterinarian, call a neighbor, and speak to Linda, too. She has got to feel right about the placement of the cat. Remember, we are not trying to get rid of cats; we want them to be placed in good, responsible, forever homes.

Karen got up from behind the desk, walked over to the prospective adopters, and said, "The cat is yours." It was a wonderful moment; one of our babies has a home. The couple filled out an adoption contract. A portion of the contract had the shelter policy on it, and the other half had the cat's medical history. On the bottom of the contract the adopters had to fill out their name, address, etc. The cost of the cat was only fifty dollars at that time. Karen gave them a copy of the contract and she kept a copy. One of the cat's new parents ran out to get their cat carrier. Karen took the cat out of the cage and started hugging and kissing it. I joined her saying good-bye to the cat. The cat was put in the carrier and off it went to its new home, and another life was saved.

Karen and I were the only ones left in the shelter. We looked at each other with that special feeling of accomplishment and success. It was the same special feeling I had when I saved Alex, the dog. It was a moment of gratification and joy. All the hard work, love, and nurturing the volunteers give these animals paid off. Karen had one more official act concerning the newly placed cat She went over to the desk, picked up a pen, went over to a piece of paper that was taped on the wall, and wrote the name of the cat on it. The title on the piece of paper was "Adoptions," and under the title was the month, and then there was the list of animals placed during that month. When the volunteers come into the shelter from week to week, they see which animals have been placed. Believe me, the volunteers get a lot of pleasure seeing those names on the list. Unfortunately, we did not have a large turnover at that time.

It was closing time. Karen and I said good-bye. I learned a lot my first time at adoptions, and there is so much more to learn. To this day Karen does not know how wonderful a teacher she was concerning adoptions. I decided to make frequent visits during adoption hours. I am fairly new to the shelter, so I am not sure if Linda wants any more help with adoptions. Linda and Karen are good friends, and Linda has a lot of confidence in Karen's judgment and put her in charge. Linda made it clear to everyone; she does not have the patience or the time to work with the public, when it comes to adoptions. Of course, Linda places many animals to people she knows personally. I must go slowly and carefully towards my pursuit to help with adoptions.

Almost every Friday during adoption hours, I went to the shelter. To my dismay I discovered the shelter was closed too many times. Karen had to work and nobody else did adoptions. No wonder we had a small turnover placing our animals. That disturbed me very much. Somebody should be at the shelter receiving the public during scheduled adoption hours, even if they are not permitted to make an adoption. If someone is there, people can come in, view the animals, have someone to talk to, and get information. If they are interested in a particular animal, they can make out an application. Karen or Linda can review the application, and then at a later date get in touch with the interested party. This way we are way ahead of the game, and we do not lose a prospective customer. The shelter is a business and there should be continuity. One of my questions has been answered; help with adoptions is desperately needed.

One Tuesday evening my partner could not come in to clean, so Linda helped me. It was too much for me to do alone. While we cleaned, we talked about many things. Somehow we got on the subject of adoptions. It was a good opportunity to tell her how I felt about somebody always being there during adoption hours, when Karen had to work. We advertise the shelter is open certain days and hours for adoptions, so we are obligated to open. Linda listened and kept very quiet. However, she did not disagree with me. I told her I would be happy to do adoption hours, when Karen wasn't available. I would receive the public, give them any information, and refer them to either to Karen or her. I also reassured her, I would never place any animal without permission. The thing that is most critical is that animals are losing their chance to find a good home just because the shelter is closed during adoption hours.

Linda was very hesitant and responded by saying that she would give my idea some thought. She told me most of the volunteers did not want the responsibility of doing adoptions. They were afraid of making a wrong decision. That never even occurred to me. I could not wait for the day when I was ready to do adoptions on my own. I was glad we had this talk. Everything I told her was plain common sense.

Two or three weeks had gone by since Linda and I talked. She had not said a word about our conversation. It was Friday, so I went to the shelter during adoption hours, and found it was closed. This was so disappointing and frustrating. I was about to go home, when Linda came by to open the door to the shelter. Maybe she was going to do adoptions? She told me to come in, so I did. She was just there to pick up a few things. To my surprise, she asked if I wanted to cover today because Karen had to work. I was taken back and blurted out, "Yes!" Well, that was Linda—unpredictable. She picked up her stuff and left. I immediately grabbed the A-frame sign, which said, "Open for Adoptions." I put it in front of the building, and the shelter was open for business. Some people came in to look at cats, some people just needed information. There are a host of reasons why people come into the shelter, and I was there to help them. The conversation was always about animals, which is my favorite subject. I was like a child in a toy store who could pick out any toy I wanted. I was having fun. There are only two other places I would rather be than the shelter. I love being with my beautiful family, and I love my home.

I do not know why, but something mysterious brought me to the shelter and guided me in the direction of adoptions. As you will see in the next chapter, God works in strange ways and there is a reason for everything.

TROUBLE

Chapter 3

Summer is approaching and it is the busy season at the zoo. Children are off from school, it is vacation time, and families like to go on day trips. What better place to visit than the zoo? The zoo staff and zoo volunteers love it when there are swarms of people visiting. I think the animals like it too.

This season new people were hired to manage and coordinate the zoo volunteers. One of their requests was that established volunteers retake the zoology courses with new incoming volunteers. That was fine, but it meant I would have to go back to the zoo extra days and nights. That did not include the meetings I had to attend, which were scheduled in the evenings. These new requests were going to be difficult for me. Geography was my biggest problem. It takes me one hour each way to travel to and from the zoo. Most of the volunteers live much closer. Evenings are the worst time for me to travel. I am afraid to travel on Route 128 in the dark. Route 128 is a very dark highway, a virtual speedway, and the quickest route to the zoo. Every time I go on that road, I feel as if I just entered the Indianapolis 500 Speedway. The possibility of getting into an accident or getting stuck is worrisome.

I had a long talk with the new coordinators and was up front. I told them my problem about traveling back and forth to the zoo. I told them I will do the best I could to attend classes and meetings. They could count on me to continue my regular duties on my usual days. Between my family, the zoo, and the shelter, I had worked out a schedule that worked perfectly for me. The new managers understood where I was coming from, and we left it at that.

I am the type of person, when I make a commitment, I will work hard to keep it, do it right, and give it a hundred percent. If I cannot keep up with my obligations, it would bother me enough to do something about it. I will cross that bridge when I come to it.

The shelter is also a very busy place during the spring and summer seasons. Not with swarms of people, but with swarms of animals. This is the season a lot of stray and abandoned animals come into the shelter. They seem to come out of the woodwork. It is also the season pet owners want to surrender their pets. Curiously, this is the season we have fewer adoptions. Many people and families go on vacation. Marblehead and the surrounding areas are beach and boating communities. It is the season to play and have fun. It is not the season to take on new obligations such as a shelter animal.

On top of everything else it is kitten season. Most people do not realize there is a kitten season. Generally kitten season is from the end of April to the beginning of October. On occasion we do get a litter out of season but, it is rare. During this season we take in many litters of kittens and mothers with kittens. Those mothers with kittens were not spayed because they either were abandoned or were strays.

If abandoned, nursing, motherless, infant kittens come into the shelter, we try giving them to a nursing mother that is already in the shelter. Not all nursing mothers will accept orphaned kittens. Before we give them to the mother cat we rub the orphaned kittens and the mother's kittens together. We take a towel or blanket the mother cat has been lying on and wrap it around the orphaned kittens. Chances are greater the mother cat will accept the kittens with her scent on them. From my experience I have witnessed several mother cats generously accepting orphaned babies. Cats are pretty receptive about that.

The suspense is unbelievable, when you finally put the orphaned kittens in with the mother cat and her own kittens. Will she accept them as her own or will she ignore them? You wait and watch. First, the mother cat gets up and smells each kitten individually. That is why putting her scent on the kittens is critical. She then looks a little puzzled. She originally had four babies, now she has more. Where did they come from? If she starts to clean them, you know they are on their way to being accepted. When they start to nurse on the mom cat, you know they have been accepted, and everything is going to be fine. What a wonderful happening to observe. Female lions share in caring for baby lion cubs. I think the domestic cat has inherited that quality.

If there are no nursing mother cats at the shelter, it could be a problem, except we have some very special volunteers who care for motherless nursing infant kittens. These exceptionally dedicated volunteers take the kittens home, care for them, and become their surrogate mothers. Their task is not an easy one. As you all know, human babies have to be fed every four hours. Baby kittens are no different. You can buy kitten baby formula at any pet store. Most of the surrogate mothers work full time. Some of the volunteers work close to home, so they run home during lunch hour and their break to feed the kittens. Other volunteers put the kittens in a basket, bring the babies to work with them, and care for them all day long.

After working all day long the surrogate mothers have to get up during the night to feed the baby kittens. The kittens' real mom would clean her babies constantly, and that also stimulates the kittens to eat. The surrogate moms have to wash and keep the infant clean too. The kittens have to be kept warm, so the volunteers put an electric heating pad under their bedding if necessary. Depending on the kittens' age, the volunteers will have to care for them from four to six weeks. The kittens will be ready to be brought to the shelter when they are able to eat on their own. At seven or eight weeks old they will be ready for adoption.

It is an understatement to say those volunteers have an enormous job. They do it without a complaint. They do it because they care. They are some of the most dedicated and special people at the shelter.

When pregnant mother cats come into the shelter, we try to find foster care homes for them. The shelter is not the right environment for expecting mother cats. Dogs are barking, cats are meowing, people are in and out constantly, there is no peace or quiet, which is what a mother-to-be needs. Some of the same and other volunteers come to the rescue. They take the expectant mother cat into their homes. They sometimes help with the delivery of the kittens. They keep the little family until the kittens are old enough to eat on their own. Just like the motherless kittens they will be brought back to the shelter with their mom. We will place the kittens when they are eight weeks or older. After the mother cat heals from motherhood, we will spay her and she will be put up for adoption. Foster care for a pregnant mother is a lot easier than caring for motherless kittens. The mother cat does all the work for the kittens.

Occasionally there is a weak or sickly kitten in the litter. The caregivers will bring that kitten to the veterinarian for professional care. Unfortunately with all the love and care we give the baby kittens, we lose one. It happens, and it is very sad, but it could be any number of medical reasons why these things occur. Sometimes it is called fading kitten syndrome. When it does occur, it is very hard for all the volunteers, but it is hardest on the caregivers.

We all work so hard to save lives. The volunteers sacrifice so much time from their personal life, so baby kittens and mother cats will have a chance for a good life. These volunteers are perfect examples of the kind of people who are associated with the shelter. They are true humanitarians.

There are so many unwanted animals, and thousands of them are being put down every single day. Mostly because of man's abuse, cruelty, and ignorance. It is horrible. Sadly, most communities do not have a no-kill animal shelter like ours. Most communities do not have an animal shelter period! I think there should be a law that every community be required to have an animal shelter or share one.

We have a strict policy at our shelter. We will not place any animals over the age of six months old, unless it is spayed or neutered. It is the shelter's responsibility to have the procedure completed on our animals, and believe me; we make sure it gets done! I cannot mention it enough because there are too many unwanted animals in the world that are dying for one reason or another.

There is a group of veterinarians who belong to an organization called Friends of Animals, and they will spay and neuter your pet at a lower cost. These veterinarians realize the importance of spaying and neutering animals, so they make it affordable for every responsible pet owner. I think all veterinarians should participate in this program. You could call the organization or go online to obtain a low-cost prepaid spay or neuter certificate. Then you call to make an appointment with the animal hospital that is on their list that is most convenient for you, and present them with the prepaid certificate. Your pet will get the same quality care as any other patient. Make sure your pet is six months or older and up-to-date on its shots. There are rescue agencies that alter animals at three months old. They do that to make sure the job gets done. They do not want to leave it up to pet owners. Many pet owners say, "Of course I am going to spay or neuter my pet," and they never do. I disagree with that practice. I think the animal is much too young and underdeveloped. Remember, unless you are a breeder, spaying and neutering saves lives.

Spring and summer are good seasons to give the shelter a thorough internal top to bottom clean-up. Periodically on Saturday during adoption hours, Linda rounds up her gang of volunteers for a cleaning day. Weather-wise it has to be a perfect day. All the cages with the animals in them will be brought outside and put on the lawn. Linda with some assistance will scrub down the walls, floors, and anything else that needs to be scrubbed. The rest of the volunteers stay outside to care for the animals. We socialize with each other and receive the public. Karen was there too, ready to handle any prospective adoptions.

It was a lot of fun being there. The shelter was located on one of the two main roads leading into Marblehead. There is always traffic coming and going into town. People drive by, see the cages with animals on the lawn, curiosity gets the better of them, they park their car, and come over to check out the animals. Children especially want to see the animals. All of a sudden the place is swarming with people. It reminded me of the zoo. Most people were just looking at the animals, but there were a few people interested in adopting a pet. It was impossible for Karen, the adoption coordinator, to speak to everyone individually, so the volunteers gladly helped out if anyone had any questions. If an individual was seriously interested in a particular animal, we brought them over to Karen to be interviewed. Nine times out of ten they were interested in kittens. When there are kittens at the shelter, they hardly look at the other cats. Who would not want a cute, cuddly, playful, adorable, fun-loving kitten? Two kittens are double the fun. Everybody wants the kittens.

While standing around, somebody tapped me on the shoulder. I turned and it was the Swampscott town accountant. We did not know each other well, but we were aquatinted through our town politics. My husband and I were elected town-meeting members. My husband is especially vocal in town politics. The town accountant had his children with him, and they were interested in a kitten. I brought them over to the cage with the kittens. He appeared to have very little experience with animals; however, he was interested in learning everything about caring for a kitten. I counseled him about various things like: diet, litter, vaccinations, and altering your pet. I explained the advantages of having an indoor cat. I was happy to share with him everything I knew about caring for a kitten. He and his children looked into the cage and were immediately attracted to an adorable white kitten. I took the kitten out of the cage and let the children pet it. The chemistry was there; they loved the little kitten, and wanted it badly. Their dad filled out the adoption application, and I brought the family over to Karen for the final okay. She glanced through it, told me everything was fine, and they could have the kitten. Apparently, he heeded my advice about keeping the kitten indoors. The town account is a good family man, and I believe he will take good care of that kitten. He made out the contract and paid the fee. Off they went so excited with their new precious addition to the family. I wished them luck.

It was getting late. Linda and her assistants were through cleaning. The inside of the shelter was spotless. One by one we brought the cages with the cats and dogs back into the shelter. It was good for the animals to get out in the fresh air. There is so much litter dust in the shelter. It was a successful day because there were animals placed in good homes. The volunteers had a chance to socialize with each and get reacquainted. All in all it was a super productive day.

Time passes so quickly when you're having fun. It is hard to believe a year has gone by, and I am celebrating my first year anniversary volunteering at the shelter. Working with the animals on Tuesday evenings with Joanne and filling in for Karen during adoption hours has been great. I am really enjoying myself.

Every Thursday in the towns of Swampscott and Marblehead a weekly newspaper is delivered to those who subscribe. The newspapers are similar, but different, in the sense that Swampscott has their local news and Marblehead has its local news, and everything else is the same. Mostly everyone in town subscribes because they want to know what is happening in town. Occasionally, there are some hot issues.

It was Thursday and, as usual, I went down my back stairway to the mailbox for my *Swampscott Reporter*. Went back into the house, sat down at the dining room table, and unfolded the newspaper. I looked at the front page and my eyes popped out of my head. I looked again and could not believe what I saw. I could not believe it. On the front page in bold black print, **"MARBLEHEAD ANIMAL CONTROL OFFICER CALLS SWAMPSCOTT TOWN ACCOUNTANT A MURDERER."** I was at the shelter constantly and knew nothing about this incident. I was astonished! How could this happen? I started to think back when the kitten was placed with the town accountant. It was about four months ago.

As I read the story, it went like this. One of the town accountant's children accidentally let the kitten out of the house. The innocent kitten wandered off to a main road and got hit by a car. The poor thing died instantly. The accountant's family was devastated. They loved their little white kitten. To soften the blow the town accountant promised his family he would get them another kitten.

Remember in the last chapter, I mentioned the million dollar question on the adoption application? I will refresh your memory, "Do you let your cats go outdoors?" I also mentioned Linda does not like to deal with the public, when it comes to adoptions.

The town accountant went back to the shelter with his children to see if he could adopt another kitten. It was not during adoption hours. He was quite unaware he was making a huge mistake. He went hoping someone would be there. Well somebody was there all right. Linda was there. He explained what happened to the kitten and wanted another one. I guess that is when all hell broke loose. He claimed she called him a murderer. Not only did she call him a murderer, but she called him a murderer in front of his children. He was outraged and immediately went to the Marblehead town hall and complained to Linda's superiors. Then he went to all the newspapers to tell his story. He was so furious with Linda; he was determined to have some action taken against her.

After reading the article three times, I ran to the phone and called some of the other volunteers. They knew just about as much as I did. Linda was closed mouth about the episode. All the volunteers were extremely upset about the incident. This was not the best publicity for the shelter. Not only did the weekly newspaper have the story plastered all over the place, the daily newspapers had the story plastered all over the place as well.

So many people knew my affiliation with the shelter. I started receiving calls at home asking, "Is it true? Is it true?" I would encounter acquaintances everywhere I went, and they asked me, "Is it true? Is it true?" People would come into the shelter and ask, "Is it true? Is it true?" I would cringe. Nobody was interested in the animals; they were only interested in the gossip.

Linda claimed she did not call the town accountant a murderer with or without the children present. The accountant claimed she did. This scandal went on for weeks in the news. It might sound stupid, but it was a hot issue in the sleepy little towns of Swampscott and Marblehead.

I couldn't find one volunteer who knew what really happened between Linda and the town accountant. I contacted several of the volunteers that were at the shelter at the time of the incident. I asked them if they knew if she called him a murderer and how the situation was resolved. A few of the volunteers told me that Linda told them she never called him a murderer. Some of the volunteers remembered she called him a murderer, but not in front of the children. There were other volunteers who would not put it past her to call the man a murderer even in front of his children. My guess is only Linda and the town account know the truth. All the volunteers agreed, Linda must have been reprimanded but good from her superiors.

Through this whole scandalous episode the volunteers continued to do their work, as though nothing was happening. Absolutely nothing deters these selfless people from caring for the animals. Their dedication is unbelievable. The animals always come first.

The scandal has become old news; however, I sense something far more serious concerning the shelter is brewing. Occasionally, during adoption hours, Marblehead residents would come into the shelter and tell me they heard the shelter was closing. At first I thought it was because of the scandal, and the residents assumed they were going to close the shelter. I put it out of my mind thinking it was nonsense. It became evident something was happening because too many people were coming into the shelter with the same rumor. Where did you hear this rumor? Why do they want to close the shelter? I asked these questions, but nobody had the answers. Since I was not a Marblehead resident, I was not familiar with their politics. Where there is smoke there is fire. I called several of my colleagues, who live in Marblehead. They heard the same rumor, but had no other information. The next time I saw Linda, I mentioned the rumor to her. She told me not to panic. Everything was going to be all right. When she told me that, I really started to panic. I conjured up all sorts of horrible thoughts. There are between sixty to seventy animals at the shelter. What happens to them? My deepest and worst fear was euthanasia. It would be a massacre. It would be a holocaust. It pained me to think about it. I was scared. The entire staff of volunteers was just as concerned.

There were so many unanswered questions. Why would the town want to close the shelter? We were doing such good work. How could the town conceive of doing such a thing? Is it because of the scandal with Linda and the Swampscott town accountant? Is it just a coincidence the rumor of the shelter closing was right on the heels of the so-called murder scandal? It was so frustrating and worrisome to be kept in the dark. Everything was hush-hush.

In 1993 when Friends of Marblehead's Abandoned Animals was established, I do not think the town fathers expected it was going to mushroom into a non-profit organization of this size. It started off with a few animals, and now we have about seventy. There were just a couple of volunteers, and now there are about thirty-five to forty. Every community is responsible for an animal control officer. Marblehead is responsible for an animal control officer and an animal shelter. I have a feeling some of the town fathers at the town hall are not happy with the situation. Why do I have that notion? For one thing we were forbidden to call the shelter an animal shelter. You can call it Friends of Marblehead's Abandoned Animals, but do not call it a shelter. You can call it animal control, but do not call it a shelter. It was ludicrous. It was an animal shelter. Everybody called it the Marblehead Animal Shelter.

Katie and her sister Nancy used to walk every day for exercise by the animal shelter. One day they got an ingenious idea to walk the shelter dogs at the same time, so they can exercise too, thus Katie and her sister became the first volunteers at the shelter. Sadly, Katie's sister passed away; so Katie continued to carry on their good work and became founder and director of the shelter. She is involved in every aspect of shelter business. Katie constantly reminded the volunteers to keep a low profile. She wanted us to be aware of the fact, that we were using a town building and could be evicted at anytime. We were powerless, so naturally, we were very careful not to do anything to jeopardize the shelter. Linda was the controversial one. She was a fabulous animal control officer. I watched her handle difficult animals, and she was good. She would have been a great zookeeper. There was a time the town of Marblehead gave her an award for "Town Employee of the Year." She is a very strong-willed person, who is determined to do things her way. She marches to a different drummer, and on many occasions she infuriates her superiors at town hall.

After weeks of wondering why the shelter might close some of the questions have finally been answered. The weekly newspaper revealed some of the answers. About a month or so ago Marblehead had a town-wide vote to override two and a half for a new nine-one-one system in the police station. Nine-one-one is a very sophisticated communication system for the police to enhance the safety of the town. The vote was passed overwhelmingly. The police station was going to be renovated to house the nine-one-one. What does it all mean to the shelter? It means the large garage and the attached little building, which is the shelter, will be taken to expand the future newly renovated police ptation. Now we know why the shelter is going to be closed. The big question is, "What is going to happen to the shelter and the animals?" The newspaper did not have an answer. Town hall did not have an answer. Linda did not have an answer. Nobody had an answer, yet! It was maddening!

Not long after we learned about the future of the shelter, there was a selectmen's meeting on Marblehead local TV. One of the shelter volunteers happened to be watching. The shelter was brought up as a topic of discussion. She described the discussion as being very negative. Furthermore they did not have their facts straight. It was upsetting. The next day the volunteer went to town hall with her young son in the carriage. She insisted on talking to the town manager who would take her message back to the selectmen. He welcomed her into his office. She straightened out a lot of misguided issues. She suggested he and the selectmen speak with the volunteers.

Since I was writing this book, I tried to get in touch with that volunteer for more details. She did not want to talk about it because it was too painful. It was an extremely emotional period for all the volunteers; after all, our beloved shelter was in trouble.

The week after that selectmen's meeting the local newspaper in big black bold printed a headline reading, "**SHELTER CLOSING IN 60 DAYS.**" It was horrible and heartbreaking. Nothing was mentioned about what was going to happen to the animals. The volunteers were devastated, but they continued to go to the shelter every day to care for the animals. It was hard to look into the faces of those innocent, loving animals, not knowing what the future had in store for them. We all prayed for a miracle.

Instead of sitting around moping about the shelter closing, the volunteers decided to go on the offensive and prepare to defend the shelter. Linda called the volunteers together for a meeting. There was a lot of talk, and we accomplished nothing. There were side meetings with smaller groups of volunteers, which did not include Linda. When she got wind of those meetings, she was furious. She was convinced she could handle everything by herself. She claimed she had a plan. Maybe she knew something we didn't. Several volunteers did not agree because at the moment she was in the dog house with town hall. No pun intended. No matter who did what, we all were under the perception the shelter might close. It was easy to have that notion because Marblehead residents were in and out of the shelter telling us it was going to close. We all agreed there was only one thing that was going to save it. It was public opinion. Most politicians do not want to make unpopular decisions concerning the town. They want to be re-elected. If a majority of Marbleheaders are in favor of the shelter, the selectmen might consider relocation. The volunteers were convinced public opinion was going to decide this issue.

Out of the blue all the volunteers were invited to a meeting with the town manager. The majority of volunteers attended. The town manager and one selectman was present. The town manager overheard me talking to the person next to me while waiting for the other volunteers to arrive. I said, "I do not trust politicians because they wear you down." I meant it too. He did not like what I said, and asked Katie who I was. I admit, when I went to the meeting, I was ready for combat. Maybe it was not the politically correct thing to say, but at the time I would have done anything to help save the shelter.

The meeting started and our goal was to emphasize the valuable service Friends of Marblehead's Abandoned Animals provides to both humans and non-humans in town. Remember, we cannot call the shelter a shelter. Here are some of the reasons why we think the shelter should exist.

1. When an animal comes into the animal control office and nobody claims it after ten days, we take the animal to the vet to be tested for feline leukemia, feline AIDS, a rabies shot, distemper shot, and we make sure it gets spayed or neutered. If the animal needs any other medical attention, we take care of it. When the animal has all the proper care and is healthy, it is put up for adoption. On the other side of the coin, we have pleased hundreds of families by matching and placing the right animals to their lifestyles. In a funny way we are recycling. We are saving lives and at the same time making people happy.

2. People die and go into nursing homes. They can no longer care for their pets. Should those animals be put down? We do not think so; the Friends are there to help. Animals are not disposable items.

3. Where do the people in town go, especially children, when they find hurt birds, squirrels, or other little critters? To Friends of course. We are right there to help, and we do everything we can to save those animals.

4. We help with spaying and/neutering and release program for feral cats. The town is better off because the feral cats have been inoculated and they cannot reproduce.

5. Parents and grandparents bring children into the shelter to see all the animals. They love it.

6. Many high school students have to do community service as part of their curriculum. We welcome young people into the shelter to help.

7. Most of all, the residents of Marblehead support the fact Friends of Marblehead's Abandoned Animals is a NO-KILL organization.

8. Our approach to the animal situation in town is humane. The alternative is inhumane.

The volunteers were through spilling out their gut feelings. It was time for the town manager and the selectman to talk. They did and were unhappy about the high number of animals we had in the shelter. They suggested an animal's stay at the shelter should to be limited to a certain length of time. The innuendo being the animal is put down, if it is not adopted within a certain period of time. They did not come out and say it, but we knew what they were suggesting. The discussion was very disturbing, and it got very quiet in the room. Finally, I said, "Could I take care, get to know, bond with an animal, and have it put down, if it is not placed in a certain time period?" No way could I volunteer under those conditions. It was out of the question. All the volunteers chimed in and totally agreed with me. The rest of the conversation was redundant. It was unclear if we made any progress. We left the meeting not knowing what was going to happen to the shelter and the animals. It was very depressing.

I understood the town manager and the selectman's concern about the numbers of animals at the shelter. We could improve on that very easily. We should open the shelter more often for adoptions. There should be more advertising. Linda has to be more flexible and let go of her precious animals. She has to put trust in some of the volunteers to make intelligent decisions. We all want the best for the animals.

Not one volunteer agreed with the notion the animals stay at the shelter be terminated after a certain period of time. To suggest that idea was absolutely unacceptable. It was unthinkable. A volunteer suggested, if we were faced with that dilemma, when the animal's time is up, we would continue to change its name. Nobody would ever know the difference. You know, it was not a bad idea. Let's hope we never have to go through that.

The Marblehead selectman and the town manager were considerate to take the time to talk to the volunteers. It gave us all a chance to vent; however, we still did not know what was going to happen to the animals and the shelter. We were so disgusted.

Living with uncertainty about the fate of the shelter, the volunteers devised a plan to place as many animals in good homes, as soon as possible. We decided to open the shelter for adoptions every week night and Saturday afternoon. These hours made it more convenient for the public. In order to put the plan in place, we needed volunteers to come forward to do adoptions. It was not surprising that several volunteers came through. When a volunteer was unable to meet his or her obligation another volunteer picked up the slack. It was amazing. There were even some volunteers who came out of retirement.

A pair of volunteers would be assigned every evening during the week to do adoptions. Joanne, my partner, and I volunteered to do Tuesdays because we were there cleaning. Linda felt she was losing control; however, she knew it was best for the animals. Our immediate responsibility was to get the animals out of the shelter into good homes as quickly as possible. We had less than sixty days.

As if things were not bad enough, Karen, the adoption coordinator, had a job change and was unable to do adoptions. The news was startling, especially at this time. We were all sad to hear that because it is a big loss. The pressure was on.

Remember I told you, "God works in strange ways." My dream to do adoptions was about to come true. I wish the circumstances were different; however, somebody had to step up to the plate to take charge. Hanging out with Karen during adoptions prepared me for the job. I took the job, and volunteered to do Saturday afternoons, the busiest adoption day. My partner Joanne helped me whenever she could.

Everything was in place. All the volunteers who were doing adoptions for the first time went through a quick training session. We had to start placing the animals immediately. Our new adoption hours were publicized everywhere. The whole community of Marblehead and surrounding communities were made aware the shelter was closing. The animals needed help! I only hoped we'd get the support we needed so badly from the public. We kept our fingers crossed, opened our hearts, and prayed a lot.

It was the week, the day, and the moment we put our plan in place to find homes for the animals. The A-frame with the sign "OPEN FOR ADOPTIONS" on it was put on the front lawn. We were officially opened for business. All we could do now was keep our fingers crossed and wait. From Monday through Friday we placed three cats. That was great because it was not uncommon weeks could go by before one cat was placed. This would be the first Saturday opening since the publicity about the shelter. Under normal circumstances Saturday was usually the busiest day for adoptions. It would be the first time I'd do adoptions without anyone looking over my shoulder. I was both excited and nervous. The shelter was cleaned in the morning. I spoke to the animals and told them to be on their best behavior. Joanne came in to help. We put the sign on the front lawn. Everything was ready. What happened that day was history.

During a lifetime most days are alike; however, there are special days in your life that stand out that you will never forget. That Saturday will be one of the most memorable days in my life. So much good, caring decency and unselfishness came out of the human spirit that day. It was unbelievable! Crowds of people came to the shelter that Saturday afternoon to save the life of a little insignificant animal. It was so good to see how so many people were animal friendly. Sometimes you lose faith in human nature. Several adopters already had animals, but adopted another to save a life. Others heard the news, those who never owned an animal, but wanted to save a life showed up. Other people came into the shelter offering help by donating money. The outreach in surrounding communities was incredible. The outreach from the Marblehead community was astonishing. The people of Marblehead deserve so much praise. They were especially supportive of their shelter, because they knew how hard we worked for the animals in the town. People do care; it does not always show. That Saturday was extraordinary, and we placed several cats in good homes. We met so many super wonderful people that day, even under these stressful circumstances, we were actually having fun.

It came to pass the shelter was the place to be on Saturday afternoon. People who had already adopted would hang out to see which animal was going to be placed and with whom. For several weeks people continued to come in and adopt. I can only describe the shelter as being a department store having a huge sale. We placed several animals, but we never ran out of merchandise. You see, the shelter is like a revolving door, even though animals are being placed, other animals are coming in who need to be rescued.

Many town residents brought in copies of letters they sent to the local paper for us to read supporting the shelter. There were letters in the paper with contrary opinions too. Other supportive residents came in to tell us they called the selectmen's office supporting our cause. Closing the shelter was a controversial subject in town.

Joanne and I decided to help the cause, so we each adopted a cat. Joanne already had two female cats. She chose to adopt Sylvester for her harem because he was so irresistible. He was an extra large, handsome, good, kindly tuxedo cat. She made a wonderful choice. I already had four cats, so what difference is one more cat going to make? Cats are low-maintenance pets. I chose Grayson to adopt. He was a five-year-old, good-looking personality plus brown tabby. I just love tabby tiger cats. Ever since I started volunteering, Grayson was my personal favorite. He is kind, loving, affectionate, smart, and a lap cat. My husband, Harv, did not want another pet. We already have six. He put up a struggle, but when I told him Grayson has been at the shelter for the last three years of his little life, he gave in reluctantly. We cannot understand why nobody ever adopted him because he was a super great cat. Grayson sleeps on my husband's lap all the time, and has become his favorite. This is a picture of my beloved cat Grayson.

Time is passing quickly and we have reduced the numbers of animals at the shelter considerably. The sixty-day deadline is approaching and still no news on the fate of the shelter. The volunteers continue working as though nothing is going to happen. I fear for the animals who have not been adopted. Why don't they tell us what is happening? At least give us some direction. It is all so frustrating!

The deadline is here. The sixty days have come and gone. Nothing is happening. The volunteers continue to keep up their weekly schedule and responsibilities. Another month has gone by and another and another. The shelter is functioning, as usual, but we are waiting for the hammer to drop.

There are some new developments. Is there a light at the end of the tunnel? The town residents are coming into the shelter to tell us the shelter may be relocated and not closed. It was not set in stone, but a location was mentioned. There is a run-down building on Devereux Beach that they may be considering. I was told there are issues concerning that particular building. During bad weather or storms, the building gets flooded. From what I hear it sounds like a risky place to put the shelter. The powers that be are rethinking their decision to close the shelter and are looking into relocation. We have not had official word, yet, but I am encouraged.

Finally, Linda gave us the word. The powers that be have decided to relocate the shelter. It will not be built at that Devereux Beach site that we heard about. The new shelter will be built on Marblehead town property not far from where we are now. That particular site already has a cement foundation for a building, which was never completed. The new animal control office/shelter will be constructed on that foundation.

There are two more obstacles we have to get over before it is a go. The first is the selectmen's office has to send their proposal for the new animal control office/shelter building to town-meeting. At town-meeting the town residents will vote on the issue to see if they approve. With the grace of God, they approved the proposal. The second obstacle is some of the surrounding neighbors are strongly objecting to the building in their neighborhood. Their protests go on for weeks. To make a long story short, the neighbors lost the fight, and there will be a new animal control office/shelter building on that site.

It is over. Our prayers have been answered. The animals are safe. The volunteers deserve so much credit. Through this period of adversity, we were solid; we hung in there and stuck to our convictions. There is cause to celebrate. This ordeal has been mentally and emotionally draining. We need time to unwind, reflect on the future, and put the past behind us.

Since the crisis, I still do not know if the town officials at that time had a change of heart about closing the shelter, or was it public opinion that influenced their final decision? I would like to think it was both.

I love volunteering at the shelter. Who would have believed I could get so involved in such a short time? We are doing such great work there and the focus is on saving lives. It is good! I love volunteering at the zoo, too. I have tried to do both the zoo and the shelter. It has become too much for me. I cannot do both and do it well. This will be very hard for me, but I decided this will be my last season volunteering at the zoo. It is clear traveling to and from the zoo, especially in the evening, has become increasingly difficult. My experience at the zoo has been wonderful, as well as educational. I will miss the visitors, the zookeepers, all the volunteers, but most of all, I will miss the animals. It was a joy to be with those magnificent exotic animals. It is hard for me to express, but I felt privileged when I was in the company of those fabulous creatures. They were sacred, unforgettable moments for me. I will continue working to help animals and look back on the zoo fondly.

OUR NEW DIGS

Chapter 4

It has been a little over a year since the town of Marblehead announced it was were going to relocate and build a new animal control office/shelter. The location for the future new shelter is off the beaten track, in a residential area, and not far from where we are now. We, the volunteers, are so grateful there is going to be an animal shelter we could care less about where it is going to be built or what it is going to look like. No matter what, we are determined to continue to do our job saving animals. This new building is the result of some higher authority listening to the constant prayers of a lot of caring people. It will be a special place for Marblehead residents, for the volunteers, but mostly for the animals.

When construction started, periodically, I would ride by the construction site to see how the work was progressing. Little by little I witnessed a structure grow out of a cement foundation. It grew into a mint green wooden building with cream-colored trim and looked like a little cottage. The front of the cottage has a dark green door, a window, and a handicapped access ramp. Facing the shelter on the left is a small lawn area and on the right is a wide driveway for parking. In deference to the neighbors who strongly resisted against the shelter being built in their neighborhood, no sign of any kind will be hung. There is a little ceramic plaque over the mailbox with a dog, a cat, and the number forty-four. Forty-Four Village Street will be our new address. April Frost who adopted a wonderful dog named Taz from the shelter created and thoughtfully donated that lovely plaque to the shelter.

The appearance of the new shelter building fits right in with the residential neighborhood. Unless you were specifically looking for animal control/shelter, you would never know what the building was used for. Believe it or not there are still people in town who do not know we exist.

We now have on the front lawn an arborvitae topiary of an extra large poodle. It looks terrific! Carr Nurseries of Marblehead very generously donated that sensational topiary to the shelter. Since we do not have a sign, the topiary comes in handy when you are constantly giving directions on where the shelter is located. It is an especially good landmark.

Post Script—There was a terrible drought a couple of years ago and sadly, the topiary died.

I could not wait to see the interior of the new building; after all, a lot of my time is going to be spent in there. For the first time I opened the front door and stepped into a completely empty L-shaped room. It was no different than the size of a living room-dining room area in the average home. To the left there was a bathroom with a small sink, a toilet, a washer, and dryer. There was a bathtub, which was built up higher than usual from the floor. The purpose of that was it made bathing the animals easier for us; otherwise, it would be a back breaker. That is it, folks. That is our little shelter.

At the old shelter dogs were kept in the garage and most of the cats were kept in the little building. Now the dogs and the cats are going to be housed together in the same room. It is not the best arrangement, but there is no choice. Dogs bark and stress out the cats. Cats meow and make the dogs anxious. It is all only natural.

The garage at the old building was also used as an area for incoming and sick animals. It is extremely important to have an isolation area for the animals. When an incoming animal came into the old shelter, we put it in the garage/holding area. The animal is checked out, given the proper inoculations, and made sure it is healthy. Only then would we integrate the animal with all the other healthy animals.

Let me give you an example of why an isolation area is so important. When a cat has an upper respiratory condition, which is basically a very bad cold, it is immediately brought into a holding area to be treated with antibiotics.

The animal is isolated and prevents contaminating the other animals. Without a holding area the upper respiratory spreads like wildfire to the other animals. It becomes an enormous job medicating all the animals, as opposed to just one or two. I will not even mention how costly it is for medication, when all the animals contract the bug.

Linda pushed very hard for an isolation area before the new shelter was built, but it never happened. Common sense tells you how terribly important it is for any shelter. You just do not know if there is something medically wrong with any stray or abandoned animal that come into the shelter. I am not sure if, at that time, Linda was out of favor with the powers that be, and that was the reason why the isolation area was eliminated. It would have been so easy, while the building was under construction, to put up a wall with a door at the far end of the L-shaped room. When you think about it, it was a no-brainer.

As I reflect back, I want to tell you about two incidents that happened after we moved into the new shelter because we did not have an isolation area. One of the incidents was tragic and the other comical. First, I must tell you about our extraordinary medical team we had at the shelter at that time. Stephanie is one-half of our medical team; Candi is the other half, and many other of our volunteers assist them. We pride ourselves on our medical caregivers and the quality care they give to the animals.

These two medical coordinators have many years of experience in nursing care and treatment for shelter animals, including: terminal care, senior animals, recovering animals, pregnant/whelping mothers, and orphaned kittens. They also coordinate the work of the medical team, comprised of many volunteers with experience in this area. All medical team volunteers are trained before beginning any work on the shelter animals. Their training has been provided and overseen by several veterinarians at their animal hospitals, or they have come to the shelter for hands-on classes. Stephanie is trained in holistic medicine, and Candi has trained for five years in both homeopathic and holistic medicine in addition to all their other talents. The medical team coordinators spend an estimated fifteen to twenty-five hours per week on these tasks, which include:

1. Transporting animals back and forth to the animal hospital

2. Following through with medications or other treatments

3. Changing bandages

4. Taking temperature

5. Bathing animals

6. Administering insulin to diabetic animals

7. Worming animals

8. Administering distemper vaccine

9. Physical therapy

10. Keeping detailed records on each animal

11. Take home animals, if they need more medical attention

12. They create a medical record for new adopters

13. A written medical history is sent to new owners

14. They follow up the adoption with phone calls

15. They have even made house calls to our adopters

Stephanie and Candi love caring for the animals, as much as I love doing adoptions. These volunteers are invaluable to the shelter because of all the kindly deeds they perform for the animals. Candi, Stephanie and their team are the Florence Nightingales for animals.

The first incident is about how vital a holding area is for the shelter. Everything happened so innocently. A litter of kittens were brought into shelter, which is not uncommon. The kittens did not look that well. After a couple of days Linda decided to take them home with her. They were not doing well, and it was best to get them out of the shelter, since there was no isolation area. Sadly, the poor little kittens were failing and died. We did not know what caused their death.

Not long after the kittens were taken from the shelter, I was standing with

Stephanie in front of Pierre's cage. Pierre was a lovely gray and white short hair cat. Stephanie examined him and was very concerned. He was not eating, drinking, he was lethargic, and was not acting normal. We put a sheet over his cage because there was no isolation area. We had no other defense from germs spreading throughout the shelter. He would be monitored very closely. If he did not improve overnight, he would be brought to the animal hospital. Pierre was a very sick cat and went to the hospital. He was diagnosed with distemper. Panleucopenia is the medical term for this disease. This viral disease is a great killer of kittens and unvaccinated cats. It produces symptoms of vomiting, diarrhea, fever, depression, and depresses the production of white blood cells. Affected cats may die in just a few days, so prompt treatment is needed. Some cats may have very mild signs and recover easily; they then have a lifelong immunity to distemper. Vaccines give rapid, effective protection for at least one year and must never be overlooked or postponed. Annual vaccination is recommended, especially if your pet will be exposed to other cats.

Poor Pierre was in the worst and final stage of the viral disease. He was suffering and was going to die. The humane thing to do was to put him down. It was very sad. Pierre was such a good, kindly cat. He did not deserve this.

This particular viral germ spreads through the feces in the litter box. We did not know it at the time, but we did not have the proper cleaning protocol at the shelter. We ignorantly used the same pooper scooper from one litter box to another. The proper cleaning protocol is to soak the pooper scooper in a mixture of bleach and water after you clean each litter box. When you have over twenty-five cats in one place, there is lots of litter and litter dust everywhere.

Things started to add up. Pierre had not yet been given a distemper shot. Most likely that litter of sick kittens died of distemper and contaminated the shelter. The disease could have already spread to some of the other animals. Disaster had come to our shelter. Our troubles were just beginning.

On top of everything else Candi is on a leave of absence to care for her sick stepfather, and going to a seminar on homeopathy that she had arranged months ago. It is up to Stephanie, as the medical coordinator to call the shots. Call them she did! She immediately quarantined the shelter for six weeks. Absolutely no animals were allowed to come in or go out of the shelter!

As luck would have it another litter of kittens and their mother were recently brought into the shelter. All my years volunteering at the shelter including up to this minute, I have never seen such a gorgeous litter of kittens.

Like their mother they were gray and white fluffy fur balls. It was hard to tell them apart. The kittens had not yet been vaccinated for distemper, which made them extremely vulnerable to contracting this horrible disease.

Knowing the danger the kittens were in, Stephanie, with Linda's permission, thought it best to get them out of the shelter immediately. A quarantine area was set up in Linda's cellar. Wendy lived in the apartment above Linda, and was another one of our loyal dedicated volunteers, who took turns caring for the little darling kittens. Back at the shelter Stephanie was giving all the cats Echinacea and Golden Seal. They are herbs that boost the immune system. Every precaution had been taken, and now we had to wait.

It was possible I could bring germs home from the shelter. I was concerned for my animals, especially my feral cat. All my pets were up to date with their shots except Spooky. She had her last distemper shot when she was a year old. She was feral and impossible to catch to put her in a carrier.

The very last time she went to the veterinarian's office for her shots it turned out to be quite an experience. Our veterinarian knew she was feral, so he handled her very slowly and carefully. You could see the cat was frightened, nervous, and resisted help. Suddenly she escaped! She ran wild through his office knocking everything over. She literally was climbing the walls to escape. She was hissing, growling, and spitting. My husband, Harv, was with me, and we were horrified. We were all running around his office trying to catch the cat, which made things worse. The vet got out his big leather gloves. After many attempts, he captured her, and secured the cat in her carrier.

Our vet was sweating and completely out of breath, but managed to tell us never to bring that cat into his office again! He explained, "As long as Spooky is an indoor cat, which she is, and your other cats were up to date with their inoculations, she will never have to go to the animal hospital for shots again."

I want you to know the veterinarian has been our animal doctor for many years and he and his wife used to share Passover with my family. We had a good laugh over that wild incident in his office.

My concern about my feral cat was not unfounded. It was possible I could bring the disease home with me from the shelter. The litter dust was on my shoes and clothing. You just do not know. I discussed the situation with people, who were far more knowledgeable about the subject than I was. I was advised not go into the shelter until the quarantine was over. When it is over, I should continue to take further precautions upon leaving the shelter for home.

My shoes should be sprayed with disinfectant and my clothes must be removed and washed immediately.

It was so frustrating and heartbreaking. Things were in a bad way at the shelter, and I was unable to lend a hand. I had to protect my little wild feral cat, Spooky. There was no choice; I was helpless.

The volunteers continued their watch at the shelter. I kept in close touch with them. A week and half into my hiatus, I received a call from Stephanie. The news was not good. One of the kittens came down with the disease and died. When it strikes a baby kitten, they go quickly. I could not help crying when I heard the news. Both Stephanie and I knew the other babies were in great danger. They were too young and vulnerable to fight this insidious disease.

As time went on, I received four more calls from Stephanie. I will never forget. One by one those beautiful kittens contracted the disease and passed away. It was horrible. There was only one kitten left from the litter. What an emotional time this was for all the volunteers. It must have been horrible for Linda, Stephanie and Wendy because they were doing everything in their power to save them.

I dreaded another phone call from Stephanie. Of course, there was another call. I prepared myself for the worst. It was wonderful news! Miraculously the last kitten from the litter of six survived! Stephanie named her Miracle. It was so appropriate. There was reason to celebrate.

During this dark period, Miracle the kitten, plus three other kittens from another litter, and two adult cats amazingly recovered from distemper, but not without a price. Every one of those animals has a condition called Ataxia, which was the direct result of the distemper and does damage to the nervous system. Those animals are perfectly healthy and will function normally, except they walk funny. They walk like a human who has had too much to drink. They look a little tipsy and lose their balance. It is the only way I can describe it. Once you know what the condition is from, you do not even notice it. It is not funny, but it is. One thing is for sure; they have a lifelong immunity to the disease and will never have to have a distemper shot again.

Stephanie, Wendy, Linda and all the volunteers who spent many hours caring for those sick animals put their heart and soul into their work and deserve so much credit. Why do we do it? Why do we bother? There is only one answer. We love animals and they need us. Our reward is all those animals, which survived distemper, were placed in good loving homes, and will be cared for the rest of their lives. Miracle and her mother were placed in a home together, which was really nice.

There seems always to be one crisis or another at the shelter. It is the nature of the beast. The degree of severity differs from very small to very big.

The distemper episode was big and handled calmly and responsibly. The shelter was closed for six weeks.

My second story, which also relates to not having a holding area, is a fun story. I was in the shelter doing adoptions, when I noticed some of the cats were sneezing continuously. It was a sure sign the beginning of an upper respiratory condition was about to spread throughout the shelter. We had just received two litters of kittens. Since we had no isolation area, we had to get those kittens out of the shelter fast. A couple of the kittens were so little, they still had to be bottle fed. They must not get sick! It is heart wrenching to see sick little kittens struggling to catch their breath because of stuffed noses. They have running eyes, constantly sneeze, and are unable to eat. There was no time to look for somebody to foster care the kittens. I stuffed all eight of them into a large cat carrier and brought them home with me. I kept them isolated in one of my upstairs bedrooms and made sure my five cats were unable to have any contact with them.

It is no secret a kitten is a lot of fun, and two kittens are double the fun. When there are eight kittens, you have a circus. They had the run of a very large bedroom all to themselves. Those normally active kittens were climbing on the beds, hiding under the beds, and running around everywhere. It was much better than being in their cage at the shelter. The bedroom was set up with three litter boxes, lots of kitten toys, kitty beds, and plenty of food. Kittens need a lot of protein to grow healthy and strong. I named the kittens after my grandchildren and children. Not only were the kittens having a ball, I was too. When my grandchildren and the kids in my neighborhood got wind that I had eight kittens, they came over every day to play with them. I loved seeing the children interact with the animals. It is important for them to respect all living creatures.

While doing adoptions at the shelter, individuals came in requesting kittens. I explained why I was foster caring the kittens at my home. If they were truly interested, I had them fill out an application. If I approved their application, I arranged to have them come to my home and pick out the kitten of their choice. Some adopters took two kittens. I encourage placing two kittens together, especially to people who work all day. They keep each other company. It is not good for any animal to be alone for long periods of time. I will not place any animal under those circumstances. It simply is not fair. Most animals are social and need human or non-human companionship. If an animal is alone a lot, they may develop separation anxiety, which means they could urinate, defecate, and do serious damage in the house. Many animals develop psychological problems. More and more people come into the shelter to adopt a friend and companion for their lonely pet. Pet owners are becoming aware of and beginning to understand how important it is for animals to have companionship too.

One by one the kittens were placed into wonderful homes with caring families. I will miss them very much. I will not miss the smell that hits you when you walked into the bedroom. Eight kittens in one bedroom produce a lot of feces. Kittens defecate more often than adult cats and the smell is strong. I loved having those little stinkers. They were so cute, cuddly, and fun.

The kittens were removed from the shelter in the nick of time. Not one of them got an upper respiratory infection. Unfortunately, all the cats in the shelter were sick with an upper respiratory infection and had to be treated.

Well, those are just two incidents why an isolation/holding area is a necessity. On rare occasions an animal may come in with ringworm. Ringworm is a fungus and not a worm which humans can contract. It is a perfectly round spot you treat with athlete's foot lotion. Many of the volunteers have caught it, including myself. To protect the public from catching it, we put a bright-colored caution sign on the front of the cage. We do not want anybody to put their fingers in to play and touch the animal. Strange as it may seem most people do not read the signs and do not heed our caution. I watch them very closely when they are in the shelter. Stray animals before they get their shots, wounded animals, sick animals, infected animals and recovering animals are all good reasons to go immediately into a holding area. It is like preventative medicine for the animals as well as humans. I cannot stress it enough. The powers that be were not thinking wisely when they decided not to include a holding/isolation area in the building plans. It is so frustrating!

The new shelter is far from being state of the art. We did not get everything we wanted on our wish list, but we got a shelter. For that we are thankful. I looked up the definition of the word shelter in the dictionary. The definition is: Something which affords protection or refuge, as from rain or attack; a place of refuge or safety. The building might not be state of the art; nevertheless, we are everything and more than the dictionary definition of a shelter. We are saving lives.

At last, the big day arrived. The day the shelter is moving to a new home. Moving all the animals in their cages will not be an easy task. Linda, with the help of Laura, the assistant animal control officer, is overseeing Operation

Noah's Ark. The town provided some manpower and town vehicles to help with the move.

Linda is one of those people who saves everything. The old shelter is filled with Linda's treasures; commonly known as a great deal of junk. You are not going to believe this, folks. She even saved a cat in her refrigerator freezer. Albie, an all white albino cat died while we were in the old shelter. I do not remember what he died from, but he died during the winter. The ground was frozen and was too difficult to dig a deep enough hole to bury poor Albie. It had to wait until spring. Albie was on hold in Linda's freezer until spring.

The new shelter is a lot smaller than the old one. Remember, we had the garage too. We hoped she would get rid of her stuff, but we knew Linda. She saved everything and transferred it with everything else to the new shelter.

I went to help out the day of the move. It was too overwhelming for me, so I decided to leave it to the younger volunteers. A day or two afterwards I went to the new shelter again to see if I could be of any help. Everything was done exactly the way Linda wanted it. Linda and Laura worked very hard to get everything organized.

When I opened the door and looked inside, I saw exactly what I expected. Cages with animals were on top of one another. Space was at a premium and every bit of it was being utilized. Empty walls were utilized with shelves for linens, cleaning supplies, food supplies, dishes etc. The place looked a lot like the little building at the old place with one exception. We now have dogs and cats in the same room. When you enter our new digs you are greeted with meowing and barking in unison. A smaller wooden desk replaced the large wooden desk she had in her old office, where all the cats hung out. It took up precious space, so it was put in the cellar with more of Linda's treasurers. The cellar came in handy for extra supplies for the animals. A key to the new shelter was presented to each and every volunteer.

Since the scuttlebutt the town was closing the shelter, it has been a rocky road. The volunteers never wavered, stood firm, and continued their valuable work caring for the animals. Throughout this whole episode needy animals came into the shelter, received quality care, and were eventually placed in good homes. Not one minute was wasted on feeling sorry for ourselves. The work never stops. We are like the Energizer Bunny commercial; it goes on and on and on.

We were back in business again without missing a beat; however, there was one caveat. The town officials want the numbers of animals at the shelter be limited to about twenty-five. They will allow some flexibility. It was a reasonable request. Now that I am in charge of adoptions, it will be up to me to work as hard as I can to keep that commitment.

A grand opening celebration for the new shelter was going to be planned, but not for a couple of months. We needed some time to get organized. The local paper announced the animal control/shelter moved to a new location and included our address. We did not have to plan a celebration. Many of the town residents and our supporters came by to see our new home. They brought gifts for the animals and good wishes. Even our non-supporters were curious to see the new shelter. It was a happy occasion. As soon as we settle into our new home, we will have an official open house.

Animals are amazing. They have adapted to their new lodgings very quickly. It was a quick adjustment for the volunteers as well. The future of the shelter looks very bright. It is a new beginning!

A few months have passed since Operation Noah's Ark. Both humans and non-humans have settled into our new digs. We have kept the numbers of animals in the shelter within range of our quota. Those days are gone, when there were up to sixty or seventy animals residing in the shelter. We had our open house, and it was a big success. Everything was going well, except up until recently. Linda had been absent frequently from her duties as animal control officer and head of the shelter for long periods of time on and off. I guess things were going too smoothly for us. It looks like we are going to have some problems. What would life be like at the shelter without some sort of a crisis?

Linda was out with a cold, then the flu, and now a thyroid condition. Frankly, I am still not sure what was wrong with her. Sometimes she was out for days and would come back. At times she was absent for weeks, then all of a sudden show up. Something was seriously wrong because this kind of behavior was totally out of character. The shelter was her life, and she would be there even in the middle of the night, if need be.

As leader of the shelter, Linda did not delegate certain duties; she had to do things her way, so she did them herself. Things were really backing up in her absence. At times there was a shortage of supplies and animals were not getting their veterinarian care on time. Things in general were just not getting done. Some of the volunteers were getting a little resentful of Linda, but nothing could discourage them from caring for the animals.

Not only was the shelter suffering from her absence, her first and foremost duty as animal control officer for the town of Marblehead was suffering as well. When the residents in town have need for the animal control officer, they want her on the spot. She was not available. The townspeople were becoming angry. The volunteers were at the shelter as usual doing their work. The townspeople would come into the shelter or call on the phone and give us hell because they were not getting results from animal control. We knew they needed to vent, and it was not directed to us personally. Believe me when I tell you, we took it but good. The volunteers were always polite and stood there and took the abuse. Why did we take it? We took it for two reasons. First, we did not want to get Linda in trouble. She was in enough trouble. Second, we wanted to protect the shelter. The circumstances were unusual and we did not want to jeopardize the shelter in any way. We never complained to town hall. As far as town hall knew, everything was running as smooth as silk at the shelter, and they were.

The volunteers began to rely more and more on Laura, the assistant animal control officer. An assistant ACO is a part-time position. Laura did the best she could under the circumstances; after all, at the time she had another part-time job and volunteered at the shelter during her free hours.

When I met Laura, she was in her thirties, very attractive, and kept very much to herself. She is laid back, sincere, unselfish, big hearted, dependable, and has a deep compassion for animals. She likes to work alone in the shelter, when it is quiet. She goes into the shelter at all hours to clean, walk dogs, medicate animals, does laundry, washes dishes, and whatever else has to be done. Laura is a behind the scenes kind of person, who gives her heart and soul to the animals and expects nothing in return.

When Laura had her first child, Justin, he practically grew up in the shelter. A baby was not going to keep Laura from her work at the shelter. Justin was growing up, so the dog cages served as a perfect play pen for him. When we had little kittens, she put Justin in their cage, and they played with each other. What a lucky little boy.

Laura had a second child, Brandon. It made it a little more difficult to do all the work she normally does at the shelter. Nothing seems to stop Laura; she still continues to do a great deal. When she walks the dogs, the children are with her in the carriage or one is on her back. Whenever Laura has free time day or night, she will care for things in the shelter. She takes home some of the neediest animals in the shelter. For example she took home five gorgeous kittens that were going to be put down because they tested positive for FeLV (feline leukemia). Their mother had it and died giving all her strength caring for her babies. The prognosis for those babies was not good. Laura wanted to give the kittens a quality life for as long as they had left. She is a very special person. The volunteers have great respect for her. This girl deserves so much credit, but she does not think so. The volunteers and the animals are so lucky to have her. She truly is a descendent of Dr. Doolittle.

There was no change in Linda's work behavior pattern. It was consistently bad. She would show up out of the blue one day and be absent for a couple of days or more. It would be an understatement to say something is seriously wrong. There is no doubt for a while there Linda was truly ill, but my personal feeling was she has a tremendous case of burn out.

Relief has come to the animal control department. The town hired another part-time assistant animal control officer. She was a volunteer at the shelter, a young girl in her twenties, who worked very well with animals. The extra help came at the nick of time for the Marblehead residents, and it was a great help to Laura. The job was getting done. Like magic there was much less aggravation in the shelter from the townspeople.

It was time for the volunteers to get their act together. The combination of the terrible episode of distemper and the absence of Linda has not helped the shelter. We can no longer tolerate neglect. We must take some action to introduce to the shelter new cleaning protocols for important health reasons. We must regroup and organize what tasks have to be done, while Linda is recuperating.

There is always somebody who rises to the occasion and is willing to take the responsibility. Remember Stephanie, who is on our medical team? She has taken on the job. She is a very detail-oriented person and has gone to a great deal of research to improve the current situation at the shelter. She is a stickler for detail.

The first thing we did was call an emergency meeting for all volunteers. I remember it well because the meeting was in my home. There was a large turnout. Stephanie conducted the meeting and did a tremendous job reorganizing the needs in the shelter. Her work was quite impressive. She had sought advice from several veterinarians and went to classes at Tufts University College of Veterinary Medicine for all her information. She was fanatic about details.

The object that was of the greatest importance at the shelter was to prevent contamination (to keep germs from spreading). A completely new cat care and cleaning protocol will have to be instituted. It will be a systematic way of cleaning safely and hygienically. Stephanie planned on personally going to the shelter every day and instructing the volunteers on the new protocols.

Stephanie also prepared a list of jobs that were delegated to the volunteers. They included:

1. Adoptions
2. Dog walking
3. Medical care
4. Fund raising
5. Grooming
6. Cage cleaning
7. Feeding
8. Laundry and general cleaning of the facility
9. Managing a database of hundreds of F.O.M.A.A. supporters
10. New volunteer training
11. *Paws and Claws* newsletter
12. Publicity
13. Purchase and delivery of necessary supplies
14. Socializing animals
15. Veterinary visits
16. Volunteer coordinating and scheduling
17. Volunteer meetings and communications
18. Friends of Marblehead's Abandoned Animals management

Every task was filled by a willing volunteer. I was given the title of adoption coordinator that evening, which pleased me very much. There was one more task left to be fulfilled. We voted unanimously to little by little get rid of the unnecessary junk that was accumulating in the shelter. Linda would never miss it.

The new protocols were put into effect. Stephanie was constantly policing the volunteers to make sure everything was being done correctly. She aggravated some of the volunteers because they did not like somebody looking over their shoulder. On the other hand, they forgave her because she was doing it for the welfare of the animals, and she was right. All the jobs that were delegated were getting done. We were eliminating a lot of junk too. The shelter was brought up to another level. We were a bunch of amateurs running a professional operation. There was always a lot to learn, and we must always keep an open mind. This life-saving enterprise has been a collaboration of the most wonderful, dedicated, unselfish, caring, sincere and kind people in the world. I cannot say enough about my volunteer friends.

I have a funny story to tell you about eliminating junk from the shelter. I was at the shelter, and it was rubbish day. Somebody had thrown out some of Linda's treasures. Out of the blue the shelter door swung open. It was Linda holding the articles that were put in the rubbish barrel that day. I stood there looking at her in amazement without saying a word. She had a high voice and said, "Why is this stuff in the rubbish? You never know when you might need it." Back into the shelter it came. I tried so hard to keep from laughing. That was typical Linda. She was a character.

Almost a year has passed since Linda's erratic behavior began. What we all suspected was going to happen eventually, happened. The town and Linda mutually agreed it was time for her to move on. It was official. Linda was no longer the Marblehead animal control officer and head of the shelter. It must have been a difficult time for her. The shelter was her creation, and she loves working with animals. I guess there is a time for everything. This may be the time for Linda to fulfill her dream to live in California.

Linda expressed to all the volunteers that she was indeed planning to go to California. Unfortunately, she ran into some differences with the town about her workman's comp. California was temporarily on hold until her legalities were resolved. While waiting for things to straighten out with the town, she started a dog-walking business to keep her going financially.

A little over one year had passed since we moved into the shelter and Linda was relieved of duty as the ACO. Almost another two years passed until the town came to an agreement and settled with Linda. California, here she comes!

There was one last piece of unfinished shelter business left for Linda to perform before leaving for the golden state. Albie the cat had been in her freezer for almost three years. She never got around to burying him. He was finally laid to rest in an undisclosed area.

The time had come for Linda to fulfill her dream to live in California. She packed all her belongings, hopped on a plane with her eleven animals and flew into the sunset for the west coast. Linda created the shelter and left a beautiful legacy for the volunteers to continue her work and save animals. A new chapter was about to begin for Linda, the volunteers, and the shelter.

WHOOPS!

Chapter 5

Who was going to be the next Marblehead animal control officer? That was the big question. Was it going to be a man or a woman? What changes were going to be made, if any? The shelter volunteers were all a buzz about it. Some of the volunteers were skeptical about a new animal control officer. Others welcomed a change. It really did not matter what the volunteers thought. We had no input in the selection process, even though we were directly affected. The town officials would interview and hire the person they thought best to handle the job.

While at home one day, I could not help thinking about the lucky person that will get to be the Marblehead animal control officer. Animal control in Marblehead has a rare, unique, and humane situation, compared to other communities. Most communities do not have a new animal control office building/shelter facility. Most communities do not have an organization like ours, which consists of thirty to forty volunteers who take care of the animals. The ACO in most communities picks up stray animals and brings them to a pound. The pound has to hold them for ten days. That is the law. If the animals are not claimed within the ten-day period, in most cases they are put down. The law varies in different communities. Some, if they are lucky, are brought to a rescue or a shelter like ours, and put up for adoption.

When the Marblehead ACO picks up a stray animal, there is a completely different scenario. He or she brings the animal to the shelter, the volunteers immediately start caring for the animal, and after ten days the animal if not claimed, it is put up for adoption. For any person in that line of work it is the most humane situation, plus, we are a no-kill shelter. How many ACO's have a facility they can call their own? How many ACO's have all that assistance? How many ACO's have the luxury of not having animals put down? The answer to all those questions is very few. This is why the next Marblehead animal control officer is very fortunate to have all these advantages.

I, and all the volunteers, realize without question the duties as animal control officer must always come first. We sincerely hoped and prayed this person, whomever it may be, believed in our cause at the shelter, had half of the desire the volunteers had to care and protect the animals, appreciated these deeply committed, hard-working volunteers, became a team player, and took pride in our new building. The right person could do wonders for our shelter and be a good animal control officer too. There was no question the volunteers would do everything in their power to welcome the new ACO into the shelter and make him or her as comfortable as possible.

I could not stop thinking about who will be the next animal control officer. When out of the blue a flash came to me! I thought of the current Swampscott animal control officer. She might like to apply for the position. Actually, she herself gave me the idea. While cruising around town in the Swampscott blue animal control van, the ACO would see me walking my dogs, park the van, and come out to talk to me. Our conversation was mostly about animals. The conversations always ended up with how unhappy she was with her job in town. She felt the town was not treating her well. I used to sympathize with her. I knew some of the politicians in town, and she had my sympathy. If she was so unhappy here in Swampscott, it may be a good opportunity for a job change.

I was remotely acquainted with the ACO but did not know her well. Not counting our sidewalk discussions, I dealt with her on only four other occasions. If you recall in the first chapter she helped me capture the homeless mother and her four kittens. I called her about a sick Canada goose that was on our local golf course. We captured it and got it some help. I was running one of my fun dog shows in Swampscott for a fund-raiser for animals. Being the Swampscott ACO, she had to be on the committee. Lastly, she asked me to go before town-meeting on her behalf and request a new ACO uniform. She was skunked in her old uniform and it smelled. I went before town-meeting, and she got her new uniform. That was the extent of our relationship.

I called the Swampscott ACO and suggested she think about replacing the ACO in Marblehead. The Marblehead ACO had already spoken to her about the job. The salary was much better, she would have an assistant ACO, and of course, the Marblehead Animal Shelter. There was no doubt the job had far more to offer her than her job in Swampscott. It was something to seriously consider.

A couple of weeks later the Swampscott ACO called me back to tell me she was going to apply for the job in Marblehead. I was glad. Anybody who volunteers at the shelter is a special person and is okay in my book. If she got the job, she had the advantage of being way ahead of the game. She was already familiar with our practices, protocols, and procedures at the shelter. She asked me to write a letter of recommendation for her. I never wrote one before, but I was more than happy to do it. My letter of recommendation was among others that she presented to the town of Marblehead with her application. All applicants would be interviewed one or more times. Now we all had to wait for the town to make their decision.

Meanwhile, everything was going extraordinarily well at the shelter. Things were running smoothly and efficiently. The volunteers, as usual, were giving the animals quality care and keeping the building in tiptop shape. That little facility means a lot to us, and we are very protective of it. It is our baby.

Several months had gone by and there was no word about a new animal control officer. Finally, the announcement came. The Swampscott ACO was selected. Almost all the volunteers were excited; however, some were skeptical and had bad vibes. The majority of volunteers had a positive attitude with high expectations.

Just a side note—when I heard the job was filled in Marblehead; I called another acquaintance of mine. She was currently a veterinarian technician, handles animals really well, and rescues pit bulls. I told her about the job in Marblehead being filled by the Swampscott ACO, and she could apply for the ACO job in Swampscott. My advice to her was not to delay and go right in to apply. She took my advice and got the job on the spot. I was happy for her.

I will never forget the new ACO's first day on the job. It was significant to me, and I remember it well. That particular day I had an appointment to bring five seven-week-old kittens to the animal hospital to be examined at ten in the morning. Unexpectedly, I got a call from my daughter, Tami. She wanted me to pick up my granddaughter, Haley, at school at eleven o'clock because it was an early release day. Tami had an appointment and might not be back on time to pick up my granddaughter. I was happy to oblige her. Time-wise it was going to be tight between bringing the kittens to the animal hospital and being on time to pick up Haley. If there is a will, there is a way. I got my husband, Harv, to go with me. If I ran late at the hospital, he could pick up our granddaughter and come back to get me. Everything was all set. We drove to the shelter early to pick up the kittens and make sure we were on time for the doctor's appointment. When I went into the shelter to get the kittens, the new ACO was there. I put all five kittens into one carrier, and told her where I was taking them. She wanted to go. I had no objection. The animal hospital was not far from the shelter. She drove the Marblehead red animal control van and met us there.

All five kittens were examined by the doctor, and got a good report. It is always good to hear that. We had just enough time to bring the kittens back to the shelter, and then pick up my granddaughter. It occurred to me, that the ACO may be going back to the shelter. It could save us a trip. She told me she was going back to the shelter anyway, but had to make a quick stop first. She told the girls at the desk, that she would be right back to pick up the kittens. It was puzzling why she did not put the carrier with kittens in the van, so she did not have to come back to the hospital at all. Oh well, I set the carrier on the bench in the waiting room at the hospital. We all drove off to our perspective destinations.

The day worked out well, I thought. At five o'clock that evening I received a call from the animal hospital. The new ACO had not picked up the kittens and the office closes at six. I cannot express how sick I felt at that moment. I was fuming! As I was hanging up the phone, I told them I was on my way to pick them up. I grabbed the keys to the car and made a quick exit out of the house. My husband is used to these quick exits. He knows it has to be an animal emergency.

While driving to the animal hospital, I could not help thinking about those five baby kittens left in a small carrier for seven hours. They had been without food and water. Those babies must be so hungry and thirsty. Baby kittens need to eat more often. There was no litter box in the carrier, so they must be lying in their urine and feces. My stomach was tied up in knots. What could have happened to the ACO? Was the animal hospital trying to locate her? Why didn't they call me sooner?

When I got to the hospital, the ACO drove up right behind me. I got out of my Jeep and looked through the glass door of the hospital. The carrier was where I left it. She came over to me with a big smile on her face giggling. She was all apologetic in her innocent childlike voice and said, "I forgot all about it. I will take them back to the shelter now."

The kittens will survive this experience. Unfortunately, it was totally unnecessary for them to have been put through this. The problem was I was put in a bad position. It was the ACO's first day on the job. We had to work together, and I wanted to have a good relationship with her. She deserved a good talking to, but the timing was all wrong for me to say something. I was angry and disappointed with her because she did not think she did anything wrong and it was funny. It was not funny to me. I was fuming. I turned around, went back into my Jeep, and drove home without saying a word. I never even went into the animal hospital.

All the way home, my thoughts were on today's events. I counted on the new ACO, and she did not follow through. She proved to be unreliable. Everybody deserves a second chance, so I was going to try very hard to put this incident behind me and not prejudge her. I prayed with all my heart this was not a precursor of what was yet to come. It was not a good beginning. I am not ready to say, "WHOOPS, I made a big mistake."

The next time I saw her, I was pleasantly surprised. I walked into the shelter and did not believe my eyes. She cleaned up the place, rearranged everything, and discarded a lot of junk. The volunteers were delighted. Remember that large desk from the old shelter, where the cats hung out? Well, she had it brought up from the cellar and put it right in the middle of everything. It took up a lot of valuable space. What is it about that large desk? It must make some sort of a statement. It is especially peculiar she had it put there because her office is officially in the police station.

The volunteers got another surprise that day. The lock on the shelter door was changed. Our present keys to the shelter were useless.

When Linda was ACO she was under the supervision of the Marblehead selectmen. That has changed. The new ACO was now under the direct supervision of the Marblehead police chief. The volunteers assumed it was the chief's decision to put a new lock on the shelter door and present the volunteers with only ten keys to the shelter. They were not just any keys; they were the type of key that cannot be duplicated. There were approximately between thirty and forty volunteers and ten keys. It certainly did not add up.

Everybody was curious why the chief suddenly changed the keys. We were told it was for security reasons. For almost two years we had been going in and out of that building at all hours without a problem. For two years, the word security was never mentioned. That building was so special to us. It was our baby and we took darn good care of it. The volunteers were shocked with this new revelation. It was really strange. We were all curious to know what or who was behind the chief's decision to change keys. It was just another obstacle we had to overcome. They sure didn't make it easy for us, but we love a challenge.

How do we handle the distribution of the ten keys? Who is going to get a key? How are the volunteers going to get into the shelter without a key? This is how it was resolved. Naturally, the ACO and the assistant ACO each got a key. Katie, the director of the shelter got a key. Our medical team each got a key. I received a key because I was the adoption coordinator and volunteer coordinator at the time. Dede and Nancy shared a key because they were the first cleaning team ever and were involved in many other things. Margo a dog walker was in and out of the shelter all the time walking dogs, and she also got a key. The other two keys belonged in the police station for the other volunteers. When a volunteer had to get into the shelter, they have to go to the police station, where there was a volunteer list, ask for the key to the shelter, sign their name and exact time on a sheet, and then they would be given a key. When they were through at the shelter, they brought back the key to the police station and on the same sheet put in the exact time the key was returned. It did not matter if you were at the shelter for five minutes or five hours. It was so inconvenient, but we had no choice. You might think this business with the keys would turn off some of the volunteers—no way! The commitment to the shelter by these exceptional human beings was stronger than ever. We were wondering and waiting for the next bomb to fall. Whatever it was, we would deal with it.

The ACO often called me at home. She was new and needed to learn the ropes. I wanted her to know I was in her corner, and she had my total support. When she asked for advice, I advised her as though she were my daughter. It was also for the good of the shelter. She constantly told me she preferred being out in the field. To be out in the field for an ACO is to ride around town in the animal control van looking for humans and critters breaking animal control laws. She was new and I think she felt insecure dealing with the volunteers.

Two or three months passed since the ACO was on the job, when an unfortunate incident occurred at the shelter. Many individuals come to the shelter to volunteer or want to help out in some way. Occasionally, a person, who wants to help us, needs our help more. Let me explain. A family brought their daughter, who was in her teens, to the shelter to see if she could volunteer. She wanted to help the animals. Their daughter looked like she was a little slow.

The shelter is a wonderful setting for this girl. Animals do not care what you look like, what religion you are, or what color your skin is. Animals only see the good inside of a human being. They ask for so little and give so much. It will be a blessing to allow this young girl to volunteer, so we signed her on. We arranged for her to walk dogs on Sunday mornings, providing another volunteer accompanies her. Some dogs are more difficult to walk than others. For her protection, as well as the dogs', it was important somebody be with her.

The arrangement was working out well until one Sunday morning. This particular Sunday the young girl was dropped off at the shelter, she went into the shelter, and her companion had not arrived as yet. The Sunday morning cleaning team was diligently working caring for the cats and their cages. The cleaning team knew the girl because she routinely came to walk the dogs on Sunday morning. I am not sure if they were not paying attention, or if they were unaware she needed a companion.

There was only one dog at the shelter to walk. It was Gemma, a black brindle and white Staffordshire pit bull. She was under a year old and had been in the shelter for several months. Little Gemma had never really known another home. The volunteers were quite attached to her. We screen people very carefully. We wanted to place Gemma, but the right person had not shown any interest in her as yet.

The young girl's companion still had not arrived, so she took it upon herself to walk the dog. She took Gemma out of her cage, put on her leash, and proceeded to go out the door. Just as she went out the door a neighbor, who lived across the street, was walking his two Great Danes to the path next to the shelter. Gemma spotted the Great Danes, got territorial, pulled away from the girl, and went after the Danes. A skirmish ensued. It was a terrible scene. Another neighbor across the street doing yard work heard the horrible sounds of the tussle. He ran over to help, grabbed Gemma's leash, and pulled her away. Just as it suddenly started, it was suddenly over. The Great Danes did not get a scratch on them. Their owner was not that lucky, he got bitten on the leg. He had to go to hospital right away to get it taken care of. Little Gemma was brought back into the shelter. She was not hurt.

This unfortunate incident was not good. It was not good at all. The volunteers were worried. We were afraid the man who got hurt may sue the town, and mostly, we feared for little Gemma. Apparently, there was another incident with Gemma before this one, which I was completely unaware of. This was not good. When the news reached the volunteers, they were speechless and an eerie silence came over shelter. We all knew it, but could not say it. Gemma's life was in jeopardy. It was now in the hands of the police chief to determine Gemma's fate.

The volunteers could not be idle. We had to be ready with a plan to get Gemma into another rescue or shelter. It is uncanny in times of need, the right person at the right time steps up to the plate to take on a difficult job. On this occasion it was a brand new volunteer, Deborah. I call her Deb.

Deb and her husband John were new to the community. On their second day in Marblehead, a neighbor where they live told them a sad story about two Siamese cats. The cats were at our shelter very sick and refusing food. They were heartbroken because their owner had Alzheimer's disease, and had to go into a nursing home, so her family brought the cats to the shelter. That was all Deb and John had to hear. They came to see me at the old shelter their third day in town. I took them into the garage, where the cats were. Missy was lying on top of BJ, as if to protect him. They were so weak. They had pneumonia. Missy lifted her little head and said, "Meow." That did it! Deb and John returned the next day and adopted Missy and BJ. They nursed them back to health.

Not long after they adopted the Siamese cats, Deb signed up to volunteer at the shelter. It was a great way to meet people and get involved with something she loves very much, animals. She became a very active volunteer.

When Deb got wind of the incident with Gemma, she immediately went to work on her computer. She searched and searched for a rescue or shelter for Gemma. She got in touch with several all over the country, but there was nothing available for one reason or another. We don't want just any place; we want a good quality rescue for the dog. At last she found the right place. It was a pit bull rescue in College Station, Texas. She emailed the rescue and told them everything about Gemma, including the incident she had with the Danes. Deb was in close contact with the rescue in Texas. While waiting patiently for an answer if Gemma was going to be accepted, Deb also contacted the police, veterinarians, and other pet-related institutions in the vicinity of College Town. She wanted to make doubly sure the dog was going to a reputable place. Everyone spoke well of the rescue. Finally, after a couple of weeks, the rescue emailed Deb. They would take Gemma. We were all excited.

We arranged for everything. The volunteers were going to chip in and purchase an airline ticket to fly Gemma to Texas. Coincidentally, one of our volunteers had family living in the area and was willing to pick Gemma up from the airport and bring her to the rescue. Everything was all set. All we needed was the okay from the chief.

We waited with bated breath for the chief's decision on Gemma's destiny. The word finally came to us. It was horrible. She had to be put down, and it was not negotiable. That was that. The chief did not make his decision without seeking advice from veterinarians. He weighed everything and came to this decision.

Words cannot express how crushed the volunteers were. We loved little Gemma and were very attached to her. All of us believed without a doubt, if Gemma were another breed of dog, she would have been given another chance. It was so hard to be in the shelter with little Gemma knowing her fate. Thank goodness Gemma was unaware of what was happening around her. She was her usual self, a happy-go-lucky pup.

The awful day came for Gemma to be destroyed. It was a black day for the shelter, and one we will never forget. The ACO offered to take Gemma to the animal hospital, but Katie would not hear of it. Katie used to walk and care for Gemma, and she loved Katie. I do not know where Katie got the courage to take Gemma to the animal hospital and stay with her till it was over. I know it was emotionally draining. Later that afternoon Katie called me, and we cried on the phone to each other for two hours. We kept asking ourselves, "What could we have done different to prevent this horrible thing from happening? We are just going to have to work harder and learn from our mistakes." Some of the volunteers were critical of the new ACO because she was not forthcoming and showed little support to save Gemma throughout this episode. That might have been so, but I also felt we, the volunteers, failed Gemma. We got too complacent and did not work hard enough to get her into another shelter that specialized in finding her breed the right home. This picture is of little Gemma.

The neighbor who was bitten by the dog was reimbursed by the town for his medical bills and the two days he missed work to recuperate from his wounds. He is still walking his dogs to the path by the shelter.

Individual volunteers and volunteer teams work at the shelter on different days of the week at different times of the day. We rarely get together in a group, unless we have a volunteer meeting. On many occasions we make excuses just to get together. Somebody found out my birthday was coming up. The volunteers used that as an excuse to plan a get-together. Of course, I was delighted. We have a ball at these gatherings. We talk and talk about what we all have in common and love, the animals. This evening was no different, when out of the blue, one of the volunteers was critical of the ACO. Another volunteer chimed in then another and it went on from there. It seems as though they all shared an unrelated unfavorable experience with the ACO and wanted to share it with the other volunteers. These volunteers want nothing but the best for the shelter and intended no harm.

I sat there listening to my friends for whom I have the utmost respect. I started to cringe and wanted to crawl under the table. If you remember, I sent in a letter of recommendation on the ACO's behalf. Not to get into a lot of minutia, it appeared she had been unreliable on several occasions, careless in many ways, did not use good judgment, lacked common sense, and showed little consideration for the volunteers. Her actions were counter productive to our protocols, policies, and safety procedures in the shelter. Listening to my colleagues, I started to reproach myself. To this day, whenever she does something wrong, the volunteers kid me about that letter of recommendation. Naturally, it is all in good fun. It certainly had not been a good start. Is it time for me to say WHOOPS?

The ACO continued to call me at home. I never mentioned to her what I learned at the get-together that night. The next time we spoke she said in her innocent childlike wining high voice, "I don't think the volunteers like me. I want to be out in the field." I was still hoping she would take some good advice, so I continued to counsel her. Maybe I was naïve, and was optimistic for better things to come; however, I was talking to deaf ears. The calls I was receiving from her were fewer and fewer until there were none. She did not want to hear what I had to say. As time went on, things were not improving. The volunteers were getting impatient with her, including myself. There were personality clashes, and the atmosphere at the shelter was unsettling. Something had to be done.

I cannot recall how it came about, but the town manager announced he was going to have a meeting with the police chief, the ACO, and the volunteers. The purpose of the meeting was to define our roles at the shelter. Possibly other issues would be discussed too. This was a positive start to help straighten out our internal problems in the shelter. There was nothing unusual for an organization or business to have these kinds of problems.

The meeting was called for during the day and most of the volunteers worked and were unable to attend. Those of us who did attend quickly discovered we were ill prepared. The volunteers strongly felt the town manager and the police chief did not have a clue what we were trying to convey. Maybe we did not articulate our concerns well enough. It was very hard to get our points across with the ACO sitting there. We found ourselves in a rather awkward situation because we did not want to hurt the ACO's feelings. We expressed ourselves delicately. I think the town manager and the police chief knew that. It was considerate of them to take the time from their busy schedules to meet with us. They also mentioned there would be another meeting. When we left the meeting, the volunteers sensed both the town manager and the police chief thought we were a bunch of fanatic whackos.

Katie and I wanted to personally express our concerns to the town manager before the next meeting. He was very gracious and gave us some time one morning. During our discussion, somehow, it came to his attention the ACO office/shelter telephone was out of order for three weeks. He got out of his chair right on the spot, asked for the telephone number to the ACO office/ shelter, dialed the number, and sure enough it was out of order. He was noticeably angry and for good reason. The animal control office is there to serve the Marblehead community, and it is up to the town manager to make sure all departments in town run efficiently. He made another call while we were sitting there. To whomever he was speaking to in a stern voice he said, "I want a new phone in the shelter today!" and hung up. This was precisely the sort of disruptive kinds of things that were happening at the shelter that we were trying to convey. He did not say anything one way or another, but he understood. He came back to the table and started to kid me about my letter of recommendation for the ACO, which he had on file. I guess I will never live that down. All I can say is WHOOPS!

The animal control/shelter is in a town building. The ACO works for the town and in a sense that building is in her care. The up-keep of the building, such as the telephone, plumbing, lighting, garbage, etc. should be taken care of by the town through her. I only wish it were that simple. More often than not it does not get taken care of until it is out of control. The volunteers are very resourceful and will try to fix whatever is in their power. For example: We were having another problem with the telephone. A new volunteer went out and purchased a new telephone. She solved the problem like magic; otherwise it might have taken a while before it got done. Another example is fluorescent light bulbs burn out and have to be changed. Days and weeks could go by with poor lighting in the shelter, especially at night. The volunteers have important work to do, time is of the essence, and we cannot wait for someone to get around to it. Two of our volunteers came into the shelter with new fluorescent bulbs. They had had it with the lighting conditions in the shelter and were going to replace the bulbs by themselves. I begged them not to do it because it was too dangerous. The ceilings are pitched and extremely high. They needed a tall ladder, which we did not have. It was really a job for a couple of men who work for the town. They were determined, so one of the volunteers stood on a table. The first try was a disaster. A bulb fell and glass shattered all over the place. They tried and tried and finally, got the job done. Thanks to those two volunteers we had light! It was difficult working in the dark.

Actions speak louder than excuses. Now when the light bulbs burn out and the garbage starts to accumulate in front of the shelter, we call on another devoted volunteer, Jane. She used to be a dispatcher at the police station. She knew how to get things taken care of sooner than later. If something had to be done at the shelter and done right, you could always count on the volunteers. They are so special and amazing how they adapt to every new situation.

Katie and I had the opportunity to address some of our concerns to the town manager. It was only right the police chief hear them too. A side meeting was arranged at Katie's house. The chief, Katie, Candi and I were present. As adoption coordinator and volunteer coordinator, I wanted to address an annoyance about the condition of the shelter when I arrive at four P.M. to do adoptions and when the cleaning teams arrive after working all day long. To give the chief a better insight of my annoyance, I wanted to tell him about an experience I just had two days prior to this meeting.

I proceeded to tell him I went into the shelter last Monday to do adoptions. The ACO is usually gone by the time I arrive. This particular Monday she had not left yet. I walked into the shelter and there was blood smeared everywhere. It was on the floor, the cabinets, the walls, the dog cages, the doors, the washer, the dryer, and on the furniture. We had a lovely stray English setter who had a sore on the tip of his tail. He constantly wagged his tail, opened the sore, and it started to bleed. Whatever his tail touched while he was out of his cage, there was blood on it. I suggested having liquid bandage put on his wound. As she was going out the door and leaving for the day, she mentioned liquid bandage was put on the dog's tail a couple of days ago. Thinking to myself, *Is that the end of it? She should at the minimum make an effort to get the dog another treatment or try to solve the problem another way!*

Well, here I was with no exaggeration left in the middle of a bloody mess. The shelter was in no condition to receive the public and was due to open in fifteen minutes. It was an understatement to say I was fuming. Quickly, I rolled up my sleeves, got out the bucket, and started scrubbing the place. It is not nice to leave a mess like this for somebody else to do. If I didn't do it, the cleaning team would come in tonight, and they would have to do it. They had about two or three hours' worth of work ahead of them, and they did not need any more. It was not fair.

The next day I went into the shelter at the same time. The ACO already left for the day. I walked in and the place was worse than the day before. I was steaming! The shelter looked like a slaughter house. We, the volunteers, are not her lackeys! At that very moment the chief instantly interrupted me. He was angry with me for being so blunt. While telling him the story, I was reliving my experience and getting angry all over again. Yes, he was angry with me, but understood what I was trying to communicate to him. True, I am no diplomat; however, I am honest, dependable, a no-nonsense person, and considerate of my fellow volunteers. The chief may call my comments blunt; I call it straight talk.

The ACO is in and out of the office during the day. When she is there, she lets the animals out of their cages. I have no objection to that. The animals are stuck in their cages, and they need to get out and exercise. I strongly objected when I discovered she was letting cats out of their cages who have not had their shots or been tested for FIV and FeLV. She was integrating them with cats that had all their medical work done. Katie and I discussed it, and she was advised this was a health issue, and not to integrate cats, unless they were checked out by the vet. It was careless of her, and she should have known better. While the animals are out of their cages, on many occasions they trash the place. I do object to leaving volunteers the additional work. She should be more considerate of the volunteers and clean up after the animals trash the place while she is in the shelter. It is not right to burden the cleaning teams with her mess and for the public to walk into a filthy shelter. The volunteers are not there for the ACO; they are there for the animals. This also was what I was trying to convey to the chief. Not a very good start. All I can say is, "WHOOPS!"

The second volunteer meeting with the town manger and the police chief was rapidly approaching. This time we were going to be prepared. Two very committed volunteers, Deb and Stephanie, prepared a comprehensive report about Friends of Marblehead's Abandoned Animals. It was an enormous effort. They put many long hours of work into it.

A few days before the meeting Deb had to go on a business trip to New Jersey with her husband. The report needed some last minute touches, so she took it with her to New Jersey. A day before the meeting she discovered she was not going to make it back in time for our meeting. She called me to tell me about her dilemma. We needed that report for the meeting tomorrow. I had a fax machine, so she went down to the lobby of the hotel, where she was staying and looked for a fax machine. She found one and faxed page by page to me. It was a wonderful piece of work. She also advised me to go to Staples and have copies made for everyone at the meeting, including putting a jacket on every copy. It would look more professional. The morning of the meeting I went to Staples and had fifteen copies collated with a green jacket put on.

The title on the front of the jacket in black letters was, **FRIENDS OF MARBLEHEAD'S ABANDONED ANIMALS**, and under that, **PROCESS SUMMARY.** On the inside there was everything you needed to know about the shelter in detail.

That afternoon the volunteers convened at Abbot Hall in the conference room of the town manager. I remember it so vividly. The ACO was sitting between the police chief and the town manager at one end of the conference table, and the volunteers were sitting at the other end. I passed out a process summary to everyone at the meeting. I watched everyone perusing it. Since I had been to the prior meeting, I wanted to give the other volunteers an opportunity to express themselves. I had my chance to vocalize, so it was just listen and observe time for me.

We were well into the meeting when from nowhere the ACO turned to the chief to tell him, "They, the volunteers, take back animals that were placed from the shelter." She turned to the town manager and told him the same thing. We were not even on that subject when she brought it up. It came out of the blue. It was the manner in which she told them that was disturbing. It was like she was tattling on us, or playing gotcha. We were not doing anything wrong or keeping a big dark secret. Right there on page two in the process summary under F.O.M.A.A. principles in black and white for everybody to see it said, "We maintain a return policy for unsuccessful adoptions." The policy is a good one. Circumstances can change in one's life, and one can no longer care for the animal. We want the animal back. We put so much into our animals to get them adopted in the first place; certainly, we are not going to turn our back in their time of need. What are we there for? It was something that only happens periodically. Fortunately, nothing came out of her announcement.

I was no longer focused on the meeting. The ACO's comments were astonishing to me; especially when she adopted an adult calico cat from the shelter and returned her some months later. She also adopted a dog from the shelter and brought him back. She never ceased to amaze me. It had not been a very good start and called for a double WHOOPS! WHOOPS!

The meeting was over and the volunteers left the conference room. We converged in the lobby to talk. All of us were astounded by the ACO's announcement about our animals coming back to the shelter. The big question was did we accomplish anything? I guess time would tell.

The next round I personally had with the ACO was a doozey. It was deja vu. Eight o'clock in the morning I received a call from the vet's office. They told me the ACO had an appointment to bring in a cat for shots, and she had not shown up. They tried calling the assistant animal control officer and Katie, but they were not around, so they called me. I was still in my nightgown preparing breakfast for my dogs. I make eggs for them every morning because it is good for their coats. Normally, I would have told the vet to forget it, but the cat in question was going to be placed that afternoon. If the cat does not get the shots, it cannot be placed. There was no need to disappoint the adopters, so I quickly changed my clothes and ran out of the house. The cat got the shots and was placed that afternoon.

The medical team usually handles these things. Someone must have been unable to keep the appointment, so they arranged for the ACO to do it. My mother taught me a long time ago never to be late for an appointment. If I was going to be late, I should call to let them know. If I could not make an appointment, I should call and cancel or try to arrange for somebody else to handle it. I taught my daughters the same basic rules, and hopefully they will teach my grandchildren. What does it take to make a phone call to say you cannot make it? The veterinarian was running a business and could have filled that slot with another patient.

Needless to say, I was annoyed with the ACO for a change. This was not the first time this had happened. On the contrary, it had happened on many occasions. I decided to talk to Katie about it. She was the liaison between the ACO and the volunteers. She was away in New Hampshire. To let this incident wait until Katie got back would have little impact. It should be called to the ACO's attention, so I called her. I knew it was not my place to call her, but I did it anyway. There were things I had to get off my chest. She answered the phone, we started to talk, and it did not take long before we were engaged in a heated quarrel. It was an opportunity to relieve some of my frustrations. She was no shrinking violet. You could tell she had been through this before. We both let each other have it, and just like that it was over.

Nobody likes to get into confrontations, but it is not good to let things fester either. There had been a build-up of one thing after another. To tell you the truth I felt cleansed.

The ACO was in close contact with the police chief and would waste no time to tell him about our altercation. I called the chief to tell him my interpretation of the story. He listened to me and was very understanding. When I got off the phone with him, I do not know what came over me. I got into a fit of crying and could not stop. It was not because of my argument with her; it was because the shelter deserved better. She was the complete antithesis of what we hoped for.

There is so much to do for the animals at the shelter we do not have time to dwell on negatives. The volunteers are the most forgiving human beings you will ever meet. If we get angry over something, it is only temporary. We get over it until the next time. No matter how mad we get we treat each other civilly. It is an understatement to say it had been a rocky start between the new ACO and the volunteers. This called for an extra-large WHOOPS!

There was a time forgiving was not so easy. The volunteers' sacred purpose to the animals and the shelter was sadly put to the test. The next three events I tell you about will explain.

The first event was about our medical team, Candi and Stephanie. I have already told you in a previous chapter how deeply committed these caregivers are. The animals at the shelter are so lucky to have them. Trust me when I tell you the animals at the shelter get better care than some human beings.

The ACO and the medical team were not getting along at all. There were definitely personality problems. Things were not going well. The ACO started to question some of the medical practices of the medical team. She was going back to the police chief with her disclosures. God only knows what she was telling him. It must have been pretty serious stuff because he called a special meeting at the police station. He invited the veterinarians from both practices in town, Katie, the ACO, and only Candi from our medical team. Stephanie was conspicuously uninvited.

When the meeting was over, Katie and Candi told me what was discussed. They talked about traditional medicine and alternative veterinary medicine. What is alternative veterinary medicine? The natural holistic approach, homeopathy, chiropractic, message, and acupuncture are some alternatives in veterinary medicine. Many veterinarians have gone back to school to learn alternative methods. Some veterinarians who are already established hire associate veterinarians with both traditional and alternative medicine backgrounds, so their practice can offer their patients choices. The public is getting educated and aware of these different approaches for their animals' health. They love their pets and are willing to go to great lengths to get them well. A holding area in the shelter was also discussed. The vets agreed the shelter should not be without an isolation area for obvious health reasons. They were emphatic about that. I was glad to hear that was mentioned. Other unimportant things were discussed, too. Katie and Candi did not have a good feeling coming out of that meeting. They felt something was not right.

Well, they were right. A couple of weeks after the meeting, the chief sent an official letter to the shelter regarding the medical team. The medical team was not allowed to practice alternative medicine of any kind. The ACO was going to oversee the medical practices at the shelter. This was insulting! It was a lack of respect for these dedicated people. Candi was trained in homeopathic and holistic medicine. Stephanie was trained in holistic medicine and was a certified nutrition herbalist. They had taken our animals to the best traditional (conventional) veterinarians in our area. On occasion when traditional medicine did not help, they would take the animal to the best veterinarians for alternative medicine. They would never administer any medical without consulting and the approval of a professional veterinarian first. They had also been taught and counseled by vets and other professionals. Nothing about their work was reckless or uncaring.

Do you think Candi or Stephanie would do anything to harm the animals? Of course not! They have saved so many lives, and spared animals from pain. They took sick animals to their homes and nursed them until they were well enough to go back to the shelter. They assisted with many births. When it was merciful to put an animal down, they were the ones holding the animal till it was over. It was so unfair to treat these good people this way. If this was about alternative medicine, it was pretty ignorant. Was it about alternative medicine? What was this really all about? To the best of our knowledge, the ACO did not have any medical training at the time she took the job, which made no sense.

When this decision was made by the powers that be, did they give any thought about the quality care the animals were receiving? Did they think about the increase in costs for the shelter? Candi and Stephanie were trained in giving fluids, administering insulin, worming, etc. Did they think about the consequences of their actions? Candi and Stephanie between them volunteered fifteen to twenty hours a week at the shelter. Who was going to pick up the slack in the absence of the medical team? Was it going to be the ACO? I think not! If we were lucky, we might be able to count on her to do meds one morning a week, if we were lucky. What about the other mornings, afternoons, evenings, weekends and holidays? I will tell you who would fill the void, the volunteers, of course! The job had to get done, and the volunteers would have to pull together to do it. It was going to be quite a task for the volunteers to replace the immense job that medical team did and the quality of their work. Knowing the volunteers as I do, they would come through and get the job done.

It was no surprise Stephanie, unhappily, decided to leave the shelter because she felt she could not give quality care to the animals that she loved so much. She felt it was unfortunate that the animals were denied effective healing treatment—alternative and traditional. You could not blame her for leaving. It was difficult enough to be treated so poorly, but how could you work under these conditions with somebody looking over your shoulder all the time? Candi could not bring herself to break ties completely with the shelter, so she stayed on in a different capacity. That was a sad time for the animals, the volunteers, and the shelter. What is ironic is it is not unusual for today's excellent medical team to take an animal to an alternative medical veterinarian for another opinion, if it is deemed necessary. We also give calming essence (a rescue remedy) to animals when they come into the shelter fearful and stressed out. You can purchase a variety of different kinds of remedies at many veterinarian hospitals and health stores.

"What was this all about?" There were many occasions when volunteers got angry and had differences with each other, including myself. We'd have it out, get it off our chests, and move on. We are a cohesive group of volunteers. Never ever would we forget the most important reason why we are there—the animals, of course. The animals are depending on us. There is no way we could be that selfish to let our personal feelings stand in the way of the animals' well-being. I am no longer going to jokingly say, WHOOPS!

The second event I want to tell you about was right around the corner. Traditionally the first week in May the shelter celebrated National Pet Week by having an Adoptathon. The North Shore Animal League and Petsmart sponsored it that year. During the Adoptathon, it gave us an opportunity to adopt as many animals as we could to good, responsible people. We stayed open the whole weekend, did a lot of advertising, and offered animal-related promotions. One year two vet techs volunteered to do free nail-cutting for people's pets. When a cat was adopted, they would receive a free litter box with litter, and a cat toy, food samples, and all sorts of coupons. We had a raffle with terrific animal-related prizes like a free grooming, or a weekend free to care for your animals while you go away. The volunteers prepared a succulent refreshment table for the public. Every year the same people came in for the refreshments and had no intentions to adopt an animal. The Adoptathon has proved to be very successful.

This particular year it was decided to bring in some animals from a local pound and try to get them adopted. These poor animals were going to be put down if they were not claimed or adopted. Our shelter is a no-kill shelter, and we want to save as many animals as we can. Several of the pound animals were placed during the Adoptathon weekend. It was great! There was enough room in our shelter for the pound animals that were not placed. We never would have had the heart to send them back to the pound.

One of the dogs from the pound that was not placed was a handsome liver color lab/pit bull cross. She was under a year old and her name was Lucy. We have successfully placed pit bulls and pit bull mixes. The adoption coordinators take extra pains screening adopters for all dogs. When it comes to this particular breed, we take extra pains to screen the adopters thoroughly. Unfortunately for Lucy the right person for her had not come along. As a result, her stay in the shelter was a little longer than expected. We started talking about sending her to another rescue/shelter, where she would have a better chance to get adopted. The sad experience with Little Gemma was still fresh in our mind, and we wanted to avoid a similar happening. Getting Lucy out of our shelter and into another rescue was in the works.

Our search for another rescue for Lucy was very successful. As a matter of fact there were a couple to choose from. We were delighted and wanted to transfer her as soon as possible. Suddenly, our hopes to transfer her were dashed. Ringworm was discovered in our shelter. Ringworm is a fungus and not a worm. Incubation period for ringworm is between four days to four weeks. Symptoms are generally a circular inflamed patch from which hair is lost and crusting develops. If Lucy caught it, it would delay transferring her to another rescue.

An animal must have come into the shelter with the parasite and it was not detected. If our medical team were still with us, it would have been spotted immediately. The volunteers were totally unaware of what was happening. By the time we discovered it, ringworm had spread throughout the shelter, including the volunteers. It was my first experience having it. Ringworm can be treated, but it takes weeks for it to go away. Lucy was going to be with us a while longer because she contracted it too. She would be transferred when she was completely cleared of the parasite. If we sent her to another rescue now, she would contaminate all the other animals in there.

Laura and Katie were in charge of the dogs at the shelter. They coordinated the dog-walking volunteers, placed the dogs, and saw to all their needs. Coincidentally both Laura and Katie planned to go out of town at the same time, which was unusual. Prior to leaving, they arranged for Lucy's care in their absence. Not long after they left, I received several calls from the volunteer dog walkers. They all wanted to know where Lucy was. I had no idea. They told me there was a note on the cage saying, "Lucy went to another shelter." I was flabbergasted because her ringworm treatment was not over and another shelter surely would not want to contaminate their animals. It was puzzling! The next day Dede, a perky, kind, terrific person, a dedicated volunteer, the best friend animals could ever have, and definitely a relative of Dr. Doolittle called me with awful news. Her voice was quivering, when she told me Lucy was destroyed. All I could say was, "Why?"

The ACO went to walk Lucy, and claimed Lucy allegedly bit her. She claimed it was not the first time it happened. A friend of the ACO was with her at the time. The ACO brought Lucy back to the pound, and had her put down. Just like that. I never had a problem walking Lucy. Other volunteers walked and handled Lucy and never complained of a problem. We do not condone biting, but this whole incident was peculiar. Out of respect to the volunteers the ACO should have notified one us.

The news spread very quickly to all the volunteers. The volunteers were sick about it. Lucy had less than a couple of weeks left at the shelter. Was the bite deliberate or an innocent accident? If a dog is in a cage for any length of time, it can be stressful. When they are let out of the cage, they get so excited and start jumping. Lucy was always so excited coming out of her cage; she might have accidentally caught her hand with her teeth.

An emergency volunteer meeting was called. It was too late to help Lucy, but we felt we had to do something. We were sick. It was voted unanimously to send a letter to the police chief expressing our feelings on the matter. Here is a copy of the letter.

August 14, 1998

Chief Palmer
Marblehead Police Department
11 Gerry Street
Marblehead, MA 01945

Dear Chief Palmer:

On behalf of F.O.M.A.A., we would like to express our dissatisfaction regarding our most recent incident involving the euthanasia of Lucy, who was being cared for at the Marblehead animal control office.

It is our understanding that all pending cases for euthanasia are to be communicated through our liaison, Katie VanDorpe. It appears that no one at the shelter was informed of the alleged attack that the ACO had claimed or the undeserving fate that lay ahead for Lucy. There was no mention of this situation to any volunteers but merely a misleading note left on the cage stating that Lucy had gone to another shelter. The real truth was that Lucy was being put to death. If the note left on the cage was meant to deceive the volunteers, we find that to be truly inappropriate and unacceptable. What we can't understand is that there were no other incidences involving Lucy that would suggest her to be a vicious dog. Those of us who truly knew Lucy know she was not a vicious dog. Lucy was merely a young pup with a lot of pent-up energy and no obedience training. We would assume that the ACO would have taken that into consideration, when evaluating Lucy's behavior and determining her destiny. There was no reason why Lucy had to be destroyed. The truth is that some animals may deteriorate or become dysfunctional when left in a small cage for too long. That is why we have found it beneficial to find a temporary foster home for animals like Lucy. Unfortunately for Lucy, we could not place her in a temporary foster home due to her ringworm. As you are aware, the shelter is currently experiencing an outbreak of ringworm. Perhaps the ringworm outbreak could have been contained more effectively and treated properly if the medical team protocol was still in force. Under your request that responsibility was delegated to the ACO.

What is most interesting about this case is that Lucy was destroyed while both Katie and Laura were out of town. Could it be that this deception was intentionally done behind our backs? It seems we are revisiting the same situation that we have faced in the past. It is unfortunate that our animal control officer can't even give the volunteers the respect and decency of allowing us to say goodbye to the animals that we have cared for and loved so much! There is no excuse for the lack of respect that we seem to have to endure time and again. We as volunteers put our hearts and souls into the care and well-being of these animals both physically and financially. We are not asking for much and deserve some consideration. We were mortified, discouraged, and saddened by this episode, which could have easily been prevented if only given the chance. All we are asking is that the volunteers be given proper notification and an opportunity to network our resources when it comes to matters such as this. We need not remind you that we never had these particular problems in the past. The recent events at the animal control office, the euthanasia of Lucy, and the ringworm outbreak would appear to be a direct result of the reassignment of duties. We feel these matters, among others, warrant further discussion, preferably amongst the respective parties.

We would appreciate a response to this letter via our liaison, Katie.

Sincerely,

F.O.M.A.A. Volunteers

Well, that sums up everything. The police chief received the letter. He never communicated back to us. The ACO was furious with all us for sending it. She was not very popular with some of the volunteers. Our high expectations of the ACO turned out to be no expectations. When there are no expectations, there are no surprises of what may happen next. Nothing is left to be said about this disturbing matter.

The third and last event in this chapter was a deep blow to all the volunteers. The town officials announced they were going to move the ACO out of her office at the police station, and build her one in the shelter. The news was so depressing, it broke our hearts. The area we dreamed of eventually utilizing for an isolation area for the animals was going to be her office. What a blow! Sometimes you get the feeling the town is trying to discourage Friends of Marblehead's Abandoned Animals. We had all those meeting with the officials and accomplished nothing.

I have elaborated throughout this book on the enormous importance of an isolation area in the shelter. It is so vital. The veterinarians in town highly recommended it. Any literature about shelters will tell you it is a must. The reason is so simple—Health. Health reasons for the animals, the volunteers, and the public who visit the shelter. Frankly it is a no-brainier. Whoever came down with the decision to build the office in the shelter showed little wisdom and poor judgment.

During construction of the office, every nail hammered into the wall was a nail driven into our hearts. The shelter was no longer L-shaped. It was a square room. We lost a third of animal space, a third of people space, and a third of supply space. There was nothing we could do about it, except make the best of it, and that we did.

I took no joy in writing this chapter. Believe me, it was a struggle and brought back bad memories. My first thought was to eliminate it entirely; however, it was a big part of the history at the shelter. It would have been disingenuous of me to leave it out. Of all my years volunteering, for me it was the lowest point. Many volunteers at the time will agree with me. Some volunteers will think I completely sugarcoated this whole chapter, others will not agree with me at all, and others did not even know these events took place. During this unhappy period the volunteers endured lots of disappointment and heartache. We had to overcome one obstacle after another, but we hung in there.

What organization doesn't have their ups and downs, occasionally? Hopefully, we can all learn from our mistakes. Regardless about all that has been said, time is a great healer and adjustments have been made by all. Many of the old crew of volunteers have moved on. Their contribution at the shelter was invaluable and appreciated. New dedicated volunteers have picked up the slack, and they will never know the events that preceded them. The volunteers continue to be thankful for what we have because we have a purpose and because of that purpose there is a deep inner strength. Despite everything the shelter is flourishing, and continues to be a protective lifesaving haven for all the animals that come under our care

Yes, we had a difficult start to say the least. To use an old cliché, it's not how you start; it is how you finish. There has been much improvement in relations between the ACO and the volunteers. The atmosphere in the shelter is much better. There is harmony again. It is amiable, cooperative, and friendly. The ACO generously allowed us to build a wall and split her office in half to make an isolation area for incoming and sick animals. Her office and the isolation area are no bigger than a walk-in closet in an average home. An isolation room was the only thing lacking in the shelter. We were able to fit four cages and an examining table in there. Despite its small size, it is working out just fine and is better than nothing at all. For many years the volunteers have yearned to have an isolation room for obvious health reasons. It was desperately needed, and we are delighted to finally have one.

The police chief retired and there is a new police chief. The new police chief and his lovely wife love animals and support the shelter. How do I know this? I placed several animals with the chief and his wife and their immediate family. Our shelter has developed a wonderful reputation, and it is spreading beyond our local area. People trust us. We are a little shelter, but we do big things!

MY FAVORITE DAY

Chapter 6

The shelter is no different than everything else. There are upsides and downsides. I can assure you the upside at the shelter outweighs the downside many times over.

As adoption coordinator, I do adoptions during the week and also on Saturday afternoons. Adoption hours on Saturday are from noon to three o'clock. The cleaning team goes into the shelter early in the morning to do their work. By the time I arrive the shelter is spotless and ready to receive the public.

Depending on what time of year it is, I wear a either a sweatshirt or tee shirt with our logo on it. Wearing one of our official shirts sets me apart from everyone else as the person to speak to for any information. I love our logo because it expresses so well in a few words our goal at the shelter. Depicted on the logo is a kitten and puppy and says, "**Until There Are None...Adopt One.**"

I look forward to my Saturdays at the shelter. Saturday is the best day for adoptions. Individuals drop by for a variety of reasons. My fellow volunteers come by to visit. We don't get to see each other too often, and it is fun to visit. Those three hours the shelter is open on Saturday whiz by, and you never know what to expect.

When I get up on Saturday mornings preparing to go to the shelter, I start thinking about what the day will be like. I keep my fingers crossed and pray there will be an adoption or maybe more. The most adoptions I ever made in one day were six, which is very rare indeed. That was a very special day. Every time there is an adoption, I feel like I won the lottery. When there are six adoptions in one day, it is like winning the hundred million dollar lottery.

There are so many emotions you experience on Saturdays at the shelter. It could be sadness, frustration, disappointment, joy, stress, aggravation, confusion, kindness, concern, satisfaction, surprise, and much happiness. This is the chapter I am going to share with you my experiences as adoption coordinator on Saturdays—my favorite day.

When I arrive at the shelter a little before noon, I turn the red "Closed" sign to the "Open" sign. When inside, I make sure the classical music station is playing on the radio in the background. The animals dislike loud rock music. Classical music is soothing and calming for the animals. The next thing I do is go from one cage to another checking on my little darlings. That takes less than ten minutes. The public will be arriving directly. There have been Saturdays when not one person came into the shelter. During those awful days, I would look outside to see if I hung the "Closed" sign up accidentally. Those kinds of days are disappointing, not much fun, but rare. I end up playing with the animals and doing laundry.

Frequent Encounters

We always have approximately between twenty-five to thirty cats at the shelter. There is a large variety to choose from. You name it we have it. There are cats of all ages, sizes, colors, and personalities.

A potential adopter would come into the shelter looking for a particular cat. The same person comes in every weekend for months looking for that special cat. If we do not have it, it does not exist. After a while you get to know the players, so when they do come in, you simply ignore them. Maybe that special cat will be there one Saturday.

Here is another common experience. An individual comes into the shelter and finds a cat he is absolutely mad about. You spend well over an hour or more talking and answering questions about the animal. It appears this individual has a sincere interest in this cat. I start to get excited inside because I sense a possible adoption. When suddenly that individual turns around and says, "I have to think about it," and abruptly leaves. They usually never come back for the animal. You just take a deep breath, throw up your arms in frustration, and start all over again.

Peculiar People

There are strange people everywhere, including Marblehead. The shelter is a public place and occasionally peculiar people come in. Sometimes you wish these people would not come into the shelter, and if they do, you hope their stay is short. I treat everyone who comes into the shelter cordially; after all, I am representing the town of Marblehead. On my very first after-school job I was a salesgirl in a nice clothing store. My boss taught me a good lesson, never judge a person by its cover. Some of our best customers looked, acted, and dressed peculiar.

One Saturday afternoon a very odd woman with a little girl came into the shelter. The woman was dressed in strange clothing and carrying a medium-size canvas sack. Besides her and the little girl I was the only other person in the shelter at the time. The strange woman looked and looked in all the cages. She and the child did not say a word. I asked if she needed help. She shook her head from side to side meaning no. I had an uncomfortable feeling. I just knew something unpleasant was going to happen. Finally, she stood in front of a cage and mentioned she wanted that cat. I explained she had to fill out an application. She interrupted me and told me she did not want to buy a cat. I was taken aback and wondered what she was getting at. She explained that she wanted to trade a cat and before my eyes she pulled a cat out of the canvas sack. You have heard of the children's book by Dr. Seuss, *The Cat in the Hat*? Well, this story is about a cat in the sack. I was flabbergasted! I swear, I saw no movement and heard not a peep from that canvas sack. It was astonishing!

I was very calm and tried to explain that we did not trade animals. She was not so calm and started yelling and made little sense. What little I could understand; she got the cat in Maine, it was not working out, and she no longer wanted it. Trying to be logical, I wanted to know if the cat was up-to-date on its shots. She got belligerent and started to threaten me. If I did not take the cat, she would leave it out on the driveway. Before I had a chance to say another word, she grabbed the little girl and ran out of the shelter. There I was standing in shock and bewildered with the cat at my feet looking just as bewildered.

I looked down at the poor helpless cat; at first I felt sorry for her. She was a black and white domestic short hair under a year old. I fixed a cage for her with a soft bed, fresh water, dry cat food, a little wet food, and a clean litter box. She was hungry and tired. I named her Peek-a-boo. It was appropriate; after all, a cat does not come out of a sack every day.

As usual before I left for the day, I check on all the animals. When I looked in on Peek-a-boo, I no longer felt sorry for her because I knew for sure she was in a better place. She was a lucky cat and in good hands. The volunteers would take good care of her, and I would see to it she got a loving home.

Playing by the Rules

This experience is not an unusual circumstance while doing adoptions. A very nice family or individual comes into the shelter to adopt an animal. They choose an animal they like best. I have them fill out an application. As I look over the application, I see they have checked off certain things that do not agree with our adoption requirements. This means I am unable to place the animal with them. These people are so excited about adopting the animal, and I am going to disappoint them. I do not like that role, but I have no choice. Suddenly, I will turn into an ogre. The volunteers trust me to follow shelter policies that have been put in place for a long time. These people will not understand that they put up a red flag, and I am as disappointed as they will be. My only wish is to find good, responsible homes for these animals. We have certain rules and standards in place, which we must adhere to. These people are not bad people. They just do not agree with our policies. We are the only advocates these animals have, and I will stand my ground. I have the right to refuse any adoption.

After I explain in great length why I cannot place the animal with them, they leave the shelter very angry. I have had applications thrown at me, doors slammed in my face, clipboards thrown on the floor, and spouses brought back to give me a hard time. Other possible adopters change their minds and adamantly promise to follow our policies so they can have the animals. I have trusted people in the past, but on too many occasions there were tragic endings. Some do not keep their promises and sadly the animal control officer finds one of our shelter babies dead in the gutter or eaten by a coyote. We put too much into our animals to have them end up that way. I learned my lesson well, and I am no longer going to be taken in with hollow promises. It is time for me to go into my litany of reasons why we must stand firm and stick to our guns.

We only place indoor cats. Depending on the situation, we do make some exceptions. A good reason not to let cats go outdoors is the automobile. The automobile is the biggest predator of all because it kills hundreds upon hundreds of small animals. There are also rabid skunks and raccoons that attack cats. Outdoor cats encounter other outdoor cats, get into skirmishes, and can contract FIV (feline immunodeficiency virus) or FeLV (feline leukemia). There is a new predator in the community killing cats by the dozens. It is called a coyote. So much of the coyotes' habitat has been developed, they have to go somewhere. Not to be gross, but cats are one of their favorite meals.

We do not place cats, if the potential adopter intends to declaw them. The volunteers consider declawing inhumane. Many veterinarians will not perform the procedure to declaw a cat. According to Friends of Animals, Inc., "Cats need their claws for protection; they also push and pull with their claws to express pleasure. Declawing is painful, cruel, and psychologically damaging." There are three digits in each finger of a human. A cat has three digits in each finger also. When you declaw, the first digit is amputated. I took some excerpts out of an article written in the 1993 September issue of *Cats* magazine by Lynn Davis:

The downside of declawing: It is a painful procedure; there is no denying that the declawed cat must learn to walk again, now on the stubs of the second bones; personality disorders may also occur in pets that cannot cope with their loss. Some cats become so frenzied, they must be euthanized. Also, upon removal of the cat's primary line of defense, it may resort to its secondary defense: biting!

There are so many items on the market these days to prevent any damage from clawing. Ask the advice of your veterinarian or local animal shelter. Go into a super pet store and choose from a variety of cat-scratching solutions. Many declawed cats get mouthy and start to bite, and some stop using their litter boxes because their little feet are so sensitive when they come in contact with litter. How do I know this? The same adopters who crossed their hearts and hoped to die, promised they would never declaw their cats. They declawed their cats and ended up surrendering them back to the shelter with those exact difficulties that have just been mentioned. It happens all the time and we end up with the problem.

We do not place animals to anyone who rents, unless they bring proof their landlord allows animals in the building. We do not want to risk adopting an animal out, and having it come back because the tenant did not follow the rules.

We do not place animals if they are going to be left alone for long periods of time. Dogs should never be left alone for long periods of time. It is not fair. Animals are social and need companionship. If a cat is left alone for long periods of time, we encourage adopting two cats to keep each other company. There are cats that don't like other cats and prefer to be alone. Kittens should definitely not be alone for an extended period of time, unless there is more than one.

There are instances when a potential adopter fills out an application perfectly. I cannot find one reason not to place an animal with that person; however, my instincts tell me different. My instincts are telling me something is not right. I have made mistakes, but after so many years doing adoptions, my instincts are usually on the money. I have several excuses to delay the adoption until I can make further inquiries. It is important our shelter animals get nothing but the best.

I am not as wise as King Solomon, but just like King Solomon I am put in a position to decide, who gets a particular animal. Part of my job is making tough decisions and sometimes it is not easy.

The Best and Worst

Quiet times in the shelter, especially on Saturday, are few and far between. Before you get a chance to sit down to take a deep breath and pause to reflect on the wonderful adoption you just made, the door flies open and trouble with it. A woman rushes in with two cats in carriers. She explains she is going to California tomorrow and her boyfriend does not want the cats. There is nothing like waiting for the last minute concerning her cats.

There is limited cage space in the shelter. We have a waiting list for surrenders and need cages for strays. Our policy requires surrendered animals be up-to-date on their shots and medical history from their veterinarian. None of which this woman had.

For certain, if I do not take those cats, this woman will leave them behind to fend for themselves. It happens all the time. A neighbor or someone will eventually call animal control to pick them up. What choice do I have, but to take them? Those poor cats deserve much better anyway. The woman signed the surrender forms, gave us the names and ages of the cats, promised to send us a large donation, and ran out without saying as much as a good-bye to her beloved cats. It was no surprise we never received that large donation.

Karen, a new volunteer, was in the shelter at the time this all happened. She could not get over how I contained myself. I explained to Karen these incidents are common. I meet the best and the worst people. The worst people have the attitude animals are disposable items. Inside I burn because they make me so mad. I would like to do what they did in western movies. Remember when a misbehaving cowboy was tossed out on his ear through the swinging doors of the saloon? Well, that is exactly what I would love to do with some people who come into the shelter. We are in a town building, and I represent the town. I have to keep my cool; however, those people can see and feel my disgust through my body language.

Not only did this woman dump her cats on us, one of the cats had something wrong with her hind leg. We had assumed responsibility for those cats and must care for them. They were brought to the vet and updated with their shots. They were already altered. The cat with the bad leg needed very expensive orthopedic surgery by a specialist. We dug deep and as usual somehow came up with the money for the surgery. The operation was a success. The cats were separated and placed in two different wonderful, loving homes.

This is the way it goes at the shelter. One animal is placed and two are surrendered. It is a revolving door that never stops.

~~

There is another side of the coin, which is very sad. People who love their pets dearly are forced to give them up for various reasons. Thank goodness we are there to help these people and their animals. There are two particular stories that stand out in my mind.

The first story is about a lovely young woman whose mother became ill. Her mother needed help badly. The young woman was forced to move in with her mother, so she could care for her. The problem was animals were not allowed in her mother's building. The young woman was faced with a dilemma and had little choice. She had to give up her beloved pet cat.

Arrangements were made to bring her cat to the shelter on Saturday, while I was there. The lovely young woman came in promptly at noon. I fixed up a nice comfortable cage for the cat and had her sign the surrender forms. It was devastating for her. She loved her cat dearly. The formalities were all over;

now she wanted to spend some quality time with the cat before her final good-bye. It was so sad.

There was something that looked like a sofa in the shelter. The cats thought it was a big scratching post. The woman sat on that sofa petting, talking, and hugging her pet cat. It was so sad. It brought tears to your eyes.

The woman was there the whole time I was there, which was a little over three hours. I tried to reassure her that the cat was in good hands and would be placed in a good home. Unfortunately, my words were hollow and useless. She only wanted her cat. I sympathized with her so much, and put myself in her in her position. I would be a total wreck if I had to give up any of my animals.

It was closing time, and time for the young woman to say her final good-bye. She put the cat's special blanket from home in the cage and then the cat. We were both crying. Believe me it was heart wrenching. You never are conditioned for these kinds of surrenders no matter how long you have been there.

This was a young beautiful brown and gold tabby cat. Her coloring was fabulous. She had a terrific disposition and personality. She was the kind of cat everybody dreams of having. I knew she would not be in the shelter for long, and I was right. She was placed with a wonderful couple who knew a great cat when they saw her. The cat hit it big! This is why I love being adoption coordinator. I get to see the animals leave the shelter with their new caring families and live happily ever after.

~~

The second story is about a little white poodle with a red collar. His owner was forced to move into an apartment that did not allow pets. The woman tried everything to be able to keep her beloved poodle. She begged and begged the landlord, but it was futile. When she finally resigned herself to give up her friend, she called the shelter. Again arrangements were made to surrender the dog on Saturday.

The owner and her six-year-old adorable dog came into the shelter. The atmosphere in the shelter changed dramatically and became extremely emotional. They did not want to part with each other. The owner tried to leave as quickly as she could, but the dog kept grabbing on to his owner's legs weeping. He knew something was wrong. He can't talk, but was saying, "Please don't leave me!" It was just like what a child would do. The owner was sobbing bitterly. Jean, a devoted volunteer, was with me on that day. We both had to walk away because we started sobbing, too. It was a real tear-jerker. Finally, Jean and I pulled ourselves together and pulled the dog away. The owner ran out of the shelter distraught. Jean, the dog and I were all stressed out. We couldn't bear putting him in a cage, so we let him run free in the shelter while we were there, but he just stood at the door waiting for his owner to come back for him. I sat down to unwind and noticed a message on the desk. I read the message. A family was looking to adopt a dog with a description of the kind of dog they wanted. It was uncanny. They described a dog exactly like the poodle. I had to have Jean read the message and tell me I was not seeing things. I immediately called the family about the dog. They lived in Marblehead not far from the shelter. They were interested and were coming in to see the dog.

The husband, wife, daughter and son came in and saw the dog. He was still upset, but the family understood why. They liked him very much, but did not want to be impulsive. You could just tell this was a good, loving, responsible family. I don't usually push adoptions, but I simply did not have the heart to put this dog in a cage. I suggested the family take the dog on trial over the weekend with no obligation. They went outside to talk it over. When they came back, they all agreed to take him. I was delighted.

We gave the family whatever supplies they needed for the dog, they signed the temporary release form, and off they went. The family did not know it yet, but Jean and I knew this dog was going to become a permanent member of this family. He was a sweet little guy who was irresistible. It was a match made in heaven.

The family had made their decision and called me after their trial weekend. They decided to adopt the dog. What a surprise! The dog was in the shelter for a total of two hours. The next time I saw him he was on a New Year's picture postcard with his adopted brother and sister.

Wasn't that a good story? Our work at the shelter serves a dual purpose. Not only did we find a good home for the dog, we brought much happiness into the life of a lovely family.

I wear many hats in the shelter. One of the most difficult is the hat I wear as a social worker. When owners come in to surrender their pets, it is very distressing and tense. Some of the surrenders are worse than others. I do everything in my power to make it as easy as possible and reassure them that everything is going to be all right. When you see men, woman, and children cry for their beloved pet, it does not take much to start crying too. Sometimes I ask myself, "Why do I this work; I don't get paid for it?" The answer is, I have a passion for animals and want to be there for them. I also want to be able to give them a second chance for a new life.

Chaos

Except for those rare Saturdays when it is very slow at the shelter, it is usually chaotic. The animal control officer does not work on Saturdays. The assistant ACO's are paged, if needed, so we take all the calls during adoption hours. While trying to attend to the visitors in the shelter, we have to answer the incessant telephone calls. Some of the calls are for animal control and some pertain to shelter business.

Here are some examples of animal control calls I have taken: A bat flew into my house; a wild animal is in my garage; there is a mouse in my drawer; my neighbors' dogs are constantly barking; there is a dead animal in my driveway; a rabid raccoon or skunk has been sighted; a seal has landed on the beach; an injured seagull or duck was spotted; an animal was hit by a car; an animal has been lost; etc. If it is about a lost animal, we take all the information and post it so in case it is picked up, we can contact the owner. For all the other things we direct them to the police station, and the police will page animal control.

Shelter calls are not as urgent. Most callers want directions; to inquire about a particular animal; to see if we have puppies or kittens; to find out how much it costs to adopt; to surrender an animal; etc.

People come in and out of the shelter other than wanting to adopt. Some come in with donations. Parents and grandparents bring their children and grandchildren in to see the animals. A good samaritan picks up a stray or hurt animal and brings it into the shelter. Saturday is a good day for volunteers to visit. This busy little building is jumping on Saturday afternoons.

The activity at the shelter does not stop. We must be there for those animals because there is no alternative. The shelter is providing a wonderful service for people but mostly for the animals. I thank GOD we are there for them.

A HUGE MIRACLE

Do you believe in miracles? I certainly do. Through the course of my life, I have experienced tiny, medium, and big miracles. The miracle I am going to tell you about was huge.

My husband, Harv, and I received a phone call from my oldest daughter, Tami. She called to tell us they were getting a new computer and wanted to give us the one they were replacing. It is important to know we never remotely gave a thought to purchase a computer. We did not want to appear ungrateful, but why do we need a computer? What are we going to do with it? Where would we put it? This is what I told my daughter. You have to know Tami; she does not take "no" for an answer. She and my son-in-law, Richie, knew what we did not know because at the time we were computer ignorant. They knew we would start using it, love it, and eventually could not live without it.

Tami was quite persuasive and insisted we take the computer. Finally, she convinced us. Once the decision was made, we had to decide where to put it, buy a special computer table, and rearrange some furniture. Everything was in place to receive the computer we did not want.

Tami, Richie, and my grandchildren, Harry and Haley, all marched into the house with the computer and all the equipment that goes with it. They set it up, put in our email addresses, gave us a quick lesson, wished us good luck, and left. My husband and I stood there looking at this thing scratching our heads. We hate to admit it, but we were actually afraid of the darn thing.

Little by little we gently started to play around with it, and little by little we started to get the feel for how it worked. At first whenever we got in trouble, we panicked and called my other son-in-law, Jeff, for help. Besides being in the computer business, he was so good and patient with us. We still call him when we need help. Jeff taught us a lot. Jeff, for all your help, thanks.

This is how the miracle began. One Sunday afternoon I sat down at the computer and tried to go into an interesting website. I will never forget this as long as I live. You already surmised my passion for animals, so naturally I started to search for pet/animal-related websites. A website called Petfinder.com came up, and I went into it. I started scrolling through the site and could not believe my eyes. I was mesmerized. I did not realize anything like this existed. It was amazing! I saw hundreds of hundreds shelters and rescues from all over the United States listed in this website. Each shelter had their animals, which were waiting for adoption, listed individually with a profile, and some had digital pictures of the pets. To me this website was a grand and a beautiful thing. Thousands of pets have been saved because this website exists. I was truly awestruck and so impressed.

That night I could not sleep. I could not get Petfinder.com out of my mind. It was a joyous discovery. It inspired me to add our shelter in the website. I want to do it so very much. It was a big project for me to undertake because

I was a novice with the computer and unsure of myself. What the heck, I was going to give my best effort. Our shelter and animals would have much more exposure, and it would broaden their chances for adoption. The most important thing was the animals would benefit most.

Very carefully, and slowly, I went into the website and read the directions on how to go about including our shelter, Friends of Marblehead's Abandoned Animals, in Petfinder. The directions were not hard to follow, and I was on my way. After filling out the preliminaries and the cover page, one by one I methodically put every animal in the shelter with their profiles in the site. As adoption coordinator it was my business to know everything possible about all the animals. We had about thirty-five animals at that time. It took me about a week to complete. This was a big accomplishment for me, and I felt good about myself. I had officially joined the information age.

Instantly great things started happening because of the website. Changes have dramatically taken place in the shelter. Adopters interested in our animals started to contact me. We were placing many more animals than we ever did before. Saturdays were busier than ever. The reason why the turnover was much larger was because we were not just drawing potential adopters from the neighboring communities; we enlarged our horizons and were drawing adopters from almost everywhere. I even got an application from Kuwait. Having the computer and putting the shelter in Petfinder was a major turning point for us. It was a huge miracle.

Not only have things changed in the shelter; my life has changed dramatically also. I am on the computer for hours daily communicating with so many people, constantly updating the website, making appointments, keeping the volunteers informed, and best of all placing animals into quality homes. I took on a huge job. It is like running a little business. I love every minute of it. Petfinder.com is a glorious gift to homeless animals and is sponsored by the Petsmart super pet store.

It is hard to believe I did not want to have anything to do with a computer. Now, I am on it constantly and cannot live without it. My daughter, Tami, was so right. The computer opened up a whole new world to both my husband and me. All I can say is, "Thanks Tami, for insisting we take the computer."

Even though I truly enjoy the responsibility caring for our shelter in the Petfinder website, there is still room for improvement. I would love to be able to put pictures of the animals along with their profiles. A little more experience on the computer would help; besides, I don't even have a digital camera. We already took a giant step and would continue to try to improve adoptions.

On a Saturday afternoon Cliff came into the shelter with a special purpose. Who is Cliff? He is a good guy, who adopted a cat named Oslo from us. Oslo, who is now called Ozzie, was a handsome all white cat, that was tested positive for FIV (feline immunodeficiency virus). Cliff and Ozzie were real soul mates.

While walking through Marblehead one day, Cliff noticed a printout of one of our shelter animals from Petfinder taped on a storefront window. He thought it would be great if the shelter had its own website. That was the purpose of Cliff's visit that Saturday. He volunteered to get it started, design, and maintain a fantastic website for the shelter. This was one exciting development! I spoke with my colleagues, and it did not take long to tell him to go ahead and do it. Our homeless animals were going to appear in Petfinder, and on our very own website.

It is history now. Cliff did an outstanding job putting the website together. It is beautiful, informative, colorful, interesting, and fun. The most desirable object of the new website is it motivates individuals to adopt from our shelter. What could be more important than that?

The new website address is **www.marblehead-animal-shelter.org**. Our new website includes our pets with their profiles. It also includes other interesting pages such as:

About Us
Adopt a Pet
How to Volunteer
Alumni Report
FOMAA News
Memorials and News
Directions to the Shelter

Cliff did not miss a thing. He also included volunteer and adoption applications, which can be filled out right online. It makes things more efficient and convenient. The volunteer coordinator and I, the adoption coordinator, are able to screen the applications ahead of time and move the process along. He even incorporated a link from Petfinder to our website. You can even make donations to the shelter on line. Cliff did a professional job, and we all appreciate all his hard work.

Things are really coming together. Another one of our volunteers, Margo, who worked with rabbits at the shelter, offered to take pictures of the animals with her new digital camera and send them to Cliff to put in the website. My dream of having pictures of the animals along with their profiles has come true. I feel as though I rubbed a magic lantern, a genie came out, granted me three wishes, and they all came true.

Cliff, Margo, and I collaborated on both websites. I would put the information, personality, and description of each animal in the Petfinder website. I would inform Cliff which animal to add to our pet list and which animal to delete after it has been placed. Cliff would than transpose it from Petfinder to the shelter website. Margo took the pictures of the animals and sent them off to Cliff to punch them into both websites. How is that for teamwork?

We were a great team and worked well together. Things were going along smoothly until Margo's allergies to cats were getting to be a hardship. She suffered every time she came into the shelter. We did not know how much longer she could continue. Anticipating Margo's career as our photographer was coming to an end, I considered buying a digital camera and start taking the pictures myself.

I swear there is an angel looking over the shelter. Just before I went shopping for a camera I came home and found a large package on my front door stoop. It was around my birthday, so I assumed somebody sent me a birthday present. I took the package in the house and could not wait to open it. To my surprise it was a Polaroid digital camera. I was puzzled. Who would be sending me a digital camera? I did not have a clue. I emptied the box and did not find a card, but I did find a form letter. The mystery was solved. Polaroid donated four-hundred digital cameras to Petfinder.com to give to shelters and rescues in their website. Our shelter was one of the lucky ones to be chosen. Maybe it was because for the longest time we had no pictures of animals in there. It was just recently we started putting in pictures. Timing could not have been better. It was awesome! I was so grateful for the new camera. Margo no longer had to suffer from her allergy to cats. I quickly learned how to use the new camera and took over for her. Cliff taught me how to send him the pictures and I was in business.

Margo adopted three bunnies from us and did not disappear from volunteering at the shelter because of her allergies. Both she and Cliff collaborated again and produced a sensational shelter calendar for the year 2001. It was a work of art and turned out to be a profitable fund-raiser. Margo also deserves credit for giving me the idea for the second part of the title of this book. Cliff and Margo, thanks for everything.

There are so many things that contribute to the shelter's success. Without a doubt the most dramatic and beneficial change was the computer, which led to the two websites. It wasn't a big miracle; it was a huge miracle.

The Pigeon

Since we are on the subject of computers, I simply have to tell this cute story. I was still in the early stages of my computer career when my middle daughter, Toby, who lives in Salem, Massachusetts, called me. She sounded troubled and perplexed. A homing pigeon landed in front of her house on the driveway. She tried everything to entice it to fly away, but it would not move. The pigeon might have been hurt. She was very concerned with the bird's safety. A cat or some other animal will attack and kill it. I told her to throw a towel over the pigeon, put it in her cat carrier, and bring it to me, which she did.

My first thought was to bring the pigeon to the shelter. Laura, the assistant animal control officer, would know what to do with it. Rethinking my rescue mission, I got the notion to go into my computer for information about homing pigeons. They say, if there is anything you want to know, you can find it on the computer. I thought I would give it a test.

I went into the computer and typed in carrier pigeon and clicked on search; behold, every bit of information I needed and more came up. It was like the computer was actually talking back to me. Step by step I followed the page of instructions on how to help a homing pigeon. It was fascinating. Not only was I learning to care for a homing pigeon; I was doing it in my home sitting on a chair. To me it was mind boggling!

It gets better. One of the instructions was to read the numbers on the colored band on the pigeon's right leg. I went over to the pigeon and got the numbers and wrote them down. They were AU2000GRC0026. I went back to the website, where there was a link to hundreds of racing homing pigeon clubs nationally. I selected four clubs that were closest to Salem, where the bird landed. After calling a few clubs, I finally found the club the pigeon's owner belonged to. The person I spoke with at the club told me he would notify the owner and have him call me. What do you think of that?

That same evening the owner called and was delighted we had his pigeon. He was so happy it was alive and well and he rushed over to pick up his bird. Came to find out he lived in Salem not far from my daughter's home.

The owner explained the pigeon was racing home from Ohio, got dehydrated, and landed to rest, which was not far from his final destination. The owner also brought with him six of his prize pigeons in a basket to show us. He loved his birds and was really into his hobby. For over an hour and a half he talked about his birds. My husband and I got an unexpected education on homing pigeons. We had no idea what went into homing pigeon racing, and all other different kinds of pigeons there are. This man was dedicated and loved it. Life is amazing. You can learn something every day, if you have an open mind.

Can you believe I found the owner of a little lowly pigeon? Who would've thunk it? It was amazing.

NOTORIOUS

Previously, I told you about some peculiar people. Now I am going to tell you about the courageous, daring, bold, and brave people that visit the shelter to adopt a cat. Not every cat that passes through the shelter door is a sweet little putty tat. These cats are not feral. I am talking about cats that are just plain scared or have an attitude. Cats like humans have different personalities. Mostly all the cats who come into the shelter are frightened at first. Some hide under their bedding or in boxes we provide for them. Others hiss and growl at first. Most sit in their cages and observe the activity around them. The shelter is a very stressful place for them. Some take longer than others to adjust. Eventually they adapt to their new temporary lodgings. It is not easy for these animals because they do not understand why they have been taken out of the only lives they have known and put into cages. It is pretty scary for them.

It is important these frightened cats interact with humans. If they do not come around, they will be hard to place. The volunteers would like to avoid getting scratched, bitten, and lashed at, so Laura, the assistant animal control officer, came up with a clever idea. She created a fake hand. It really is a glove that is stuffed with material and a stick is attached to enable the volunteers to pet the cats without getting hurt. Believe it or not it works wonders. When you use the fake hand, slowly trust replaces fear, and the cats come around a lot quicker because they are treated with kindness. Of course, there are always a few cats that continue to show their displeasure being in a cage and will not cooperate.

If you volunteer at the shelter for any length of time, it is inevitable you will be scratched, bitten, or lashed at by a cat. I have experienced all three several times. This is an example of an encounter I had with a cat named Rocky. Rocky was a stray. The woman who brought him in was holding him like a baby. He looked harmless enough. A couple of days later I noticed his cage was messy, so I put my hand in to straighten it out. He suddenly lashed out at me with his paw. It happened so quickly, I did not feel a thing. He caught me with his claw on the top of my left hand. You could see four little punctures. I immediately washed it thoroughly, put peroxide on it, and forgot about it

Rocky was not at fault. He had been outside on his own running loose for a long time. All of a sudden he was confined in a cage. He was frightened and felt cornered, and that is why he lashed out at me.

When I woke up the next morning my hand was swollen. My husband rushed me to the hospital. The hospital staff told me a cat bite or scratch could be very dangerous; if it gets infected it should be taken care of quickly. My fingers were so swollen they had to cut off my wedding ring. They put me on an IV with antibiotics and I left the hospital with my arm in a sling. Would you believe it?

My hand healed very quickly and did not stop me from continuing my work with the animals. Rocky turned out to be a sweet handsome dude. He was placed into a wonderful home, where he would be taken care of the rest of his life.

~~

Rocky's story was nil compared to the story about the most infamous cat we had at the shelter. Her name was Lucy Melissa, and she was nasty! She was a gorgeous brown tabby and white long hair Maine coon cat. Lucy Melissa lived on a boat with her owner and her owner's significant other. The significant other did not want Lucy Melissa around, so she was surrendered to the shelter. I am usually on the side of the animal, but in this case I was not so sure whom to sympathize with.

We will never forget Lucy Melissa because she left her mark at the shelter. She also left her mark on a few volunteers, which was no joke.

One Tuesday evening my partner Joanne and I were cleaning cat cages. All of a sudden I heard Joanne loudly yell, "OUCH." She was cleaning Lucy Melissa's cage at the time, and the cat bit Joanne's hand not once but twice. Instantly, her wound was turning blue. Infection was setting in and had to be taken care of immediately. Another volunteer was in the shelter and took Joanne to the hospital, so I could finish cleaning up.

Joanne was not the only volunteer who suffered the wrath of Lucy Melissa. There were others who went through the same thing. This is what I meant when I said, "Lucy Melissa left her mark at the shelter."

I know exactly what you are thinking at this point. Why don't we put this devil cat down? It had crossed our minds on several occasions, but we could not do it. If you looked at her and saw how beautiful she was, you would not do it either. We strongly believed it was poor cage behavior. If she were out of her cage in a home, she would be a totally different animal. We are a special breed of people and have faith there is a home for every animal in the shelter, including Lucy Melissa.

Many people were interested in Lucy Melissa because she was a sensational-looking cat, but after I told them about her poor behavior, they did not want to risk it. As a result, she was in the shelter longer than most cats. We were positive her day would come.

One Saturday afternoon a terrific couple came into the shelter. They wanted to adopt a cat. They looked at all the cats in their cages, but kept going back to Lucy Melissa's cage. The wife fell madly in love with her and no other cat in the shelter measured up to Lucy Melissa. She always wanted a Maine coon cat. I told them the truth about the cat's behavior. The wife was in love with her, but was unsure. The couple decided to go home and think about it. I did not think they would be back.

Well, I was wrong. The next Saturday the couple came back for Lucy Melissa. They deliberated and deliberated and decided to take her on trial. Inside I was bursting with excitement!

Suddenly, fear came over me because I realized I could not handle Lucy Melissa. I had to get somebody who knew how to take her out of her cage and put her into a carrier. We were not dealing with the average cat. That person was Stephanie. When I told this couple about the situation, I was afraid it would nix the adoption. I told them about my dilemma and would have to make an appointment for them to meet Stephanie at the shelter to make the transfer. You might think that would discourage them from taking the cat, but they had their mind set on adopting her. They were a gutsy couple and indeed, it was Lucy Melissa's day.

This event happened while Stephanie was still volunteering, and she knew exactly how to handle the cat. I arranged for them to get together for the transfer. I also assured the couple they could bring the cat back if it did not work out. Off they went with the cat to live happily ever after, I hope.

Every week for a month I called to see how things were. They told me everything was just fine. The trial period was over, and Lucy Melissa was a keeper and officially adopted.

About a year later I ran into the couple at the market. They were still in one piece with no visible wounds. Lucy Melissa was a permanent member of their family. It goes to show you, if you are patient and keep the faith, there is a home for every animal that comes into the shelter.

~~

Naughty cats do come into the shelter from time to time, and we deal with them. I must tell you about Nightingale, one of our shamefully naughty cats, who gave me the biggest scare of all. She was a brown mama tiger cat with kittens that was picked up and brought to a pound. She nursed and cared for her kittens until they were weaned. When they did not need their mom any longer, they were put up for adoption. Everybody wants kittens, and they got adopted quickly. Adult cats like Nightingale do not get adopted as fast. To make room for other animals in the pound Nightingale was scheduled to be put down. That was so sad.

Fate entered into the picture, and Nightingale got a reprieve. A litter of motherless kittens were brought into the pound. The kittens were too young to take nourishment on their own and still needed to nurse. Nightingale was still in condition to nurse, so they took a chance and put the infant kittens in with her to see if she would accept them. She was such a good mom and generously accepted the infant kittens. She cared for them like they were her own. Again, when they were weaned, they were put up for adoption. They all got adopted, but nobody wanted Nightingale, so she was put on that no-tomorrow list again.

This part of the story is unbelievable. Nightingale got another reprieve because more homeless motherless kittens where found. Yes, Nightingale took care of that litter as well, until they were all placed. She gave life to three litters of kittens. There was no way she should be put down.

Somebody up there was looking out for Nightingale. We got a call at the shelter from a woman who worked at the pound and networked with us to take animals whose time was up. We are a no-kill shelter and as long as we had room, we were happy to accommodate her. She wanted us to take Nightingale. After hearing her story, how could we refuse? At the time she came into the shelter, she had no name, so was appropriately named Nightingale.

Nightingale was about four or five years old. She was a pretty wide-eyed cat, who was getting impatient being in a cage. We let the cats out of their cages when the cleaning teams come in. The cats have a chance to run around and exercise. Nightingale was too afraid to come out of her cage. For some reason nobody had shown enough interest to adopt Nightingale, so she was at the shelter longer than most cats. She started to develop bad cage behavior, which was not uncommon. You cannot blame her for being unhappy. She wanted to have a home with a family who would love her. The same kind of love she gave to those three litters of kittens.

One afternoon during adoption hours a real nice lady came into the shelter to adopt a cat. She had been in several times before scouting for the right animal. She was attracted to Nightingale and kept going back to her cage. Other people had come into the shelter who were also interested in adopting. Since I was the only volunteer there, I went from one person to another to help and answer any questions. I left the nice lady to talk with the people that just arrived. My back was turned to the nice lady and unbeknownst to me she opened Nightingale's cage and picked her up. That was not good. Nightingale was very frightened and did not like to be picked up. When I turned around and saw the nice lady taking Nightingale out of her cage my heart went into my mouth, I held my breath, but kept my composure. I did not want to startle everyone in the shelter. I started to hastily walk over to the nice lady, but before I could say or do anything it was too late. The cat took her claw and scratched the nice lady's face and jumped back into her cage. It all happened in a matter of seconds. It was terrible. I was mortified. It was a nightmare. I kept apologizing. I grabbed the woman and rushed her into the bathroom to wash her wounds and put hydrogen peroxide on them. The nice lady was very blasé about the whole incident and did not seem to mind. She kept telling me not to worry. I felt terrible about what happened and hoped there would not be any repercussions toward the shelter.

Without exaggeration the woman left the shelter with four red scratches from her forehead straight down the middle of her face to her chin. It was a miracle her eyes were not touched. It was not funny. I was a wreck and went home with a throbbing headache. I don't know what happened to the other people who were in the shelter at the time of the incident. They disappeared quickly. Nothing more ever came from that unfortunate incident, thank goodness. A couple of months later that nice lady came back into the shelter and adopted two adult extremely gentle black cats. By the way, her scratches healed nicely.

Nightingale had been at the shelter well over a year and was one of our longest residents. The volunteers felt so sorry for her. We knew she would be an entirely different cat out of her cage in a home running free. After all she had been through, she did not deserve this. We never gave up hope there must be somebody out there for her.

One of our most generous shelter supporters came into the shelter with her friend, who wanted to adopt a cat. We went from one cage to another to check out all the cats. I told them the story and personalities of each cat, including Nightingale. The three of us chatted for a long while. Her friend made a decision and chose a very nice cat. The chemistry was good between them and it was a good match.

While I was making out the contract for her friend, I heard a voice say, "Make out a contract for me too." It was the generous shelter supporter. I gave her a puzzled look. She listened with great interest to my tale about Nightingale, had such empathy for her, and wanted to give her a home.

It was an emotional moment for me. It would be for the other volunteers, as well, when they heard about it. My eyes welled up with such happiness. This woman's kindness, compassion, and generosity to the shelter had always been appreciated. Adopting Nightingale was so magnanimous it left me speechless. This was one special lady. She was giving Nightingale a life, which she so very much deserved.

Our naughty cat lives in a magnificent home with lots of rooms and windows overlooking Marblehead Harbor. Nightingale sits by the window watching the dinghies, boats, and yachts sail in and out of the harbor. Nightingale paid her dues big time, and we, the volunteers, again kept the faith.

~~

I thought I was through with the naughty cat segment of this book, but while typing this chapter lo and behold the notorious Miss Kitty arrived at the shelter.

Liz, our volunteer cat intake person, received a call from a man who wanted to surrender two cats to the shelter. The excuse he gave was the cats would follow him around, wanted too much attention, and would not leave him alone. He threatened Liz and told her, if she did not come for these cats, he will throw them out on the street. Liz being a compassionate person made arrangements to pick up the cats.

It turned out one of the cats was a beautiful pure breed seal point Siamese named Miss Kitty. The other cat was a year-old gray and white medium hair domestic kitten named Little Jack. Their owner put them in carriers and off they went with Liz to the vet's office to be checked and update their shots before going into the shelter. The cats never had shots, they were not spayed or neutered, and were malnourished. It was clear these poor babies were not properly cared for and possibly abused.

The doctor had to take out the heavy gloves to examine Miss Kitty. She was vicious and fought her way through the whole examination. She was so bad, it was suggested she be put down. It must have been a real bad scene.

Little Jack was a shy thing to begin with. He was so scared, he was shaking like a leaf. Little Jack was so traumatized over this whole experience, it took him three and half weeks to recover and come out of hiding in a box we put in his cage. The shelter is a stressful place for the animals, so we put boxes in the cages upside-down and cut out an entrance so the cats can go in and out. The boxes have their scent, give them a sense of security, and a place to hide to feel safe. Little Jack was such a sweet, affectionate, loving little baby. It did not take long for him to get adopted with the kindest, nicest couple, who would give him the care, attention, and love he surely deserved.

Let's go back to Miss Kitty. Her cage behavior had been abominable. She hissed, growled, and lashed out. We had to wear thick gloves and use large tongs to clean her cage. Most of the volunteers were afraid of her, including myself. She was impossible, yet so beautiful. Ever so slowly she started to acclimate to her new surroundings. She responded to petting from the fake hand. She rubbed her head and body against the cage bars returning the affection. It led us to believe she hated being in the cage and would be much better behaved in a home environment like Nightingale.

Some weeks passed and the time came to put Miss Kitty on our website. We wanted to get this unhappy cat in a home environment as quickly as possible. When a pure breed Siamese cat is put on the website, you get many more applications. She should not be placed with children or with other pets, and has to be an indoor cat. None of the applications seemed to be right.

A sweet, older woman came into the shelter with her daughter and granddaughter. She has always had Siamese cats and saw Miss Kitty on the website and was interested. I told the woman the truth about Miss Kitty and what a bad girl she was. If she decided she wanted to adopt the cat, there would be no surprises when she got her home. The woman wanted to think about it and left. The very next day she called me and wanted to adopt the cat. The woman and her husband had a quiet home with no children or other pets, and it would be an indoor cat. It seemed like a perfect situation, so I decided to place the cat with her. I insisted she take the cat home on a trial basis. If things worked out, she could come back and fill out the official contract.

Kitty was in a very large cage and we kept a small carrier in there for two reasons. The first reason was she felt safe in it and liked to take her naps in there. The second reason was a safe way to get her out of the cage. We put food in the carrier to lure her into it, and close the door behind her. Kitty went home in her carrier with the woman.

The volunteers wanted so much for this to work out. I do not usually give my phone number out, but in this case I gave it to the woman to keep me informed. She called me the next day and told me the cat explored the whole house and loved to sit on her husband's lap. I was delighted to hear this and shared it with the other volunteers. A couple of days later she called and asked me if the cat was up-to-date on her shots. The cat bit her husband and he was a diabetic. She took him to the doctor and the doctor wanted to know if the cat had all her shots, which she did. The woman did not appear to be alarmed. Two days went by and I received another call from the woman. This time she was alarmed. The cat disliked her and would not let her go near her own husband. The woman tried to go into the bedroom to give her husband his insulin shot. The cat stood by the door growling and hissing and would not let her in. The woman was terrified.

Well, I guessed the trial period was over. The animal control officer had to go over to the house and bring Miss Kitty back to the shelter. What a big disappointment for all of us, including the poor woman and her husband. We did learn Miss Kitty liked men better than woman. Maybe we should have placed her with a single man? I changed her profile in the website, and we would see what happens.

We had no success finding a single man to adopt Miss Kitty. A couple from the Cape, who loved the Siamese breed, wanted to adopt her. We had been in contact with them. I told them the truth about her behavior. They told me they knew how to deal with it because they had misbehaved Siamese cats in the past they worked with successfully. The question was, "Should we risk placing the cat with this couple?" Miss Kitty's cage behavior had improved considerably. She was so unpredictable. "Should we give her another chance?" I spoke with my colleagues and decided to give her another chance.

The couple drove more than two hours in traffic to get to the shelter for Miss Kitty. They were quality people and so nice. I repeated everything about her behavior. They were so excited about adopting Miss Kitty, they were half listening. Miss Kitty was the cat of their dreams. She was just what they were looking for. I wanted them to take the cat on trial, but they insisted on paying for her and gave an extra donation. Off they went with Miss Kitty back to the Cape. I kept my fingers crossed and prayed things would work out.

The very next evening I went on line to check my mail and there was an email from the couple. I was hoping it was an update on how things were coming along. My hopes were dashed. This is what it said, "I have to bring the cat back tomorrow. I will tell you why when I see you." I could not wait till tomorrow to find out what happened, so I immediately emailed him back. This is what I asked, "Please tell me why? Did she do something wrong? What is it? I feel so bad." I included my telephone number for him to call me. He called later that evening. He told me he had just come from the hospital, where his wife was being treated for a very severe cat bite. She would have to be on an IV for twenty-four hours. I was sick and apologized over and over.

The next day I met him at the shelter with Miss Kitty. Her cage was waiting for her and back in she went. The man actually cried because he wanted it to work out so much. He would not accept the check he gave us and left for home. Miss Kitty missed the boat. She would have had a sensational home with these quality people. I was so angry looking at this exquisite creature in her cage and thought to myself, *Why is she so wicked?*

I went home disgusted. I decided to contact a woman who volunteered for Siamese Rescue and ask her advice about Miss Kitty. This woman lived in Connecticut and actually came to our shelter to adopt a specific kind of cat. She wanted a snowshoe cat, which is another breed of Siamese, and we had one. She emailed me back with some good ideas to help rehabilitate the notorious Miss Kitty.

Well Miss Kitty was back in the shelter for the second time. We continued to receive several applications for her, but none of them were suitable for the notorious Miss Kitty. Pedigree cats up for adoption are desirable and are adopted quickly. I only wish the domestic cats were as popular.

Since she came back to the shelter for the second time, approximately two months had passed. I went online, opened my mail, and before me was an application from a gentleman for Miss Kitty. He described himself as single, divorced, and straight; plus he was mad about Siamese cats. His application looked too good to be true. I wrote him a long letter telling him all about Kitty and emailed it back. I told him the whole truth and nothing but the truth. I even told him that if she bit him, he should go to the hospital right away because it could get infected. You couldn't be more honest than that. Nothing I said seemed to faze him. He emailed me back and still wanted to adopt her. I encouraged him to give it some thought. He said he was going to speak to his vet. His vet told him to go for it.

This would be the third opportunity for a good home for Miss Kitty. The man came all the way up from the Cape Cod to get her. I liked him immediately. He loved the cat and was going to give her every chance to make it work. I told him what I tell everybody who adopts from us, "If things do not work out or if your circumstances change, we will take the animal back." I had my fingers crossed and said a little prayer as they drove away. We all prayed this adoption was a success and would be the last time we saw the notorious Miss Kitty in the shelter.

Miss Kitty and the personable gentleman had been together for about two and half months. He changed her name to Maggie. Periodically he would send an update about the cat. This was the most recent, "**On a positive note, Maggie has settled in very well, and pretty much runs things around here. She's met all the people in my house, and responds very well. She has also met a couple of woman friends, and rubbed up against them both affectionately. More to follow.**"

I still don't believe it. Kitty has a home. Every time I see an email from the gentleman I cringe; I don't want to get any bad news. She was so unpredictable. So far so good, but I kept my fingers crossed just in case.

~~

When you have animals, at one time or another there had to be an occasion you were shocked and surprised at just how much they understand. I am convinced they understand a lot more than we know.

This naughty cat story must be told. A Russian woman surrendered a cat to the shelter because she had to go back to Russia and could not take the cat with her. The cat was a big guy, an all black short hair with a beautiful shiny coat. His name was Gypsy and he was a very nice cat. He did not like being in a cage, but most cats don't like being caged. It was quite normal and the volunteers understood that.

I went through the usual procedures when a new animal comes into the shelter. I took his picture and observed his behavior before putting his profile in the website. He was a handsome boy with good behavior. Unfortunately, there were no takers for Gypsy right away. The longer he was in the shelter his behavior became worse. His coat was no longer shiny, and he always seemed to have an upper respiratory problem from stress. He was a very unhappy cat. If anyone was interested in him, they were turned off after meeting him.

We treated him when he was ill. He was put in the largest cage in the shelter. We thought he would be happier there because it was right next to a window. We tried putting rescue remedy in his water to relax him. We even tried letting him run free in the shelter. Nothing seemed to help. Some of the volunteers were afraid of him, including me because you would never know when he would lash out. The volunteers felt so bad for him. We knew if he were in the right home, he would be fine. We were beginning to have our doubts, but we don't give up that easy.

Every day I go into my computer to check my mail. On this day I opened up an application and it was for Gypsy. I didn't want to get too excited. I reviewed the application. It looked real good except for the fact there was a young child in the family. I was disappointed. It was too risky to place Gypsy in a home with a young child. I emailed them back with an explanation why the cat would not be a good placement for them. The family replied to my email and insisted on meeting Gypsy. Frankly, I couldn't understand why they didn't accept my explanation. I decided to call and talk to them instead of emailing them.

When I called the woman of the house answered the phone. I introduced myself and immediately told her all about Gypsy's unpredictable behavior and how unwise it would be to place him in a home with children. She proceeded to explain why she was so interested in adopting Gypsy. She went into our website and read Gypsy's profile. The fact that his previous owner was Russian caught her attention. It turned out they were a Russian immigrant family. The woman was very persistent and insisted on meeting and adopting Gypsy. I wasn't adverse to this Russian family coming into the shelter to meet the cat. To be honest I was extremely skeptical about the adoption. Far be it from me to discourage them from coming to the shelter. It was obvious this woman wanted to meet Gypsy and decide for herself whether he was the cat for them.

The Russian family arrived at the shelter the next Saturday afternoon. They didn't live locally and came from somewhat of a distance. We introduced ourselves, and I immediately brought them over to meet Gypsy in his cage. They wanted to spend some quality time with him alone. Again, I cautioned the family about his unpredictable behavior and told them to please try to keep the little girl at a distance.

To tell you the truth I was very tentative when dealing with Gypsy. His cage was next to the bathroom. My plan was to let Gypsy out of his cage with hopes he would walk into the bathroom and the Russian family could follow behind. As I slowly opened the cage door, I was praying my plan would work. Gypsy walked out of his cage, looked around, then walked into the bathroom. The family slowly followed him in there and shut the door. Who could know what was going to happen? It was their call.

I stood by the door for a while, but heard nothing. Fifteen minutes passed and not a sound was coming from that room. I was sure they would be running for their lives out of that room. A half hour passed and still no activity. My curiosity was killing me. What was happening in that room? After forty-five minutes of silence, I couldn't stand it any longer and opened the door. I couldn't believe what I was witnessing. It wasn't possible. There they all were one big happy family sitting on the floor of the bathroom. Gypsy was weaving in and out rubbing affectionately against each of them. There was no sign of aggression. He was one happy cat.

What was their secret? How did they manage to turn this unhappy gruff cat into a loving pussy cat? Their secret was simple, but will surprise you. They spoke to Gypsy in Russian because that was the language he understood. He didn't understand what the volunteers were saying to him. It was so apparent Gypsy was comfortable with this Russian-speaking family, who adopted him that very day.

The family and I continued to stay in touch for a while. Gypsy's progress reports were superlative. You see you just never know. This story and other shelter stories convinced us to believe animals understand a lot more than we know. We can also learn from this experience. When people who speak foreign languages come into the shelter to surrender an animal, we might have to hire interpreters for those animals—just joking.

~~

WOW, I did not realize how much takes place during adoption hours until I wrote this chapter, and I am not through. I just deal with everything as it comes. Saturday is the day I wear many different hats. I deal with all kinds of personalities. Some people are reasonable and are a joy to deal with. Some people are not so reasonable and are difficult to deal with. There are hard decisions to be made. I must always stay focused, stand my ground, and make sure the animals come first.

MY FAVORITE DAY PART II

Chapter 7

The shelter is like a police station for animals. We are there to serve the community, and the Marblehead community knows they can depend on our help. There is no small emergency at the shelter. Every emergency is monumental.

Wild Life Emergencies

Accidents happen all the time, but especially during spring and summer, when wild animals are nesting and reproducing. Birds, squirrels, raccoons, skunks, etc. They get injured, fall out of trees, and are displaced. Marblehead residents call animal control or bring injured wild animals to the shelter for help. We once had a baby skunk. It was so cute and did not look real. It looked just like a Beanie Baby.

Very often while I am on duty at the shelter, a child or an adult will come in weeping with a wild animal that needs help. It may be a baby bird or a squirrel that has fallen out of the nest. I explain, "There is no need to worry because the animal was brought to the right place. This shelter helps all animals." After we reassure them, a great burden is lifted from their shoulders. They leave the shelter relieved and confident the animal will be taken care of properly.

We do everything in our power to help these wild animals. There are very special people who take these animals and care for them. Two of whom are Laura and Dede. They are the two assistant animal control officers. There are others who occasionally help out too. These terrific people might have to nurse baby animals, fix small injuries, or take them to animal hospitals that specialize in wild life. When the animals get well and are strong enough, they are released back into the wild.

Those wild animals whose injuries are going to take longer to heal or will disable them for life are also taken care of too. We do not give up. We go a step further and take the animals to special rehabilitation centers for the different kinds of wild animals. The people who run these centers are dedicated and work just as hard as we do to help animals.

If an animal injury is going to take longer to heal, these dedicated human beings will care and rehabilitate it, until it is ready to be released. The unfortunate animal, whose injury was too serious for it to go back into the wild because it could not protect itself and would not survive, will also be protected. The centers for these wild animals will put them in a confined area similar to the kind of environment they were accustomed to living in with some of their own species. These animals will be cared for and safe from any danger to live out their lives.

Those animals whose injuries are life threatening and cannot be helped are put down humanely. There is no need for them to suffer.

Back to Back Emergencies

I vividly recall two extraordinary emergencies one week after another on Saturday afternoons during adoption hours. The first emergency was on a beautiful summer day. I was alone in the shelter. It was close to closing time and the animals were quiet and content in their cages. While standing looking out the screen door enjoying the peaceful day, out of the blue, a beat-up red pick-up truck with smoke coming out of the radiator turned into the shelter driveway. I knew immediately a problem was coming my way.

A small, slender, rugged-looking man with a cigarette hanging from his mouth jumped out of the driver's seat. The man in the passenger's seat came out too. He had missing teeth, and they were both dressed poorly. It was obvious these two men had not had an easy life. They both rushed into the shelter all upset.

The rugged-looking man proceeded to tell me his sad story. The apartment building he lived in burned down. He went to live elsewhere, but they did not allow him to have his dog and cat. His pets were living in the pick-up truck. This was obviously not a good living situation for his pets he loved dearly and he was forced to give them up. He went from one shelter to another. Most of the shelters refused them, and others would take them and put them down. This was a terrible ordeal for this man because he wanted his pets, but circumstances changed everything. The last shelter he was at recommended our shelter because we are a no-kill. This poor man was beside himself, desperate, and at the point of having no hope of a safe place for his beloved animals.

I listened to his sad story and felt terrible. I wanted to tell him, "Of course we will take the animals." Unfortunately it was not that easy. There are rules and protocols at the shelter, which must be followed for good reason. I was put in a terrible position. My job is to adopt out animals. Laura and Katie are in charge of intake. At the time of this incident we were only supposed to take animals in from Marblehead. These animals were from a different community. I have in the past used good judgment and taken the liberty of accepting a cat into the shelter, if there was cage space available. Dogs are a whole different story. Dogs require more maintenance. They have to be walked three times a day. It means we have to round up our dog walkers.

The two gentlemen listened politely while I explained I needed the proper authority from the assistant animal control officer to take in the animals. If it were up to me, I would be preparing their cages because this kind of emergency is precisely why we are here. An okay from Laura or Katie would make me feel so much better. The men did not want to hear my flimsy excuses. You could feel things were getting tense. I asked them to be patient and wait while I made a few calls. Knowing his beloved pets might have a safe place, he would do anything.

I first called Katie and there was no answer. I remembered she had gone out of town. I called Laura and there was no answer. I was getting nervous and my mind was racing. You see I had already made up my mind to take the animals without anybody's permission. Just then Jean, my dedicated sidekick, came into the shelter. I was so happy to see her and explained my predicament.

We were trying to buy some time until I could get in touch with Laura. I kept calling, but there was no answer. I knew she was on duty. I was a total wreck, and not thinking because I knew I was not going to follow the shelter protocol. There are times you have to make an exception, and this was one of those times. Suddenly, I felt so stupid. Why didn't I think of it before? I called the police to page Laura and have her call the shelter as soon as possible.

The gentlemen were getting antsy waiting for Laura to contact us. Five, ten, fifteen, twenty minutes went by and no call. Suddenly the little, rugged-looking man with the cigarette in his mouth completely fell apart and started crying like a baby. When Jean and I saw a grown man weep like he did, we started crying. I could not wait any longer and was about to tell him to bring in the animals, when at that very moment the door to the shelter opened and it was Laura. It was like seeing an angel from heaven. We told her the whole story. She could not help noticing everybody's tears. She smiled, as if to say, *Everything is going to be all right.*

We all went out to see the animals in the pick-up truck. The dog was a young, medium-size short hair black and tan mix. His name was Axel. He was well behaved and very adoptable. The cat's name was Pinball. She was a very frightened beautiful calico cat hiding under the seat of truck. The living conditions for the animals were pretty pathetic. It did not take long for Laura, who is a compassionate person, to give the okay to bring the animals into the shelter. We were all so relieved. I personally felt so much better because that was her job and not mine.

The animals were put in nice, comfortable, clean cages with food and water. Their new accommodations were quite an improvement. The rugged-looking, little man was not so rugged after all. When it came to his animals, he was a softie. It was a bittersweet good-bye. On one hand he was happy they were in a safe place and going to be well cared for. On the other hand he loved his pets and did not want to leave them. Before his last good-bye he reached into his pocket and took out all the money he had. He appreciated what we did for him and his animals and insisted we take the donation. It was about twenty-five dollars. You just knew he really could not afford to give us that amount of money. We did not want to take it, but he insisted. His last good-bye was extremely emotional; he wept and wept. The two men drove away in the beat-up red pick-up truck knowing his babies were in good hands.

Not long after arriving at the shelter, the dog, Axel, was placed with a lovely family. They lived on an island off Rockport, Massachusetts. Pinball the cat was not as lucky. When she was brought to the animal hospital for a complete physical, she tested positive for FIV (feline immunodeficiency virus). What a bad break! Most people do not know enough about FIV and are afraid to adopt a cat with it. She would be hard to place. It was too bad because she was so nice and so beautiful. She had been in the shelter for too long, so Laura decided to bring Pinball to live with her grandfather in New York.

Two years later Laura's grandfather passed away, so Pinball had to come back to the shelter. She was not well and was taken to the veterinarian to see what the problem was. She was diagnosed with diabetes and would have to be given insulin twice a day. Poor Pinball was FIV positive and now a diabetic. She did not deserve this.

On a Monday night, when I was on duty at the shelter, and it was also New Year's Eve, I was about to leave for home when the cleaning team came in to do their thing. Yes, even on New Year's Eve they come in to care for the animals. Just as I was going out the door, Jean, who was a nurse, noticed Pinball looked strange. I thought she was in a deep sleep. She yelled out, "Pinball is in diabetic shock! She needs immediate emergency attention!" The situation was serious. It was six o'clock in the evening on New Year's Eve. Most of the animal hospitals were closed by now. I threw my stuff down and instantly started making calls to animal hospitals closest to us. They were not open and all emergencies that evening were directed to a hospital a good distance away. Pinball was in a life-threatening condition and there was no time. I tried contacting one more hospital, which was not too far. I caught the doctors just as they were leaving for the evening. I told them about Pinball, and they told us to bring her in right away. What luck! They were so kind to stay for us.

Jean wrapped the cat in a blanket and held her in her arms, George went along to help Jean, and Sue drove. The cat was near death and was having seizures. It was a horrific trip to the hospital. They were praying they would get to the hospital on time. When they got to the hospital the veterinarians and vet techs were there waiting. Jean, George and Sue would not leave the hospital until they knew about Pinball's condition. The staff worked and worked on Pinball for a couple of hours and somehow brought her back to life. She was one sick cat and needed lots of care. Jean, George and Sue could have used some doctoring as well after their ordeal with Pinball.

Once again Pinball was brought back to the shelter. She was one sick kitty. The shelter environment was not the best place for her to recover. It was unlikely a ten-year-old cat who was FIV positive, diabetic, and could hardly walk on her hind legs would be adopted, although stranger things have happened. Putting poor Pinball down was suggested by some. Laura would not hear of it! She took Pinball home with her. She was another addition to Laura's extended family of animals. Whatever time Pinball had left, it would be extended in Laura's care. Laura is a saint and a descendant of Dr. Doolittle. Pinball's future was iffy, but the fact of the matter is Pinball miraculously stayed alive for many years living with Laura.

~~

The very next Saturday afternoon I was faced with another startling dog emergency. This time I took the bull by the horns and handled it myself. To tell you the truth it was a no-brainier.

It was another exceptionally perfect summer day. Everything was quiet in the shelter. I was doing some paperwork when a woman flung the door open. She was excited, out of breath, and notably upset. I got up from the desk to see what I could do for her. Believe me when I tell you things are never dull at the shelter.

The woman calmed down a little, grabbed my hand, and took me to her car. Her daughter was in the car holding a very little black and white dog. The dog was a little too big to be a Chihuahua, but looked like one, and too small to be a Jack Russell. It looked like a Chihuahua mix. The poor thing was shaking, it was so scared.

The woman proceeded to tell me how she acquired the dog. She and her daughter were enjoying the day on Preston Beach walking along the rocks, when these strange people walked passed them holding the little dog. The strange people were foreign because they were conversing in another language and walking further and further out on the rocks with the dog. The mother and daughter suspected they were up to no good and followed them. They all walked as far as you could go unless they wanted to jump in the ocean. The woman asked the foreigners what they were going to do with the dog. She could hardly understand what they were saying. What little she did interpret was shocking. Those foreigners did not want the little dog any longer and were going to throw him in the ocean.

I was appalled to hear such a thing! The woman somehow communicated to those horrible people that she would take the dog. Right on the spot the foreigners handed the dog over to her and took off as fast as they could. The mother and daughter headed right to the shelter with the dog. How was that for a story? It was a chilling! There are all kinds in this world.

While I was in the driveway talking, Jean drove up. Jean always pops up at the right time. We told her the story. She was furious and picked up the dog to comfort him. The poor thing was shivering because it was so frightened. I

132

thanked the mother and daughter over and over. They did a good deed and saved a life.

We took the dog into shelter without anybody's permission this time. How could you not? We fixed up a dog cage for him, but the dog was too small for it. We never had that problem before. It was so funny. To make him comfortable we found a basket, made it into a soft bed for him, and put in fresh food and water. He felt secure in the basket and started to settle down. I named him Paco because it fit him so well.

If you think Paco's troubles were over, wait until you hear the rest of his story. It happened two days after Paco was rescued. Somebody carelessly left the shelter door unlocked and left. An individual walked into the shelter and helped themselves to little Paco. That individual left a note. The note was muddled. We couldn't make out who the person was who took the dog. The signature looked something like, *Jo*.

At first we thought a volunteer took the dog. We called every volunteer, but nobody had a clue who took the dog. We all started to panic. What kind of person would come into the shelter and take an animal without permission or without speaking to someone? How could anybody do such a thing? We were crazy with worry. We notified the police. Another volunteer, Alice, and myself called every animal hospital in the area with a description of little Paco. Nobody knew where Paco was. He just disappeared.

Five days later a woman casually walked into the shelter like nothing monumental had happened and mentioned she took Paco. She really came in for a cat, but when she saw Paco, she had to have him. Just like that she took him. She had no idea all the worry and trouble she caused. She was unable to keep the dog, so Paco was back in the shelter safe and sound in his little basket in the big dog cage. It takes all kinds.

It did not take long for a little fellow like Paco to be placed with a wonderful family. The year we did the shelter calendar as a fund-raiser, Paco was one of three dogs that were adopted from the shelter chosen to be in the calendar for the month of October. The three dogs were dressed in Halloween costumes. There was Josie, a small wire hair mix. She was dressed in a south-of-the-border costume with a sombrero. Grace was a Sheba Inu and dressed in a devil's costume. Little Paco was dressed as Dracula from Transylvania. To get the real effect of Dracula his owner painted his white forehead black with a point down the middle, and he wore a black cape. The dogs and children were adorable and colorful. The month of October was my favorite picture in the calendar.

Well, another emergency was dealt with, and another happy ending to a shocking story.

Desperate

When an individual is up against it and forced to give up their pet, it can become a devastating situation. Throughout this book I have mentioned a multitude of reasons why people have to give their pets up. The owner of the pet, who has to give it up, starts looking for a family member, a friend, neighbor, or an acquaintance to adopt his pet. If he has no luck finding someone, he starts calling shelters to surrender his pet, but is rejected for one reason or another. He certainly does not want his perfectly healthy pet to be put down. He is stuck and has no solution. Desperation starts to set in.

Some of these desperate individuals leave their pets behind on the street to fend for themselves. It is horrible for the animal. Left behind without the basic things they are accustomed to, like food, water, care, shelter, and love. Most of those animals are unable to cope and do not survive because there are just too many dangers out there. If they are lucky, a neighbor or someone will call animal control to the rescue. Those sorts of calls to animal control are not uncommon.

If the individual does not want the pet to fend for itself, what other options are there? There are none. The situation becomes increasingly hopeless. They think about it all day long. They stay up nights thinking about what they are going to do with the pets they care for. Suddenly a thought crosses their minds. The thought is clandestine. Should they do it? Do they dare do it? Yes, occasionally they do it.

Secretly during the darkness of night or before morning daybreak an animal is left on the doorstep of the shelter. There have been dogs tied to the banister, cats left in carriers, kittens in boxes, injured birds left in the mailbox, and even dead animals in boxes are left on the stoop. Now their emergencies becomes our emergencies, and we handle them.

When I walked into the shelter one Saturday morning, Laura was checking out a mother cat with six infant kittens. She found them in a box on the shelter doorstep. The mother cat was still nursing the kittens. She was so thin and hungry. I prepared a cage for the little abandoned family and gave the lovely gray and white mother cat a whole can of food. She gulped it down so quickly and we gave her another and another. She needed her strength to care for the kittens. Her belly was full for the first time in a long time. She felt so much better and lay down to rest while her babies were nursing.

I was sad to see the hungry mother and her babies. It must have been a terrible struggle to find food to keep her babies and herself alive. On the other hand I was glad the mother and kittens were left at our shelter door. They would be cared for properly and placed in good homes.

I named the mother cat Patsy after the country singer Patsy Cline. The six kittens were named after country singers too: Garth Brooks, Willie Nelson, Loretta Lynn, Crystal Gale, Tammy Wynette, and Dolly Parton. They were all placed in sensational homes.

~~

The most unforgettable story about an animal left at the shelter door was Sara the cat. She was a fourteen-year-old, pretty, orange and white short hair cat and appeared to be in good condition. Along with Sara was a note which said, **"Please put this cat to sleep—her name is Sara—she is fourteen years old—my wife and I are divorcing. She would not be able to live with anyone else."** Was that unbelievable! To suggest we would put an animal down for no good reason was revolting. To suggest she could not live with anybody else showed ignorance. We had bigger challenges than Sara and successfully found super homes for them. We do not give up that easy on any animal.

Sara was taken into the shelter. It was obvious she was depressed and she hid under her linens. She went to the vet for a check-up and we discovered she had severe dental problems and was in pain. That explained a lot. Sara ended up having quite a few teeth extracted. Some of you maybe thinking, why spend so much money on dental surgery for a fourteen-year-old cat who may never be adopted? Wrong. Throughout this book, I have also tried to convey, we truly believe there is a home for every animal that comes through our shelter door. We also wanted Sara to be free of pain.

When Sara completely recovered from her surgery, it was time she was put up for adoption. Her picture and description was put in the community newspaper, including a copy of the note that came with her. The community newspaper comes out every week on Thursday.

The following Saturday after Sara's picture was in the paper, a lovely lady was waiting in her car for the shelter to open. I arrived early and welcomed her in. She was teary eyed because her twenty-one-year-old cat she loved so much had passed away. She explained she had no intention of getting another cat until she saw Sara's picture in the paper and felt such empathy for her. This so sweet, compassionate woman looked at all the cats in the shelter and only wanted Sara. Need I say more?

Sara went into a new home that day with her new big-hearted mom. It was a perfect match. The lovely woman was a senior citizen and Sara was a senior citizen. A couple of days later I called to see how things were. Sara's new mom told me everything was great. Sara was a little shy and did not like to be picked up too often, although, her new mom put her on her lap every day, and she was starting to like it. She slept on the woman's bed and did not like to get up early. Sara was good with the grandchildren when they came to visit. Who said Sara could not live with anyone else?

When Sara was settled in her new surroundings, I went to the house to take a picture. I wanted to put a follow-up story of Sara and her new mom in the community paper. The story was a warm one and the readers loved learning about Sara's happy ending.

The Worst

The worst emergency is when an animal is in a car accident. If it happens on a Saturday afternoon in Marblehead the animal hospitals are closed, so where do you bring the victim for much-needed help? Unfortunately, in most animal-related car accidents, the perpetrator does not stay around to help. It is usually a hit and run. When the perpetrator does stop to help, he or she contacts the police, and the police will quickly contact animal control. Animal control has the authority to call a veterinarian when there is an emergency and a doctor will immediately go to the hospital to care for the injured animal.

Recently a cat was hit by a car on the same street the shelter is on. Several witnesses came running into the shelter to tell me an injured cat was coming in. I must admit I am not good when it comes to this sort of thing. I am a little squeamish, but you got to do what you got to do. Before the cat arrived I called the police to page animal control because a cat was hit by a car and they were bringing it into the shelter. Dede was on duty that day. On the way to the shelter from her cell phone she notified the vet to meet her at the hospital for a seriously injured cat.

The injured cat was put in a box and brought into the shelter. It was an adult female calico cat. She was in shock and looked in pretty bad condition. The person who accidentally hit her came along. He felt terrible and was in tears. There were several other curious people gathered around.

My right hand man on Saturdays was Jean and thank goodness she was with me. She was a nurse and took charge of the situation. She took the cat into the bathroom away from the crowd and covered the cat to keep her warm because she was in shock. She also stayed by her side to comfort her until Dede arrived.

It was not long before Dede arrived to take the cat to the hospital, which was a short distance from the shelter. The doctor was there waiting for them. The cat was in serious condition. They preformed emergency surgery and did everything possible to save the animal. Dede stayed at the hospital until nothing more could be done. It was now a matter of wait and see.

The next morning Dede called to find out the cat's condition. The news was bad. The poor little cat did not make it through the night. The only consolation was we did everything possible that could be done for the cat. At least the little calico cat did not die alone in the gutter.

The Needy

Early in my career as adoption coordinator, I learned there are people who need animal companionship as much as the homeless animals in the shelter need human companionship.

I received a call from a director of an assisted living home. She told me about a resident in the home who was in her late twenties, confined to a wheelchair, and blind. She further explained the resident needed a friend to keep her company. They thought a lap cat would be just the thing.

Surely I could not refuse her request. I needed a little time to consider all the cats presently at the shelter and find the best lap cat for this woman. I told the director I would get back to her with my choice.

There I was in the shelter looking in one cage after another methodically searching for the perfect cat for this special situation. When I came to Rambo's cage, I stopped. My search was over. Rambo was an all black, kindly, gentle, loving, affectionate, and most definitely a lap cat. He was surrendered to the shelter with that name. It certainly did not fit his personality; he was quite the opposite from being a Rambo.

I immediately returned the call to the director of the assisted living home and told her we had the perfect cat for the resident. Arrangements were made for the resident to come to the shelter to hold and feel the cat. If all went well, she could take him home with her.

Katie and I were anxiously waiting for the young resident and the director to arrive at the shelter. We knew it was going to be a happy/emotional occasion. We prepared a bundle of supplies for her to take home. It consisted of all the cat's needs such as: a bag of dry food, some canned food, litter, a litter box, toys, and a soft cat bed. We even put a break-away collar with a bell on Rambo, so she would know where the cat was at all times.

They finally arrived and we all helped her into the shelter. After all the introductions were made, it was time for the most important introduction. Rambo was in his cage and gently we took him out and put him on the resident's lap. It was just like Rambo to make himself comfortable on her lap. She started petting him, and instantly there was love for each other. The match was perfect! Rambo did not move from her lap until it was time to put him in a carrier for a safe trip to his new home and new life. Words cannot describe how happy the blind girl was to have her new companion. There was not a dry eye in the place.

This is what our volunteer work at the shelter is all about. This is how we get paid. Not monetarily but through deeds. Money alone could never pay for the gratification and pleasure we received this day.

~~

A couple of years later a brand new huge assisted living complex was built a block away from my home. On a Saturday afternoon I received a call from the woman who was in charge of the Alzheimer's floor in the building. Someone recommended our shelter to her. The woman was representing the assisted living home to adopt a cat. They wanted a cat to live on the floor with the Alzheimer's patients. There were individual patients living in the home who brought their own pet cat or dog to live with them. The cat the home wanted to adopt would have the freedom to roam around the whole floor and be every patient's pet.

Again, it had to be the right cat for this kind of circumstance. It had to be friendly, even tempered, able to mingle well with people, and another lap cat. As usual, I told the woman I needed a little time to find the right cat and would get back to her.

That same afternoon an English couple came into the shelter to surrender their cat. It was a seven-year-old, handsome, silver tabby male cat named Alex. They were moving back to England and thought he would be adopted quickly because he was such a wonderful cat. They did not want him to be quarantined in a cage for six months. You see in England there is no such thing as rabies. Any animal brought into the United Kingdom from another country is quarantined for six months. Rabies is a deadly virus, so you cannot blame the English for taking every precaution to keep rabies out of their country. I believe they have relaxed their rules since then.

Suddenly I got a hunch! Alex was perfect for the assisted living home. My thinking was, if I could place Alex in the assisted living home right away, he would only have to adjust to one situation and not two. I have already told you how fatiguing it is for an animal when they come into the shelter. I wanted to save him the stress of acclimating to shelter life. He would have to adjust to life in the assisted living home, but it would not be as threatening.

I called back the woman and told her about Alex the English gentleman. She wanted to meet him. As advocate for these animals, I wanted to check out the home and make sure it would be a good placement for the cat. I arranged to bring him to the home right after adoption hours.

Alex and I went into this beautifully decorated, state-of-the-art assisted living home. A receptionist greeted us, and I told her the name of the woman I was to meet. The woman came down the elevator to greet us. The Alzheimer patients were housed on the second floor, so Alex and I followed her back into the elevator to the second floor. When the elevator door opened, we stepped into a really huge living room. There was a television set, overstuffed chairs, sofas, and rockers. Alex could cuddle up and nap on that kind of furniture. There were lots and lots of windows that Alex could look out of. There was a big corridor leading into a lovely dining area where Alex could have his meals. The patients' bedrooms were off of other smaller corridors. Alex could visit with them.

The elevator was my biggest worry. I was afraid one of the patients would open it, Alex would go in and might get hurt or lost. My fears were alleviated when I was told only the professional staff had keys to use the elevator.

Of course my thoughts were for Alex alone. There was a lot of activity on that floor. He would never be bored. The area was very large and he would have complete freedom to go where he wanted to. The woman assured me a person on the day and the night shift would be assigned the responsibility for the cat's needs. After speaking with the woman at length I was convinced he was going to get excellent care. If the woman wanted Alex the English gentleman, I decided it would be a good placement. I just happened to bring a contract with me. Alex was adopted into the assisted living home. He only had to adjust to one new surrounding, and it would not take him long to acclimate to his new life. Animals are amazing because they adapt so quickly.

Alex brought much happiness into the lives of the patients. The few times I visited, he was on a patient's lap. Another time he was visiting with a patient in his bedroom. Sometimes he was in the dining room eating tasty treats the patients save for him. Patients come and go, and Alex was at the home affectionately bringing joy and comfort to the lives of the Alzheimer patients who were currently living there. Alex was a shining light on the second floor in the assisted living home and doing a superlative job. Jolly good show, Alex!

I thought Alex would spend the rest of his life in the home comforting the patients, but things did not work out that way. There were some extenuating circumstances that came to my attention.

I mentioned Candi in a couple of my previous chapters. To refresh your memory she was once on the medical team at the shelter. Coincidently she was engaged by a family to take care of their mother's cat in the same assisted living home and on the same floor where Alex resided. She knew Alex was there from volunteering at the shelter, so she looked in on him as well. He appeared to be doing well.

Some time later she called me with a very disturbing report. She told me Alex was not eating well, had lost a lot of weight, and was lethargic. There was hardly any food and fresh water in his dishes. Some discharge was coming from his mouth and nobody seemed to care. He was also very afraid and did not want to leave the room of a patient who was fond of him. He refused to go out in the common area on the second floor. This piece of news was upsetting to me. It was obvious something was terribly wrong. He could be ill. Something must have frightened him so badly that he would not come out of the room. I wanted it looked into right away. Candi is a capable person, who is right on the spot and knows whom to deal with. We decided she should handle it. I would intercede if necessary.

As it turned out the woman I dealt with originally moved on to another assisted living home. Candi went to the new woman in charge to discuss Alex's problem. She recommended he be taken to see the veterinarian right away, and offered to take him. The woman had to get permission from the director of the home. It took some time for permission to come. If it weren't for Candi's persistence, it might not have come at all.

The cat went to the hospital and was given a complete examination including blood work. It turned out Alex had kidney problems and a bad mouth infection. He needed mouth surgery on his teeth. They gave him fluids for his kidneys and antibiotics for his mouth infection. Candi went back with the diagnosis. The director of the home would not appropriate money for surgery on the cat's teeth even knowing he was in pain. They signed a contract to be responsible for this cat's welfare. I hate to say it, but they dropped the ball on poor Alex. They were getting big bucks in that assisted living home from their residents, and they could not come up with a measly sum of money to help the cat. It was disgraceful!

Alex was back in the home and still would not come out of the patient's room. Candi arranged to have his food and litter box put in there. She also looked after him whenever she was there and felt he had improved somewhat. God bless Candi!

Sadly, the patient Alex roomed with was dying. For weeks Alex stayed by this woman's side and comforted her while she was dying. Finally, the end came. The room needed to be prepared for the next patient and no other patient was willing to have Alex room with them. He was thrown out of his room into the common area with nobody to nurture him. All he did was run around crying. What a sad state of affairs.

I spoke with Candi and suggested she approach whomever was in charge to surrender the cat back to the shelter. The shelter would give him the care he needed. Let's face it they did not want him any longer. If it weren't for Candi, he would not be in this world. Candi did what I asked with one difference, she was going to take him home with her and not back to the shelter. That was just like her. Of course it was no surprise the home agreed to release the cat.

I personally went to the director of the home to sign the surrender form and got up the nerve to ask him for a donation for the shelter. I deliberately made the point the donation would go toward the cost of fixing Alex's teeth. He reluctantly gave a donation. I had the hatred feeling for him because of how poorly Alex was treated. Alex was leaving and this same nasty man acquired a dog for the home. When I heard that I was distressed. I prayed the dog would be cared for better than the cat was.

Alex went to live with Candi and her extended family of many cats. The shelter paid for his mouth surgery, and he felt like a new cat. Candi gave him fluids for his kidney problem. He is living the good life now. Alex being an English gentleman and so appreciative asked me to thank Candi for saving his life. Thanks Candi, Alex loves you!

~~

Inspirational is the word for this next story of an exceptional man. While working at the computer, I received an email from our website. It said, "Hi folks, I'm a disabled guy, who works as an engineer on my PC all day. I would be privileged giving Oreo a warm, peaceful, and loving home. Can u get us together? (I'm willing to pay for your gas and parking). I'm in downtown Boston."

Oreo was a sweet, slender, ten-year-old, black and white, declawed cat that was pictured on our website. She was brought into our shelter because her owner passed away. We never found out what her real name was, so she was given the name Oreo. She was in excellent health, up-to-date on her shots, and spayed.

Anytime I receive an inquiry for an animal, I reply by telling them to go back into the website and fill out an application for me to review. As I have told you time and time again my main concern is for the animal. I want it to be the right placement and cared for in a responsible home.

The gentleman filled out the application. It looked good, but I wanted to be absolutely sure the cat was going to get the proper care, especially because I was unaware of how bad the gentleman's disability was. On the application was the telephone number of his veterinarian, so I called him. He told me the gentleman was a quadriplegic. My immediate thought was how he was going to care for Oreo. How naïve I was. The veterinarian assured me the cat was going to get the best care. The gentleman had several care-givers and he, the vet, lived in the same apartment building.

After my conversation with the vet, I was confident Oreo would have a wonderful home and a quality life with the disabled gentleman. I contacted him and made arrangements to bring the cat to him.

It would be nice to have company on this trip, so I asked Jean to accompany me. We got excellent directions, parked in a car lot, and walked with the cat in the carrier to the address he gave us. It was a brand new, enormous, round-shaped building in downtown Boston.

The place was gorgeous. I must confess I was a little nervous walking through the corridor to the elevator and down another long corridor to his apartment. I just did not know what to expect.

We got to his apartment and the door was ajar. We knocked and a voice told us to come in. It was the gentleman in his wheelchair. He was anxiously waiting for us to arrive. He especially could not wait to meet Oreo, so we let her out of the carrier. When he saw her he yelled out, "I'm your new daddy!" Oreo was so frightened from the trip, her new surroundings, and the wheelchair. She jumped up on the top of his kitchen cabinets over the sink.

I told the gentleman I brought food and supplies along with Oreo. He would not hear of it. The litter box, litter, food, food dishes, and cat toys were all there ready for Oreo.

While waiting for Oreo to calm down, the gentleman invited us into his living room/office. The apartment was geared for his disability, immaculately clean, and had big windows with a beautiful view of Boston.

It did not take long to see we were in the presence of an extraordinary person. There were all sorts of degrees and diplomas hanging above his desk. He was working as an engineer for a well-known company. He was also a doctor of psychology and still saw patients. From then on we addressed him by his title, Doctor.

Dr. B had a remarkable attitude. He was determined his disability was not going to stop him from doing what he wanted. He told us he was going to live to be a hundred. Dr. B was truly an inspiration.

Oreo was still up on the kitchen cabinet. She has a big job ahead of her. She had to acclimate to her new home and the wheelchair. It would take a little time. It is amazing how animals adapt to all kinds of situations.

It was time to go. There was a hundred dollars on the corner of Dr. B's desk. He wanted to give a donation to the shelter and pay for the garage, tunnel, and gas. We did not want the money. He was very firm and insisted we take it. We took it because it made him happy. You experience many different moments in your life, most of which are forgotten. Jean and I will never forget our experience with Dr. B. It was emotional, uplifting, and inspiring. We will cherish it forever.

Dr. B and I still keep in touch by email. At the beginning hardly a week went by that I did not receive updates on Oreo's progress and pictures also. Her name was Rain now. Dr. B loved the Spanish people and their culture. He told me Rain is a popular Spanish feminine name. Rain took her sweet old time adapting to her new life. I would like to share three progress reports with you:

9/25/02: *Hi Linda, Rain'n me are on the verge of a breakthrough. She is down off her perch 20 hours per day and she stays in the same room with me and my wheelchair. She sits beside my bed and stares at me at night.*

10/5/02: *Hi Linda, Gosh!!! Me'n Rain are soul mates. She sits with me when I am on my PC and she meets, greets, and of course enjoys a petting session with each of my patients. She has officially adopted me and her new home.*

10/24/02: *Hi Linda, at night Rain brings her toys to my bed and plays while I read. When I kiss, hug, and call her pretty baby she becomes kittenish, talkative, and rolls on her back, and hiding her eyes with her front paws.*

Oreo/Rain was Dr. B's shining little star. She provided him with lots of amusement. She was his constant companion and loving pal. The cat brought a new dimension into Dr. B's life, which enriched it so much. This is a true heart-warming story. It was a privilege to have placed one of our homeless cats with this special man. The devoted, selfless volunteers have a dual purpose. We want to find good responsible homes for our animals. We also want to bring happiness into the lives of our adopters.

~~

There are so many examples of how animals help people in need. Here are more brief examples. A teacher came to the shelter with her family to adopt a dog they saw on the website. The dog was a Shiba Inu, a Japanese breed of dog. His name was Sly, who looked like a little fox and was about the same size as one.

The teacher discovered she had breast cancer and was operated on, but needed to have chemo treatments. She decided to take a leave of absence from teaching for a year while she was getting the treatments. She and her family were animal lovers and thought a dog would be a comfort to her while she was going through this stressful period.

There were many applications to adopt this particular dog. I simply could not refuse this woman. It was a lovely, responsible family. I truly felt the dog would fit right in with them, so I placed the dog with her.

The teacher emailed me how Sly had become her constant companion and seemed to understand how much she needed him. I would like to quote two sentences from her email: "**Sly has spent many hours with me while I rest in the family room after chemo treatments. He still recognizes me without hair or in my wig (I was hoping that wouldn't scare him).**" After reading that, my heart went out to this woman. It makes me feel so good I placed the dog with her. She is getting so much comfort and joy from her nurse, Sly.

~~

Sons and daughters come into the shelter with a parent whose spouse has passed away. The parent is lonely and adjusting to his/her loss. Adopting a pet may help the situation. A pet will give the grieving parent something else to think about. The pets are there when they wake up in the morning and are company to have breakfast with. The parents will never come home to empty houses. The pets will always be there to greet and welcome them home. While watching TV, it is nice to have a little friend snuggle beside you. You are never alone with a pet to comfort you. Doctors prescribe getting a pet rather than pills.

~~

This information is from the website, www.healthypet.com, the Pet Care Library entitled, "Pets for Seniors."

You've probably noticed that when you pet a soft, warm cat or play fetch with a dog whose tail won't stop wagging, you relax and your heart feels a little warmer. Scientists have noticed the same thing, and they've started to explore the complex way animals significantly benefit health, and not just for the young. In fact, pets may help elderly owners live longer, healthier, and more enjoyable lives.

A study published in *The Journal of the American Geriatrics Society* (Jags) in May 1999 demonstrated that independently living seniors that have pets tend to have better physical health and mental well-being than those that don't. They're more active, cope better with stress, and have better overall health. A study showed that elderly pet owners had significantly lower blood pressure overall than their contemporaries without pets. In fact, an experimental residential home for the elderly called Eden Alternative, which is filled with over 100 birds, dogs, and cats and has an outside environment with rabbits and chickens, has experienced a fifteen percent lower mortality rate than traditional nursing homes over the past five years.

There are a number of explanations for exactly how pets accomplish all these health benefits. First of all, pets need walking, feeding, grooming, fresh water, and fresh kitty litter, and, and they encourage lots of playing and petting. All of these activities require some action from owners. Even if it's just getting up to let a dog out a few times a day or brushing a cat, any activity can benefit the cardiovascular system and keep joints limber and flexible.

Consistently performing this kind of minor exercise can keep pet owners able to carry out the normal activities of daily living. Pets may also aid seniors simply by providing some physical contact. Studies have shown that when people pet animals, their blood pressure, heart rate, and temperature decrease.

Pets are an excellent source of companionship. For example, they can act as a support system for older people who don't have any family or close friends nearby to act as a support system. The Jags study showed that people with pets were better able to remain emotionally stable during crises than those without. Pets can also work as a buffer against social isolation. Often the elderly have trouble leaving home, so they don't have a chance to see many people. Pets give them a chance to interact. This can help combat depression, one of the most common medical problems facing our seniors today. The responsibility of caring for an animal may also give the elderly a sense of purpose, a reason to get up in the morning. Pets also help seniors stick to regular routines of getting up in the morning, buying groceries, and going outside, which help motivate them to eat and sleep regularly and well.

~~

I would like to add that there are children who do not do well socially or might be ill, who need a friend, too. Doctors highly recommend getting a pet for them as well. A loving pet can become their best friend, help build their confidence, and comfort them. There is no end to how pets help humans. Animals help the blind, the deaf, the disabled, etc. They are trained in police work to protect. The tireless, hard-working search and rescue dogs are truly a wonder. Let's not forget the fantastic, sensational, and amazing war dogs, which have saved so many soldiers' lives in combat, and sacrificed their own lives in the process. I would like to honor and give praise to all these extraordinary creatures.

Special People

Anyone who adopts a shelter animal is special. Most adopters want a perfectly healthy young animal, which is normal. This is the segment I tell you about adopters who reach out to an animal who is overlooked because it is not so perfect. It could be because of age, a disability, or an ailment. I consider those people utterly fantastic.

Animals are no different from humans. They are born with defects. They develop illnesses. They have accidents and suffer with disabilities. They grow old and are no longer wanted. Many of these animals I have described come through our shelter doors and are welcome. We call animals with issues, *special-needs*. The special-needs animals may not be placed as quickly as the other animals; however, we have lots of faith and patience. We know at any time an utterly fantastic person with tremendous compassion is going to come through our door and adopt one of our special-needs darlings.

I have been at the shelter several years and have placed many animals with afflictions. Here are some of the afflictions: deaf, blind, one eye, three legs, heart murmur, heart trouble, crippled for life, psychological problems, diabetes, thyroid, feline leukemia, feline immunodeficiency virus, and on special diets. We even placed the sweetest little orange female cat, which was born without the bottom half of her hind legs. Elderly animals are placed in wonderful homes, where they can live out the rest of their lives napping on a soft chair or looking out a sunny window. God bless those fantastic human beings, who adopt the special-needs animals.

~~

I must tell you the Sweetie Pie story. As I already reiterated most shelters accept young, perfect animals, which are a cinch to place. The Marblehead Animal Shelter is quite different because we accept animals of all ages and some not so perfect. Our unique shelter policy works because there are unselfish, kind, and big-hearted individuals out there who adopt these needy animals.

The story about Sweetie Pie, a beautiful, all-white, long-haired cat is a perfect example of our shelter policy. Her original owner sadly had to go into a nursing home, so Sweetie was surrendered to our shelter. She was eleven years old with a crippled paw. The poor thing had two strikes against her; age and a bad leg. Most animal shelters would reject her. The shelter volunteers will not turn our back on these animals and are resolved to find quality homes for them.

Sweetie was put in one of our high-priced cages. It was high-priced because it was located near a window. A couple of months passed when an English couple came into the shelter to adopt a cat. They fell in love with Sweetie Pie and wanted to adopt her. Her age and disability did not matter to them. It was one of those gratifying moments for the volunteers who took such good care of her. We were all so happy and happy is good.

Two years had passed since Sweetie was placed when an unexpected call came in from the English couple. They had to surrender Sweetie back to the shelter because they were moving back to England and could not take the cat with them. What an unlucky break for Sweetie.

Depending on the situation, animals being surrendered back into the shelter can be very emotional. You might think after many years of volunteering you would be conditioned to handle it. The day Sweetie was surrendered for the second time, there was not a dry eye in the place. It might take a little time; however, we were determined to find another home for her.

Shortly after Sweetie Pie's picture and profile was put back into our website, I received this email: "**How does Sweetie Pie get along with other kitties? I'd love to give a senior a home and have three critters now.** "**They are very mellow and love other kitties. We have a new big house and plenty of quiet spots to sleep or bird watch, including a cozy sun room.**"

This sounded too good to be true. I wanted to make sure she understood about Sweet's front leg, so I emailed her back…She replied, "**The problem with her leg is not worth mentioning…I'd just like to give her a home, a nice soft bed, a spot of sunshine, good food and TLC.**" I was truly touched.

I could not wait to meet this special person. The day she came into the shelter to adopt Sweetie Pie, I met an attractive woman who turned out to be a doctor. She was an anesthetist for a well-known Massachusetts hospital. What a wonderful person. It was obvious Sweetie's luck had changed for the best. Here are two of many updates from the doctor about Sweetie's progress in her new forever home:

"Well, it seemed like you all had special feelings for Sweetie Pie, so I wanted you to know she is doing well. Last night I was watching TV and looked over and Sweetie was sleeping under the coffee table. She decided she likes company, at least from a distance. Each day she gets a little more adventurous and surprises me the way she runs up and down the stairs. All is well."

"Sweetie Pie is coming out more and more and has started sleeping with me at night. There has been slow and steady progress. I don't think she will ever be cuddly with the others, but she seems more comfortable all the time. Thanks again for such a sweet girl."

Of course I do not have to tell you how gratifying it is to all the volunteers when one of our special-needs babies is placed into a good home. It means so much to us. Every time it happens it is a small miracle. Earlier in the book I referred to a sampler hanging in my kitchen. It says, "The earth has music for those who listen." It appears when one of our special-needs animals gets adopted there is music everywhere but much louder.

Post Script; another email: **Hello, I don't know if you remember me, but I adopted Sweetie Pie, the thirteen-year-old white kitty with the club foot several years ago. She lived a very quiet life here. Loved to lay on my desk while I worked on the computer. She died in her sleep this morning some time, very peacefully. I knew it was coming—she had lost an extensive amount of weight over the last month or so. She was still drinking water, and acting like her normal self yesterday. I didn't take her to the vet as she hated being "fussed" with, and since she was happy, felt she deserved to go on her own terms. Being poked and prodded would have been miserable for her, and I don't think we would have bought much time for a seventeen-year-old cat anyway.**

She is buried under a lilac bush, back by my fence. The horses that live behind me came and paid their respects to her as I laid her in the ground, wrapped in a nice soft towel. I hope she has a good retirement here with me...my initial goal was just a warm bed and plenty of food and water for as long as she wanted it. She came out of her shell after 6 months or so, and I will miss her companionship. Thank you for trusting me with this very wonderful girl.

Blessings Sweetie Pie! May the angels guide your way to the Rainbow Bridge.

I wept reading her email. It was so touching.

Reunions

Through the years hundreds of animals have crossed the threshold into the shelter on a temporary basis. Just as many are adopted and cross over the threshold again out of the shelter to start a new life. During their brief stay, the volunteers form attachments to the animals. You just can't help it. Everybody has their favorites and after being adopted we often wonder how they are doing.

Every time there is an adoption I ask the adopter to update us on their new pet's progress. Many adopters send letters, cards, emails, and pictures. The letter, cards, and pictures are hung on the bulletin board for the volunteers to enjoy. I forward the emails to share with the volunteers, so they can take pleasure and enjoy the results of their hard work. What could be better than reading about the wonderful new life of one of our temporary lodgers?

There is one thing that tops reading about one of our adopted animals. It is seeing them in person. Occasionally one of our adopters brings their pets to the shelter for a reunion. It always seems to happen on Saturdays. The reunions are so much fun. Everyone involved is so excited except the pets. They can't get out of the shelter fast enough. Their brief stays here were not the most pleasant experience, and they think their owners are bringing them back. If they only knew how lucky they were to have come to our no-kill shelter in the first place.

The volunteers love seeing the animals again. You can't help noticing how happy and healthy they look. Some gain weight and their fur is shiny again. Many animals while in the shelter get dry skin, develop dandruff, and their fur gets dull from stress. The most obvious observation is how the animal and the adopter have bonded. It truly gives us a sense of accomplishment, which makes us so proud.

The one thing we have plenty of at the Marblehead Animal Shelter are stories. Every animal comes into the shelter with a story and every animal we place continues the story. They are all unique. I have a particularly cute one to tell. It is about our reunion with the 20,000-mile cat.

During our regular Saturday adoption hours a wonderful, young-at-heart, retired couple of Marblehead walked into the shelter to adopt a cat—not just any cat, but a cat that liked to travel. I was puzzled by their request and did not quite understand. We test all our cats for FeLV (feline leukemia) and FIV (feline immunodeficiency virus), but we do not test them on how well they travel.

This adorable couple explained that they had a mini motor home and went on very long trips. Their beloved cat, Shadow, had passed away. Shadow accompanied them in their camper on all their trips. As a matter of fact, Shadow traveled about 75,000 miles and loved every minute of it. The couple loved Shadow very much and missed having a loving companion.

I went into action to see which cat at the shelter would suit their needs. I looked in all the cages and knew immediately which would be a suitable cat for that couple. It was Pickett. He was a big, beautiful, shiny, all-black cat with a super personality, who could adapt to almost any situation. The couple liked him too. There was good chemistry, and off they went with Pickett.

The traveling couple brought Pickett into the shelter for a reunion. They had changed his name to Midnight, and he looked magnificent. You could just tell he was a spoiled, happy cat. Midnight walked with a harness like a dog and went everywhere with his adopted parents. He had just come back from a trip to San Francisco by way of Texas and had been to Nova Scotia twice. As of today he has traveled about 20,000 miles. They have plans to go to North Carolina and Quebec.

This is just one of our many success stories at the shelter. These stories are what it is all about for the volunteers, because they work tirelessly for the animals. We all wish these special people and their traveling cat, Midnight, a Bon Voyage!

Periodically I put our shelter stories in the weekly paper. They are good human interest stories that people love to read about. These stories are also good public relations for the shelter. The 20,000-mile cat story in the weekly paper was a huge success.

~~

My book would not be complete if I did not do a segment on Slinky/Kitzy the cat. When Kitzy was brought into the shelter, his name was Slinky. He was a handsome, large, black and white, domestic, short-hair, tuxedo cat. A young couple was forced to surrender Slinky because their young child was terribly allergic. They loved Slinky very much, and both were in a terrible state leaving the cat in a cage in the shelter—especially the husband. I remember it vividly.

Some weeks later a lovely couple came into the shelter looking for a black and white tuxedo cat. They lived a distance away and found us on the website. It just so happened at the time we had two tuxedo cats in side by side cages. They were both nice cats. Slinky was a husky cat and the other cat was slight. I showed them both cats and answered all their questions. We talked at length, and I was convinced any one of our cats would be lucky to have them as parents. They told me they were going to think about it and walked out of the shelter. The other volunteers in the shelter at the time were disappointed they didn't take a cat. I told the volunteers because of many years of experience as adoption coordinator, my instincts were telling me the couple was going to be back to adopt one of those cats. I was right! Twenty minutes later the couple came back into the shelter and decided to adopt Slinky.

Slinky was going to live in a big house on an estate in an affluent community. He was going to be loved, spoiled, and doted over. Slinky without exaggeration hit MEGA BUCKS!

It appears Slinky was the perfect cat for them. The couple was so enthralled with him, it inspired them to write this article for their local paper and sent it to me to put in our website in the alumni section.

Kitzy is enjoying his new home, to say the least! And we are enjoying him! After our last cat passed away, we never thought that we would find a cat that would come close to taking his place. As a matter of fact, we were not "cat people" at all! When it became apparent that my husband and I would never have children, I began to suggest to my husband that we should get a cat. "No way" was always the response! Until one cold November evening when this old black and white stray cat appeared at our door...hungry and cold. He melted my husband's heart and we took him in. We came to love this cat and he loved us; but as fate would have it, he developed a fatal cancer in his jaw. We kept him going as long as possible, but finally we had him quietly put to rest at our home and buried him at his favorite spot on the estate. Totally heartbroken, we began looking for another black and white cat.

Enter the Marblehead Shelter and this terrific black and white cat that we saw on one hot August day. We went to the shelter not expecting

to take home a cat that day, but when we saw this big black and white guy, we knew that was the one! And we think he felt the same way...After discussing whether or not to take the cat, we decided "yes" he was coming home with us—he actually got into the cat carrier and was ready to go to his new home! After a few days of getting acquainted, we knew that we made the right choice. We named the cat "Kitty Kitzbuehel" after our favorite mountain town in Austria, but we call him "Kitzy" for short.

Kitzy is gentle, polite, sweet and loving. He is truly "one of us." He blends right in and knows how to be a great family member. I'm almost embarrassed to say this, but this cat is almost human! He has such feelings! For instance, one day I came home from work with the flu. Immediately Kitzy knew I wasn't feeling well, so he kept butting me with his head and leading me to the couch, he pulled up (with his mouth) a small blanket that was on the couch and covered me. Once he was satisfied that I was going to rest, this terrific guy snuggled up with me and didn't let me get up until I was fully rested! Now that's a cat!!

The stories of this cat and how he has changed our lives can go on and on (he's a great traveler in the car and loves monthly trips to our Vermont house...everyone on the estate where we live just loves this cat and brings their pets over to visit—his best friend is a three-legged white cat next door!). But, again, the stories go on and on, but it is no story that my husband and I found love and faithfulness in an unexpected place far away from our home. Which just goes to prove that you can hide in a closet, but whatever is meant to be will be and no matter how much you hide from fate, fate will always find you! Having this cat has been rewarding in so many ways. If ever anyone tells me that they are contemplating getting a cat, I wouldn't hesitate to tell them to run over to the Marblehead Shelter and get one! They won't be sorry!

Would it be an understatement to say, this starry-eyed couple adore Kitzy the cat? Well, if that article doesn't convince, maybe these amusing excerpts from email updates of the cat will:

So, this is the update: Right now he is sleeping in the sun in the family room and is stretched out a mile long! He seems to enjoy watching the Red Sox at night with us and will snuggle right up to the couch. He runs around with his tail held high and jumps up and down. He really can jump! His most daring escapade was to jump up on our granite kitchen island and snatch a piece of ham off it—whoosh!! All in one motion! You should have seen him running down the hall with that ham in his mouth!!! He's also already wormed his way into sleeping on our bed (something our last cat wouldn't do until he was ill). And I don't have to worry about dirty dishes…Kitzy likes to lick the platters clean when I'm not looking!! He's done this with a couple of ice cream and fish plates.

All is well here. Had a dinner party here last night with 12 of our friends in the formal dining room. Kitzy loved every minute of it. As the guests came in to be seated, Kitzy would jump from chair to chair and "surprise" them as he poked his head out from under the tablecloth! Then he plopped himself down at the head of the table again and wouldn't move. My poor husband had to get out a kitchen chair and sit so Kitzy could sit in the "head of the table" chair all evening and join in the conversation!" Yes, he actually looks at whomever is speaking and nods his head, like he really knows what's going on! What a character. All the guests just loved him!

Hi there: Just checking in…Kitzy is doing well and remains a terrific cat. We did leave him for 10 days to go to Florida. He had a morning sitter, an afternoon sitter and an evening sitter, though!! He was never alone too much, but every person said the same thing; that he really missed us. He would sit by the front door all the time waiting for us to return. Finally, when we came back and opened the door he looked at us and at first was confused, but then got very excited to see us. For two days he stuck to us like glue. Literally stuck to us!!! We did "call him" (i.e. left the message machine on loud and left messages for him). We played the messages back a day or two after we returned and he went wild!! He was singing and jumping in the air—so we guess he enjoyed his phone calls!

Just a quick Kitzy report. Kitzy is fine. Cute as always. Great cat. Loves tomato sauce and Friendly's Vienna Mocha Chip ice cream! He's better than an alarm clock…every morning he wakes us up with a big old butt from his big old head! And of course he loves the air-conditioned house. The other night that cat just spread himself a mile long across the bed...the AC was on and the ceiling fan and he was just letting everything get cooled off. We went and slept in another room, but the Big Boy found us and voila! He wormed his way in and took over that bed, too! He really enjoys our company and is just the kind of cat that likes to be near us, but is not obnoxious about it...except of course in the morning when we try to read the paper. WHACK! One swipe of his giant paws and that newspaper goes flying. And that cat enjoys a nice morning rubdown. He's not spoiled, though!

Greetings from the Land of Kitzy! Kitzy asked me to drop you all a note to let you know that this big boy is just doing fine! He had a nice trip to Vermont last weekend and got a tour around the complex with his female cat friend, Dibby, who lives downstairs. Dibby is quite the hunter, so we hope that Kitzy didn't pick up any bad habits. But he had a great, mellow time, as always.

Also, Kitzy is a hero—he was asked to donate blood and so he stepped up to the cause and did just that! Apparently they needed blood at the MSPCA, so Kitzy's vet asked if he would donate, since he is such a healthy guy. He made it through it just great. When I went to pick him up there was a nice big picture of Kitzy in the waiting room that said "Donor of the day." Then when Kitzy was brought out, as usual, everyone in the waiting room went crazy over him cause he is such a ham! The staff there just love Kitzy. Sigh! What a following this cat has.

Kitzy is in the dog-house, though! He gave us quite the scare last night. He wasn't coming in and finally about dusk we put out an all search. We found him behind the greenhouse having coffee with the neighborhood skunk (a pretty harmless gal)!! Were we ever mad at him! (Well, they weren't really having coffee, but they were sitting there together). Sure, she's pretty and she's black and white too, and probably has her own pad behind the greenhouse, but I doubt she'll give him three square meals a day and a comfortable big house! So, that's for Kitzy going outside after 5:00 for a while.

Right now this little romancer is in the window making eyes at the new cat that moved in at the condo complex next door last week. Don't think that cat goes out, but we'll have to keep an eye on this!

Take care everyone! Rest assured, Kitzy is a very happy guy! Someday we'll get up there to visit.

So, those are the latest Kitzy antics!! These people are infatuated with their cat. Besides the updates I have received pictures of Kitzy in a pumpkin

Halloween costume greeting children trick or treating on the estate. The other precious picture of him was sleeping in an empty Christmas gift bag under the Christmas tree. That very picture is on our website in the alumni section with the article the couple wrote. Now you know what I meant when I said Kitzy hit Mega Bucks!

The shelter's goal is to find sensational homes for all of our animals. The volunteers love to read the updates after animals have been adopted, and especially love to see them in person. The couple brought Kitzy back to the shelter for a reunion. We thought he was a big handsome dude when he was at the shelter. When we saw him again he had grown even larger, his coat was sparkling, and he was still a handsome dude. No wonder they named him after a mountain.

~~

The most festive reunion at the shelter was for a dog named Calvin. Calvin came all the way from Ohio. He was a shepherd mix with extra large ears that stood straight up. We were networking with a group that saved animals from being put down. There are areas in the country where there aren't any no-kill shelters. This group saves animals by transporting them to no-kill shelters nationally. People volunteer to drive the animals a portion of the distance to their destination, meet another volunteer at safe meeting places, transfer the animals into their car; and go a portion of the way to meet the next volunteer. It goes on and on until the final destination. Along the way animals are dropped off at different shelters. This was the transport schedule on how Calvin got to our shelter:

Ashtabula, OH–Erie, PA; 48 miles; 7:00–8:00; Filled: Darlene; Blue Nissan

Erie, PA–Buffalo, NY; 93 miles; 8:00–9:45; Filled: Shelly; Blue Isuzu Amigo 2-door SUV or Navy Blue Explorer

Buffalo, NY–Rochester, NY; 76 miles; 9:45–11:00; Filled: Mary; White Subaru Forester

Rochester, NY–Syracuse, NY; 89 miles; 11:00–12:45; Filled: Helga; Light Blue Dodge Caravan

Syracuse, NY–Utica, NY; 56 miles; 12:45–2:00; Filled: Sue; Purple Geo Tracker

Utica, NY–Albany, NY; 95 miles; 2:00–3:45; Filled: Robin; Humane Society of Rome White Van

Albany, NY–Springfield, MA; 87 miles; 3:45–5:30; Filled: Becky

Springfield, MA–Worcester, MA; 50 miles; 5:30–6:45; Filled: Cindy

Worchester, MA–Marblehead, MA; 71 miles; 6:45–830; Filled: Cindy

For obvious reasons I excluded phone numbers, cell phone numbers, and addresses. If there was a change of any kind, they could contact each other. Boxer mix puppies were transported to Sue, who was doing the Syracuse to

Utica leg. After Utica it was only Calvin the shepherd mix, who was coming to our shelter in Marblehead. All of the dogs were provided with collars and leashes. I call it a pony express for animals. Calvin was not the only animal to come to our shelter via pony express. We took in several cats too at different times.

Well, Calvin arrived safe and sound from his long pony express trek from Ohio but not without a problem. He was taken to the vet for a complete physical examine, when it was discovered he needed hip surgery. Other than that he was a healthy, sweet, loving dog. Calvin deserved a chance for life without pain. A yard sale was organized to raise money for the expensive hip surgery. The money collected from the yard sale, from some very generous donors, and from our shelter account; Calvin was able to have his hip operation.

Enter a marvelous Marblehead couple, George and Pam Derringer, who had been looking for a dog. Many of us at the shelter knew them. George was the editor for the community newspaper and his wife, Pam, used to be a reporter there as well. They heard about Calvin and came in to see him. Both the dog and the couple hit it off and took him home on trial. Well, it didn't take long for the three of them to bond. They did not even wait for the trial period to be over when they adopted him. Calvin had a grand home with the nicest people.

Not long after Calvin was adopted, I received a call from his new mom. She and her husband were so in love with their new addition they wanted to do something to thank the volunteers for saving his life and allowing them to adopt him. I told her it wasn't necessary. We do this every day because that is what we do. She insisted on giving a party at the shelter for the volunteers and Calvin.

On a Saturday afternoon during adoption hours there was a party. Calvin's mom and dad provided all the refreshments and decorations. They invited their relatives, friends, and volunteers to attend. Everybody was anxious to meet Calvin. Some brought Calvin gifts. Visitors to the shelter that day were also invited to participate. It was a super, fun, festive day. Calvin felt very special. We never had a reunion like that before or since. It was the best!

Benevolence

Here is one more reason why my Saturday afternoon at the shelter is my favorite day. As you already know, we are a non-profit organization. We depend on donations, fund-raisers, and what little we charge for an adoption, which does not cover the cost of their medical check-up.

We are most fortunate our shelter is in the town of Marblehead. The community is very supportive of our organization, and we appreciate their generosity.

There are donors who give large sums of money, who wish to remain nameless. There are those who give more than they can afford because they believe in our cause. Some people can't afford to give money and bring food and supplies to the shelter for the animals. Others use their talents. One woman sewed curtains to decorate the interior of the shelter. Another woman generously made quilted soft comfy pads for the different size cat cages. Children of all ages create projects to collect money to help the animals. Brownie troops, Boy Scout troops, and other organizations also find ways of helping. One of the most unselfish acts of generosity is when a child is having a birthday party and asks his or her guests to bring supplies and food for the animals at the shelter in place of presents for themselves. That is pretty praiseworthy. All these acts of generosity are greatly appreciated.

Saturday afternoon during adoption hours appears to be the most convenient time for these kind, charitable people to come into the shelter with their donations. I am so glad to be the one to receive them. It gives you a good feeling.

~~

This story will show you how humans who care have compassion, and will go to great lengths to extend themselves for animals in need. One of our devoted volunteers, Sue, heard about a six-month-old German shepherd who was going to be put down because she needed surgery on each of her hind legs. She has a debilitating health problem that affected the bones and ligaments behind both of her knees. The problem restricted her from running and she was in constant pain. The operations were going to cost at least two thousand dollars or more for each leg. That was a lot of money, which none of us could afford. Sue made arrangements with the rescue that had the dog, not to put him down. The dog would become the responsibility of the Marblehead Animal Shelter. Sue needed a little time to find a foster home for her. After she found a foster home she was going to try to raise the money for the dog's surgery through our shelter. This would not be an easy task, but if anybody could do it, Sue would. She is a kind person and has such compassion for animals and will literally go to the ends of the earth to help save them.

Sue emailed me explaining the whole situation. She requested I send out an S.O.S. email to all the volunteers to help find a foster home for the crippled German shepherd pup. I did what she asked and thought it was a reach, but you never know. Lo and behold another volunteer, Andrea, answered the call and offered her home to foster the dog. Chloee was the dog's name. She was immediately released and transferred to her foster home. Thanks to Sue and Andrea, Chloee was going to be saved.

Sue and Andrea became partners in their pursuit to raise money for the two absolutely necessary cruciate-ligament operations. Chloee would not be able to walk normally if she did not have that surgery. Their first attempt to raise money was to organize a yard sale at the shelter with help from the other volunteers. I don't think Andrea realized at the time what was going to happen when she advertised the yard sale in the newspaper with the story why we were having the yard sale and also a picture of the puppy.

Well, talk about doing for others! The public had such compassion for little Chloee. It was overwhelming! People were sending money, small, medium, and large checks to the shelter. There was such an outpouring, it was unbelievable. A church collected money from their congregation. Children collected money from their teachers and classmates in school. Generous people from surrounding communities also contributed. Of course, our most special shelter donors, who are always overly generous, helped too. It was astonishing! It was incredible! It was wonderful!

The weather on the day of the yard sale was horrible. It was cold, raw, and raining. It couldn't have been worse. In spite of the weather the public came out to help Chloee. They bought things they didn't need just to help. There are not enough adjectives to describe this experience. There are lots of good, kind, big-hearted people out there.

Remarkably enough money was raised to cover the cost of both operations. While fostering Chloee, Andrea got attached and fell in love with her. Yes, you guessed it; Andrea adopted her, and Chloee was no longer in foster care. She became a permanent addition to her new home. Over time Chloee had both operations, and they were successful. She would be able to walk normally the rest of her life and not be in pain. This warm-hearted story about a six-month-old puppy captured the hearts of so many. Compassion, kindness, and generosity from so many good, caring people gives you reason to pause.

The shelter on many occasions has helped with medical expenses for people who can't afford to take care of their animals. Their animals need medical care desperately because the alternative for the pet is not good. We just helped a single mom and her little boy with their kitten, which had heart problems. The little boy didn't want his kitten to die and wanted to donate part of his own heart to the kitten he loved so dearly. Without our help the kitten's death was imminent. The operation cost three thousand dollars. The story was put in the paper, and we ran one of our famous yard sales. The donations started pouring in, and we exceeded far more than the cost of the operation thanks to the generosity of people of all ages in the community. The kitten's operation was successful, and the little boy would have his kitten for a long time to come. Jean, my sidekick, spearheaded this emergency. She took the bull by the horns and made it happen. Jean has a big heart!

Genuine acts of kindness and charity are performed throughout the year at the shelter. During the Christmas holiday season the acts of kindness are enormous. Beautifully wrapped gift packages with an assortment of supplies, food, and toys for the animals are brought to the shelter. Hundreds of joyous cards with checks enclosed are mailed to us and brought to us personally by our sincerest supporters. They all truly believe in our cause.

One year a thoughtful mom and her three little daughters came into the shelter with a unique Christmas gift. It was a ten-inch cat doll dressed in a spectacular glittering gold angel costume. This lovely angel belonged on the top of a Christmas tree. Since we did not have a tree in the shelter, we found a very special spot in the shelter to hang the angel. The little family wanted the cat angel to look after the animals in the shelter all year long.

You have to believe in Santa Claus when you see so many people taking the time to remember the homeless shelter animals over the hectic holiday season. There is a special feeling you get, which is hard for me to describe. I feel like Jimmy Stewart felt in the last scene of the classic movie *It's a Wonderful Life*.

If you are not familiar with the movie, I will try to capsulate a little of what it is about. Jimmy Stewart was a hometown boy, who wanted to travel and see the world. His father died suddenly, so reluctantly he took over his father's savings and loan business. His father was a good and fair man, who went out on a limb to help the townspeople. The only other bank/loan office in the town was run by a greedy heartless tyrant played by a great actor, Lionel Barrymore. The tyrant disapproved of the way Jimmy Stewart and his father before ran the business. The townspeople hated him.

There is so much more to this movie, but I'm only telling a small portion of it. Jimmy's best friend, who worked in the loan office with him, carelessly misplaced a huge sum of money from the loan office. The loss of this money was going to deplete his friends and neighbors of their savings, as well as ruin the business his father worked so hard to maintain. It was a disaster!

When Jimmy learned about the careless mistake, he knew he was in big trouble. More than anything he did not want to let his friends and neighbors down. He panicked and ran and ran until he came to a bridge. Looking over the bridge, he contemplated committing suicide. Suddenly a jolly little elderly gentleman appeared from nowhere. He was an angel. He convinced Jimmy to go home and face the crisis and indeed he did.

It was late when he finally returned home. All the lights were on and crowds of people from the town were there. He thought the people were there to castigate him. He courageously walked into the house and was bewildered and surprised. The townspeople had learned about the costly mistake and were donating whatever money they had to help make up the shortfall.

For many years Jimmy's father had helped the people in the town and Jimmy followed in his father's footsteps. This time the people turned the table and came to his rescue. Can you imagine how he felt at that very moment? He was overcome with emotion. Jimmy had a lot of friends who supported him. The shelter also has a lot of friends who support the animals.

If you have never seen that movie, I strongly suggest you do. My point of telling you about that movie was the only way I could describe how I feel during the holiday season and beyond. I sometimes become emotional witnessing so many of our supporters remembering the animals with their generosity and kindness. It is a wonderful life!

The animals and volunteers want to take this opportunity to say thank you for all you do to help the shelter. Believe me, it is truly appreciated.

MOSES

While writing this chapter, I had the heart-breaking task to say good-bye to my beloved Bernese mountain dog, Moses. He was a month shy of eleven years old and was stricken with bladder cancer.

Moses was seven weeks old when we adopted him. He was so special and very much a part of our family. He grew up to be an absolutely handsome, magnificent animal, who weighed well over a hundred pounds. When we walked together, people continually remarked about how regal he was. They all said the same thing, "He does not look real." Moses was my precious jewel.

No person or animal could come near our home without Moses's bark to warn us. He was our loyal protector, yet, he was gentle with our grandchildren, whom he loved dearly. He was also gentle with our cats, and his best friend, our bloodhound, Annie. What I would not give to put my arms around his big head and hug and squeeze him again. He was my own personal big teddy bear.

I used to sing to Moses to show my affection. The melody is unimportant. Here are the words: *You are my baby boy, my living toy, my pride, and joy*. He loved when I sang to him and would roll over on his back for a belly rub. I will treasure every moment he was with me. Moses was my dream dog and so special. He will live in my heart always.

This quote by Will Rogers expresses my sentiments. "If there are no dogs in heaven, then when I die I want to go where they went."

It was so very hard to say good-bye.

HODGEPODGE

Chapter 8

This chapter contains a mixture of various short stories and events that occurred at the shelter through the years. Some of the stories are sad, humorous, serious, and surprising. I know you will find them all interesting.

Names

What is in a name? Well, you will be surprised. A name can conjure up all kinds of emotions and memories. A particular name may remind you of a friend, a romantic interlude, a wicked person, an unforgettable experience, an admirer, and much more.

On every animal's cage in the shelter there is attached a pink or blue card to distinguish the animal's gender. The card also has the date the animal arrived, its medical history, when it was spayed or neutered, and of course its name. Visitors who come into the shelter love reading the cards. They always ask me, "Where do the animals get their names?" I explain when the surrendered animals come into the shelter, they already have their names and we won't change them. When a stray or abandoned animal is brought into the shelter, the volunteers on duty at the time share in the naming process. We all have our individual ideas on naming the animals. The selection of names could be creative, common, or ridiculous. I personally like people names for the animals such as Agnes, Eddie, Lucy, Harry, Cleo, Stanley, Louise etc. I am sure you get the idea.

Let me cite some of the inventive imaginative names given to the animals. Since I was a little girl I have loved westerns. When a litter of six kittens came into the shelter, I named them after my favorite cowboys. There were three boys and three girls in the litter. The males were named Hopalong Cassidy, Roy Rogers, and Gene Autry. The females were named Annie Oakley, Calamity Jane, and Belle Star. Very often we name the kittens after all the endless Disney cartoon movie characters. There are also the old favorite cartoon characters from Warner Brothers and Hanna Barbara such as Bugs Bunny, Porky Pig, Elmer Fudd, Yogi Bear, and Scooby Doo. A good source of kitten names are from the newer cartoon shows on television like *The Rugrats*, *The Powerpuff Girls*, and *Pokemon*. The children especially love the names of the kittens because they can relate. You have to have a sense of humor and it makes things fun. Whatever or whoever is most popular at the time the kittens arrive will likely be used for names. It could be rock stars, country singers, movie stars, authors, dancers, etc. There are an abundance of names out there, and we never seem run out.

The adult animals usually get people's names or cutesy names like Bubbles and Spunky. A lot of names are aristocratic (Princess, Queen, Duke, Duchess, and Sultan). Then there are ethnic names (Angelo, Pepe, Pierre, Katja, etc). What about colors for names (Sterling, Blue, Buffy, Ivory, and many more)? Let's not forget food names (Hershey, Chili, Cinnamon, Vanilla, Mousse, Muffin, and Dumpling). Other popular names are after cities, states, and countries (Nevada, Dakota, India, Alaska, Tennessee, and Dallas). These are just a few examples and the list of different names is endless.

Some other interesting adult names come from specific events. A cat was named after Picabo Street, a fabulous skier who was in the Winter Olympics. After the 2000 presidential election we named some of the animals after our new president and his cabinet. A stray brown tiger cat was found on the local golf course. Yes, you guessed it! He was named Tiger Woods.

The most humorous name story is this one. Two lovely female adult cats came into the shelter during the sex scandal of one of our United States presidents. I wanted to have some fun and named the cats Monica and Paula. The cats were up for adoption. Their pictures and names were put in the local paper. You would not believe the response we got. So many people came to the shelter to adopt those cats. There were over twenty other cats in the shelter at the time, but they only wanted Monica and Paula. People are funny sometimes. I was hoping for more scandals, so I could place more animals.

If you were a fan of the sitcom television show *Seinfeld*, you were not alone. More animals placed from the shelter had been named after one of the *Seinfeld* characters (Kramer, Cosmo, Newman, or George). They were unbelievably popular at the time.

Believe it or not, animals have been adopted just because of their names. The name obviously connotes something very special to the person. Some people feel it is an omen of some sort.

Occasionally, animals at the shelter happen to have the same name. It could be confusing. We had a Tigger in the shelter and another Tigger came in. I called the second Tigger, Little Tigger because he was younger and smaller. We had a Sally. When another Sally came into the shelter, we called her Sally II. We try to keep it simple. Names are important because it is the only source of identification on all shelter medical records. Only when an animal is placed, the adopter will decide whether to keep or change their name. The new pet will have a new loving family, a new beginning, and possibly a new name.

Boomer

Who is Boomer? Boomer is a medium-size tan and white dog. He was one of the most loveable affectionate, friendly, fun, comical, and intelligent dogs I have ever encountered. Please, don't tell my dogs I said that. Boomer was between two or three years old.

He used to escape from his home, get picked up by animal control, brought to the shelter until his owner picked him up. Every opportunity he had, he would escape. He even jumped out of the second floor window to escape according to his owner. Boomer was so smart that every time he escaped, he went right to the shelter. He didn't wait for animal control to pick him up. If no one was at the shelter at the time, he waited on the front stoop for someone to let him in. Boomer loved being at the shelter. There were lots of people, animals, and so much going on. He wanted to be where the action was.

Everybody loved Boomer. You just couldn't help loving him. He was a real charmer. One day I pulled into the shelter driveway and there was Boomer on the stoop with the neighbor who lived across the street. She was one of the neighbors who had vehemently opposed building the animal shelter there. They were together waiting for someone to open up. She befriended Boomer and they became good friends. A little birdie told me the police chief at the time also loved Boomer. He was a very special dog.

It was apparent Boomer had a bad case of separation anxiety. He did not want to stay home. It got to the point his owner could not afford to pay for all the citations. They added up to a great deal of money. The dog would rather be at the shelter than in his own home. His owner loved Boomer, but had little choice and reluctantly surrendered him to the shelter. He was our responsibility now and we loved having him. It was not going to be easy finding him a proper home. Remember, he had that separation anxiety problem and had to be where the action is. Secretly, the volunteers wished he could stay at the shelter and be our mascot.

Boomer got his wish—the shelter was his new home. Most animals want out of the shelter as soon as possible. Not Boomer, he loved it. He was never caged and ran free in the shelter. He got along with the cats and the dogs. He thought it was his job to be the official greeter when we had visitors. The children especially loved him. When it was nap time for Boomer, he would go into the laundry room, cuddle up in the laundry basket, and take a snooze.

Some months had passed before the perfect owner for Boomer came along. It was a perfect match. The gentleman was a courier and Boomer would go everywhere with him. There would never be a separation anxiety problem with him any longer; however, there would be separation anxiety with the volunteers. We got very attached to Boomer and missed him terribly. It was best for the dog to have a real home and a loving family. A couple of years later Boomer came back for a visit. He was still a very happy, special dog.

Why am I telling you about Boomer? If you recall there were two unpleasant segments in this book; about Gemma, a pit bull terrier, and Lucy, a pit bull terrier mix. Both dogs were put down and in my opinion, unjustly. This breed has gotten a bad reputation. I never did mention what breed of dog Boomer was. Well, Boomer was also a pit bull terrier and so very special.

Telling you this warm story about Boomer might alter any fears you may have about this breed. There are good and bad in humans as well as in animals. There are also bad dog owners. Do you remember the old-time children's movies *The Little Rascals*, or the *Our Gang* movies? Do you remember Petey, that wonderful dog with the black circle around one eye, who was always with the children? Well, Petey was a pit bull too. Boomer and Petey were so much alike—sensational!

Shock and Awe

It was a Saturday afternoon and the shelter was jammed with potential adopters. Jean, my right hand was unable to assist me that afternoon. I was alone going from one potential adopter to another. Adopting an animal is a major decision to most individuals, and they deserve quality attention. It is important the animal and the adopter are compatible.

Another couple came into the shelter. They were dressed very nicely and the woman had beautiful, black, long, curly hair. They mentioned they had no intension of adopting because they were from Vermont and came to town to go to a wedding. Their family lived up the street, where they were staying, and wanted to take a walk to the shelter to visit the animals. I welcomed them and went back to attend to the other people.

The Vermont couple didn't get far in the shelter when they spotted Siam. Siam was a pedigree Russian blue cat under a year old. He was regal, handsome, active, something to behold, and a little devil. The couple summoned me over to get the background on Siam. I told them he was a stray picked up and brought to the pound. Nobody claimed him and he was going to be put down in ten days. We had cage space and took him in. I sensed the Vermont couple, who had no intention to adopt, fell head over heels for Siam.

I went back to the other potential adopters. They needed input from me. While I was talking with them, from the corner of my eye I was observing the Vermont couple. They did not move away from Siam's cage and were having a vigorous conversation with each other. As if I didn't know what they were discussing. I've been there before. They were considering adopting Siam.

The Vermont couple summoned me over again and wanted to ask me more questions. Wow, was I busy that day. They told me they had a Persian cat and two Bengal cats. Their concern was how Siam would get along with other cats. I told them he gets along well with the other cats when they are out of their cages exercising. I also provided them a sheet of paper with directions on how to introduce a new cat into a multi-cat home. I personally followed those same directions many times and they work. There is nothing but harmony in my home with six cats and two dogs. I returned to work with the others.

One more time the Vermont couple summoned me over. They wanted to know, if they adopted Siam and it did not work out, could they bring him back. Absolutely, we want the cat back. It is our policy. We put too much into our animals to let them go anywhere else. They also wanted to know, if they could pick him up tomorrow before driving back to Vermont. We are closed on Sundays, but I would make an exception and come in. Right at that point they expressed their wish to adopt Siam. I excused myself from the others in the shelter and would get back to them directly. The Vermont couple made a decision and had my complete attention.

They had to fill out an adoption application before anything was finalized. I gave the woman the clipboard with the application. While she was filling out the application, I started asking a lot of questions. There was no time to screen them, and I did not want this adoption to be just on impulse. The woman abruptly stopped filling out the application and slammed the clipboard on the desk. I was stunned by her action and knew I hadn't said anything to offend her. Her voice was stern and she asked me if I wanted to know if they were going to be responsible owners. I said, "Yes I do." Again, she asked me if I wanted to know if Siam was going to get the love and the quality care he required. I replied, "Yes I do."

She proceeded to say, "Well I will show you!" I couldn't imagine what she was going to show me. At that very moment she unbuckled her pant belt and pulled down her slacks. My face turned red and my eyes popped out of my head. Everyone else in the shelter was flabbergasted and their eyes popped out of their heads as well. It was a shock and awe moment for all of us. On both her thighs down to her knees were tattooed her beautiful beloved Bengal cats. It was one of those rare occasions I was totally speechless.

I am at the ripe young age of sixty-four and in my generation we thought only sailors got tattoos. Frankly, I can't understand why anyone would want a tattoo; however, I must admit her tattoos were beautiful. They looked like a very expensive, beautiful tapestry. When I got my composure back, I asked her if it hurt. She said, "It sure did!" She researched and researched for the right person to do the work. It took three sittings at seven hours a sitting for a total of twenty-one hours. Can you imagine? She did not call them tattoos; she called them "cattoos." There was no question about her love for their cats.

The Vermont couple passed the screening test with high marks and adopted Siam. We met on Sunday next. They brought their whole family and friends with them to check out and meet Siam. It was a happy occasion. Both Siam and the couple took off for Vermont, while an entourage of family, friends and I were waving good-bye.

The very next day the couple emailed me. Their trip home went smoothly. They changed his name to Sammy and assured me things were going well. They sent me many pictures of him, and continue to update me on Sammy's progress.

The other people in the shelter that day adopted animals too. Not only did they bring home a new pet; they brought home a story they would never forget.

The shock and awe story was fun to tell. After telling the story everyone asked me the same question, "Is she going to have Siam tattooed on her?" It was a fair question and I was curious myself, so I emailed her and asked. This is what she emailed back to me:

Oooh! Thank you for reminding me. I've already begun conceiving my next tattoo. Sammy has become quite a jumper. Tonight, he jumped from the top of an antique cabinet to the top of the cat tree, a 5.5-foot span, with no difficulty. So, I'm thinking it will be Sammy, jumping from one side of my torso to the other, either on the front (jumping over the tattoo around my belly button) or on my back (jumping over the round tattoo on my sacrum). But these things are a long time in the making, so they will come out just right. You can bet I'll come and show you, and leave a photo, when it happens. It could be at least a year though.

Lethal

The story I am about to tell you is a serious one. It must have been serious because several newspapers picked it up when they got wind of the story. It was also on local and national television news programs. Some of the newspapers reported a lot of misinformation, which made me angry. All our years of hard work building a superb reputation at the shelter was at stake. I personally called one newspaper to inform them of the true story. They understood our position and kindly printed a retraction. When you deal with living things, things happen. It is so very important the public continues to trust in our animal shelter.

The story started the day I walked into the shelter and noticed a large, tall corrugated box. My curiosity led me over to the box to look inside. Two absolutely adorable silver gray tabby infant kittens were nestled together in the box. The kittens were really young and needed a mom to nurse. Laura came in shortly after me. She told me the kittens were from a feral colony located in town. She went on to say a neighbor witnessed a skunk attacking the litter of kittens. The neighbor was horrified and called animal control.

When the skunk left the premises the neighbor went out to retrieve the kittens. One of the kittens was severely injured and she wrapped the poor thing in a towel. The other two kittens didn't look like they were harmed. The concerned neighbor put all three kittens in a basket and waited for animal control to arrive. When animal control arrived the kittens were immediately taken to the veterinarian's office. The injured kitten was barely hanging on to life. The poor little thing was not going to make it and was humanely put down. The other two kittens were carefully examined and not a mark was found on them.

Not long after the kittens were attacked and picked up, animal control got a report of a peculiarly behaving skunk. It was picked up in the same vicinity of the kitten incident and thought to be the same skunk that attacked them. The skunk had to be destroyed because of his peculiar behavior and sent to the lab to be tested for rabies. It takes a little while for the test results. The kittens in the meantime were brought to the shelter to be bottle fed. As soon as those nurturing volunteers saw those sweet helpless kittens, they went into active duty caring for them.

The results of the skunk's rabies test came back. It was not good. It was positive. Rabies is transmitted through cuts, scratches, or saliva. Was there a chance the kittens were exposed to this deadly disease? Yes, there was. Is it possible the volunteers could have been exposed? Yes, there was a possibility. The kittens were behaving like typical normal kittens; eating, pooping, and playing. They looked so healthy. It is hard to believe they might have been exposed to this horrific disease. I wasn't privy, but knew there were discussions on what to do with the kittens. They could be put down. It was decided they be isolated and put on a six-month quarantine.

The volunteers continued caring for them for at least a week or two. A volunteer came forward and offered to take the kittens into her home and foster care them until the quarantine was over. This volunteer was a very competent, compassionate, and educated person. She also knew the kittens' history. She had a brother in another country who was a veterinarian. She consulted with him before bringing the kittens home with her. I assume he gave her the go ahead because she took the kittens. She was given lots of precautionary measures. She was told to wear rubber gloves when handling the babies, keep them in a separate room, and be the only person to handle them. Absolutely nobody else in the family should handle them including her husband and daughter. She also signed a release form.

The kind volunteer communicated with me regularly after bringing the kittens home with her. She loved caring for them and was having a lot of fun. Things were going well until one afternoon I received a call from her. She was quite upset. I immediately thought the worst. While bottle feeding one of the kittens, he bit off the top of the rubber nipple and swallowed it. She was worried it was going to get lodged somewhere in his body and get sick. I advised her to contact the vet's office, which she did. I also advised her to be sure to tell the doctor about the kitten's history.

The doctor examined the kitten and told her the kitten would pass the tip of the nipple in twenty-four hours and she took the kitten home. After twenty-four hours passed the kitten was not eating and the nipple did not pass through his system. Back to the animal hospital he went, and the kitten was kept for observation overnight. The next day the volunteer received a call from the hospital. The kitten was fine and she could pick him up sometime in the afternoon. Something came up; she was unable to make it to the hospital and would have to pick up the kitten the next day. Early the next day she received a call from the vet's office. She was told not to come in for the kitten because he was acting peculiar. She feared the worse. The next call from the veterinarian was most disturbing. The doctor thought the kitten might have rabies. It is something you cannot take chances with. There is only one way to find out if the kitten has rabies. Tragically, the kitten would have to be put down. His remains would be sent to a special laboratory where they performed the most reliable and conclusive test for this horrible disease. We patiently waited for the results.

The volunteer was crushed and notified the shelter immediately. This turned into an extremely dangerous situation. Rabies is not only a deadly disease to animals; it is also lethal to humans. The shelter volunteers, the animal control officer, the two assistant animal control officers, the vet techs, the doctors, had all been in contact with the kitten. We all waited with bated breath for the results of the test. The stress level at this time for everyone was high. Believe me when I tell you there was a lot of anxiety and many sleepless nights.

The result from the laboratory was POSITIVE. Damn! Damn! Damn! Everyone who had contact with the kitten could have been exposed to rabies. Thank goodness there are a series of six shots a human can take to prevent this devastating disease. Laura, the assistant animal control officer, called every volunteer who was in contact with the kitten, the veterinarians, and the vet techs who handled the kitten and alerted them. We all had to have the series of shots.

This is the information I got off the **Rabies: Prevention and Control** website. **Postexposure prophylaxis** (PEP) is indicated for persons possibly exposed to a rabid animal. Possible exposures include animal bites, or mucous membrane contamination with infectious tissue, such as saliva. PEP should begin as soon as possible after exposure. There have been no vaccine failures in the United States (i.e. someone developed rabies) when PEP was given promptly and appropriately after exposure.

Administration of rabies PEP is a medical urgency, not a medical emergency. Physicians should evaluate each possible exposure to rabies and as necessary consult with local or state public health officials regarding the need for rabies prophylaxis.

Post exposure prophylaxis regimen: In the United States, PEP consists of a regimen of one dose of immune globulin and five doses of rabies vaccine over a twenty-eight-day period. Rabies immune globulin and the first dose of rabies vaccine should be given as soon as possible after exposure. Additional doses of rabies vaccine should be given on days 3, 7, 14, and 28 after the first vaccination. Current vaccines are relatively painless and are given in your arm, like a flu or tetanus vaccine.

Those who already had rabies shots had to have booster shots. The vet tech who originally took care of the kittens after the attack was pregnant. She had no choice but to take the shots. It was a matter of life and death. The kind volunteer who fostered the kitten did not follow the precautionary measures, which were given to her. She allowed her husband, daughter, her friend neighbor, and her daughter to handle the kittens. Without a doubt they had to have the series of shots too. It was a mess!

Everybody involved rushed to get their shots. Some health insurance companies cover rabies shots and some do not. There were those who did not have insurance and couldn't afford to pay for the shots. The shelter picked up the bill. The shots are very costly. Fortunately, my insurance company covered the shots. Everyone did what they had to do and thank God nobody contracted rabies. It was an isolated case. The shelter never experienced anything like this before. I hope and pray it will never happen again. When you deal with living things, stuff happens. Through this whole nasty business, every volunteer except one continued to volunteer at the shelter. I thought that was telling. The volunteers are the most dedicated, wonderful human beings.

This story is not quite over. Remember there was still the other sibling kitten living with the volunteer. The kitten was behaving normally—happy, playful, energetic, and loving. It was possible this kitten could contract rabies too. The kind volunteer wanted to continue caring for the other kitten until the six-month quarantine was over, even after all that had transpired. She received a call from the program rabies coordinator in Boston. He insisted she bring the kitten in to be put down and tested for rabies. It broke her heart to have to do it, but she had no choice. I remember her telling me how sick to her stomach she was that day. It must have been so emotional and hard for her to bring that innocent sweet kitten to the animal hospital. She also told me how poorly she was treated by the staff in the hospital because of the previous events with the first rabies positive kitten. She left the hospital distraught and empty inside. She was made to feel like a criminal. The only thing she was guilty of was being too kind and compassionate.

The results of the rabies test for the other sibling kitten came back NEGATIVE. How sad is that? This is a true story that happened in our little shelter. It is also a story I want to forget.

A Little Love Story

It is a luxury to live in a world where we are free to choose. We can choose the kinds of food we eat, the kinds of clothes we wear, what kind of car to buy, etc. There are a variety of animals to select to have as a pet. It is a matter of selecting the proper pet that is suitable for one's lifestyle. People come to the shelter requesting a particular animal. If we can't accommodate their request, we have them fill out an application, keep it on file, and contact them in the event we can fulfill their request. There is no unreasonable request because you never know from day to day what may come into the shelter.

This little love story started with Margo before she became involved in volunteering at the shelter. The same Margo I spoke about, who was our photographer for the website and the shelter calendar fund-raiser. The first time she came into the shelter, she inquired about adopting a bunny rabbit. It was the very first time we met. She was allergic to other animals except bunnies. She really wanted to have a pet and adopted a rabbit and named him Edward Hopper. She felt he was lonely and needed a companion. There were no rabbits in the shelter at that time, but they do come in occasionally. I had her fill out an application and kept it on file.

As fate would have it, shortly after Margo requested a rabbit, a woman named Mary had a rabbit she wanted to relinquish to the shelter. How she came by this rabbit was quite a story. At Mary's place of work a gal went to her, knowing very well how Mary felt about bunnies. The gal told her about a friend who purchased two live rabbits for Christmas dinner from an elderly man that lived in Swampscott. Mary, a devoted rabbit lover, was appalled and filled with horror listening to the story. She was not going to let this astonishing disclosure pass without doing something. She found out where this old man lived and went to see for herself. The place was filthy and the rabbits were living in deplorable conditions. Mary spoke with the elderly man and it was obvious he was a little senile and unable to properly care for the rabbits. Mary wished she could purchase all the poor little rabbits that were there, but it was not realistic. She wanted them to be in a better place in the worst way. She had her own family of rabbits to deal with, but did purchase two. The elderly man pointed to a rabbit that was going to be somebody's Christmas dinner, so she grabbed that rabbit. She couldn't help noticing a pregnant rabbit living in a cage that was so small that she couldn't turn around, so Mary grabbed that rabbit also. She threw the man twenty dollars and quickly took off. They were not going to be anyone's Christmas dinner. She did one more thing; she reported the horrible living conditions the rabbits were living in to the proper authorities.

One of the rabbits she confiscated was named Clementine. She was all black with a tan underside and very pregnant. A good friend of Mary's gave Clementine a home. The other rabbit was called Sophie. Her coloring was called agouti (tan with other colors mixed in) and her breed was a Rex. Sophie was welcomed into the shelter. Mary appreciated our help and volunteered to care for Sophie as long as she stayed in the shelter, which was really nice of her.

Doing my job as volunteer coordinator, I went to my files and contacted Margo about Sophie. She was so excited and rushed to the shelter in a flash to see her. I told her the story about how Sophie got here. She was sick to her stomach. Margo liked Sophie a lot, but before making a decision to adopt her, she wanted to bring Edward Hopper in to meet her. If they got along, they would make a beautiful couple. The big day arrived and Edward was brought to the shelter to meet Sophie. We were all holding our breath. Our fingers were crossed. You could feel the tension in the air. Margo carefully put him in the cage with Sophie. At first the rabbits just looked at each other, then Edward made the first move, did not waste any time, and went at it with Sophie. Sophie was very receptive to Edward's overtures. It was love at first sight! What a love story! Margo was going to adopt Sophie and change her name to Hedda Lettis. We didn't want any more little bunnies running around, so an appointment had to be made to get Sophie spayed before she went home with Margo and Edward. It was going to be about three weeks to get an appointment for Hedda's spay, so Margo offered to share with Mary the responsibility of caring for Sophie/Hedda. We could always use a hand at the shelter and this is what I call great teamwork.

On a Monday afternoon when I arrived at the shelter for adoptions, I always checked the animals in their cages. When I got to the rabbit's cage and looked in, I noticed some very peculiar behavior. The rabbit was actually pulling the down fur out of her chest and piling it into the corner of her cage. Knowing very little about rabbit behavior, I continued to go on my rounds. I couldn't help but thinking what strange behavior it was. On Tuesday when I arrived at the shelter, I did my usual routine and checked all the animal cages. When I arrived at the rabbit's cage, somehow it just looked different. I took a closer look and questioned what I was seeing, so I got a little ladder and took an even closer look. The down fur that Hedda pulled out of her chest was moving. It was wiggling. I was totally shocked at what I saw. Underneath the down in the corner at the back of Hedda's cage were six new born baby bunnies. It was quite unexpected and exciting at the same time. I had never seen baby bunnies before. I ran to the phone to announce the birth. There was so much excitement in the shelter. We don't often have adorable baby rabbits. Sadly, one of the babies did not make it, but the other five were healthy and strong. It was so much fun watching them grow, and they do grow quickly. Things changed dramatically concerning the bunnies. Their stay at the shelter was going to be extended because Hedda had to take care of her babies. Mary and Margo fulfilled their commitment and cared for the rabbit family until they were weaned from their mom. Edward Hopper was patiently waiting for Hedda and was not at all upset about her infidelity.

While waiting for Hedda to complete her commitment to her babies, Margo got the idea of ideas. You have to know Margo. She is full of humor and quite imaginative. She was going to plan a wedding for Hedda and Edward. I am not kidding. First she put an announcement of their engagement in the local paper. Margo mailed invitations to friends, family, and acquaintances. There was also an article in the newspapers welcoming anyone who wanted to attend. It was the event of the year.

The wedding took place in the groom's back yard. The Reverend Patricia Long, who recognized this for what it was—a celebration of the happy stories in our lives, was going to perform the nuptials. At the wedding Edward presented the ring, which consisted of twenty-four carrots. Several people showed up at the wedding and brought gifts and donations for the shelter. Children were encouraged to bring their own pets too, which they did. There was a small reception that followed the ceremony. Carrot cake, bunny cookies, and other light refreshments were served. It was a lot of fun for all.

This humorous human interest story I loved because so much good came out of it. Two bunnies and their babies were saved. Every one of them found wonderful homes. Edward Hopper agreed to adopt one of Hedda Hopper's baby bunnies and named her Kaddidle Hopper. The shelter got some positive publicity. Mary and Margo became volunteers. Margo even had a fifth anniversary party for Edward Hopper and Hedda Hopper, which I attended. She has quite an imagination. What would we do without Mary? Her title at the shelter is now Bunny Lady because she is so knowledgeable about rabbits. When a rabbit comes into the shelter, Mary takes it home to foster care until it is adopted. Thank you both for all your generosity and dedication to rabbits. This is a picture of Margo's family of bunnies: Edward Hopper, Rosa Parks, their daughter Kadiddle Hopper and Hedda Hopper.

Holly

Holly was a lovely long-hair diluted calico cat. She was hit by a car and found on the side of the road with a lump on her head. Linda, our first animal control officer brought her to the vet's office to be treated. This poor cat had trauma. If that wasn't bad enough, it was obvious when Holly woke up she was a feral cat. Being feral coupled with her medical condition justified putting her down, but Linda wouldn't have it.

Holly was brought to the shelter to recover. She was terrified and cowered in the corner of her cage. We thought in time she would relax a little and come around. Her behavior kept us guessing. She was so unhappy. Some of us thought she was unresponsive because she was feral. Others thought it was because of her head trauma. As time went by, you kind of thought maybe putting her down might have been wise, just to get her out of her misery. That kind of thinking was unheard of at our shelter; besides, nobody would do it anyway.

We continued to care for Holly and there was no change in her personality. She just huddled in the corner of her cage. Almost two months had passed since Holly arrived at the shelter. When I went to do adoptions, as usual, I checked on all the animals in their cages. When I got to Holly's cage, I noticed things were different. She wasn't huddled in the corner of her cage cowering. She was lying down cleaning herself. At first I couldn't make out what was different. Something seemed peculiar. I left to finish my rounds and do some of my work in the shelter. My curiosity got the best of me because it was apparent something was up with Holly. I went back for another look. I simply couldn't make out what was going on in there. I looked closer and saw something quite unexpected. I was in a tremendous state of shock. Holly was a long-haired cat and under all that fur were two new born kittens nursing. Who would have believed this? Holly had kittens and was doing an excellent job mothering them. Again I ran to the phone to give the volunteers the birth announcement. We were godparents again! None of us had any inclination Holly was going to be a mother. Will wonders never cease!

Shortly after Holly delivered her kittens, a motherless infant kitten about the same age as Holly's kittens was brought into the shelter. It needed mothering desperately. We were all hoping Holly would accept the motherless kitten as one of her own. Still huddled in the corner of her cage with her babies, she accepted the infant without a fuss. Holly was full of surprises.

181

When I think back that conversations considering having Holly put down were even held gives me the willies. Most of the animals in the shelter get spayed or neutered within two to three weeks. We didn't know what was to become of Holly, so a spaying was never scheduled for her. Holly, herself, answered our question. She gave life to two beautiful babies and adopted another. Now we were going to do our job and try our very best to find a life for her. With her personality it would n't be easy, but we'd had tough challenges before.

Holly's beautiful kittens were ready to be placed in super homes, and they were. It was time for Holly to be spayed and put up for adoption. Her personality had not changed one bit. She stayed in the corner of her cage and did not respond to a thing. She had been in the shelter for quite a while. A gentleman with an Irish brogue came into the shelter looking at the cats and felt sorry for Holly. He had two cats, but wanted to give her a try; the Irish gentleman took her home. All the volunteers were excited for Holly because it was her chance for a new life. Six to eight months later the gentleman called to tell us he was moving and could not take Holly with him. His two cats were picking on Holly and she was so unhappy. Things were not working out. Candi came to the rescue again. She went and picked up Holly and brought her back to the shelter. It was so very sad and disappointing.

Flyers with a picture of Holly were posted everywhere in town. A letter was put into the local newspaper about Holly. Finally, we got a response. A flight attendant was moved by Holly's sad story and adopted her. After six months of Holly hiding under the bed; she wanted no part of her. Candi was called upon again to pick up poor Holly. This time she was not going to be brought back to the shelter. Candi was given an offer she couldn't refuse. If she would take Holly and care for her as though she were her own, the shelter will pay her expenses. It was clear she was not adoptable and we did not want her to rot in a cage. Really, there was little choice. Candi being the animal angel that she is took Holly home to live with her and her multi cat family. At first she lived alone in a front room for many months. Candi changed her accommodations to a bedroom where she lived alone for several months. Candi got frustrated with her and finally opened the door to the bedroom to see how Holly would react. She was now out of the front room and out from under the bed in the bedroom after all this time. She was mingling with all the cats. Any animal under Candi's care lives in paradise. It took some time and lots of effort, but Holly now has a life.

Controversy

We are an obscure little shelter in a bedroom community. The volunteers have one interest, taking care of the animals. We have enough problems to deal with and don't need more. Whether we liked it or not the shelter got involved in quite a controversy in town because of an infamous young lady. This young lady was the talk of the town, the state, the nation, and England. The young lady was Louise Woodward, the British au pair who was convicted of first-degree murder and sentenced to life imprisonment for the 1997 death of eight-month-old Matthew Eappen. She was accused of shaking him, which caused his death. You might remember the case that was splattered all over the newspapers. Louise Woodward's legal team included Marblehead Attorney Ms. Elaine Whitfield Sharp.

Louise Woodward lived with Attorney Sharp while working on her appeal. Louise was bored waiting for the legalities to commence. Attorney Sharp suggested she volunteer at the shelter taking care of the animals. She filled out an application. All volunteer applications are checked by the Marblehead police chief, because he oversees the shelter. Police Chief Palmer (he has since retired) turned down her application. He knew the town would not be able to keep the hungry media sharks away from Woodward at that time.

WOW, this started a contentious debate in town. Everybody had an opinion, including the volunteers. Some were in favor of it; some were not. The volunteers were told not to discuss it with any visitors to shelter. I answered several phone calls from people expressing their opinion. Some of the residents agreed with the chief. Others did not and were pretty angry.

When I researched this story for this segment, I went straight to an editor at *The Marblehead Reporter* (the local newspaper). George helped me and went into the archives for the information on the Woodward incident. He gave me the body copy of everything that occurred in sequence. It told the whole story. It was quite interesting.

This is an editorial from the local community paper, *The Reporter*:

The town of Marblehead is getting a bad rap from people who charge it with being callous for denying Louise Woodward the opportunity to volunteer at the animal shelter. Word has come from as far away as Cleveland, Ohio, that Marblehead must lack a sense of decency.

What we wonder is who in their right mind would want anyone in

Woodward's circumstances to hold even the most remotely public position in their town? Marblehead may appear flinty to some, but it's not foolish.

We do not pretend to know whether Woodward is guilty or innocent of murder or manslaughter. Nor do we think anyone should who has not been in the courtroom for all the testimony in her trial and appeals. We also have no objections to her Marblehead residency while her status is sorted out. She is here under perfectly legal circumstances.

Yet the facts remain that she has been found guilty in the death of Matthew Eappen by both jury and judge, and that her final status is not decided.

Only after she is found to have paid whatever debt she may owe society should the town accept her offer to volunteer for it. We certainly see no problem with accepting the services of people found not guilty of a crime, no matter how sensational. We also approve of hiring people convicted of crimes who have served out their sentence, for what is, indeed, about the most remotely possible of public positions.

But the very doubt surrounding her case—in these weeks as the Supreme Judicial Court weighs her and the prosecution's appeals—as well as the intense international interest these circumstances generate, mark her candidacy as wholly unsuitable.

The animal shelter is, after all, under the auspices of the Police Department. Who cannot foresee the kind of circus atmosphere that could result from her checking in for her first day at the cages? Police Chief Jon Palmer says he rejected her application out of concern for the safety of Woodward herself and others. These are eminently reasonable concerns.

Chief Palmer's decision also eliminates the possibility of Marblehead being used to rehabilitate the reputation of a notorious figure. There is an old journalism adage that if you want to increase sales of a newspaper or magazine, put a furry creature on the cover.

We do not know that a media circus would result from her working at the animal shelter, or that her motives are anything less than noble. The point is, why should Marblehead risk the possibilities? The town just isn't that hard up for dog walkers and cat groomers.

This is an article from the same local newspaper, *The Reporter*:

Marblehead's Police chief believes he acted in the best interest of the town when he denied Louise Woodward a volunteer position in the Animal Control Department.

Woodward, who is living with her attorney in Marblehead while she awaits the out come of her appeal on a manslaughter conviction, applied for the position in January. Police Chief John Palmer responded to the letter immediately, turning down the request and apparently setting off some bad feeling.

The request to work walking dogs and grooming animals at the local shelter became the source of published reports last week, days after Woodward's appeal was heard by the state Supreme Judicial Court. Palmer's January response to the request stated that he did not feel it was in the best interest of the Police Department for Woodward to be a volunteer in the Animal Control Department.

No specific reasons were given in the letter, but Palmer said he received a call from Woodward's attorney, Elaine Whitfield Sharp, a couple of days ago after mailing his response. During that conversation, Palmer said, he felt that his reasons were self-explanatory.

"She said, 'This isn't the last you've heard of this,' and slammed the phone down," Palmer said this week. "That was on or about Jan. 14 or 15. Then, two months later, I hear this."

Palmer said he didn't feel it was necessary for him to explain his reasons in the letter, and he also said he didn't think it was necessary for him to explain his reasoning to Woodward's attorney. Palmer said he had addressed his response to Woodward herself.

Sharp, however, was not satisfied with the chief's response.

"When I called and asked him to explain," Sharp said, "he very nastily and curtly told me the letter spoke for itself. I find it fascinating that he is willing to give his reasons to the newspaper, but he refuses to give me a reason on the phone. If that's the case, why didn't he say it in the first place?"

Sharp insisted the original request was not a public relations move for her client, and she added that she did not release the response to reporters last week. She also maintained her position that she found Palmer bigoted.

"I think what he says has to do with public relations and not public safety," she said. "I think he's a bigoted individual if he thinks having a convicted person groom and walk dogs reflects badly on the Police Department.

"Even if you believe Louise did it, shouldn't the Police Department, as part of its mission, be willing to help rehabilitate that person? Isn't that what

a Police Department is all about? I think he sees himself on one side of the fence, and that's why he's bigoted."

Not true, said Palmer.

"The safety and the security of the individual is paramount in my mind," he said, "and I don't see how we could guarantee the safety of any high-profile figure who wanted to do that. Should something happen to her while she's acting on behalf of the town, that could create a serious problem for the community and the Police Department.

"Even if she's inside, the building is open during certain hours. And if she's outside, things could happen."

Palmer said he had approved six other such applications since taking over the Animal Control Department. As a matter of procedure, he reviews each application with the Animal Control Officer, and it is either approved or denied. He did not believe he had denied the request of anyone else.

"I can't recall denying anyone, nor would I expect to deny anyone," Palmer added. "She made a request, I responded, her attorney responded back in a threatening and rude way, and two months later I hear this."

Despite the controversy, this latest situation has not soured Sharp or her client on the town of Marblehead.

"I think Marblehead is great," Sharp said. "I've has such a large number of calls about this story, and a lot of people think (Palmer) is wrong. It confirmed that there is positive support for Louise. In this getting out, I think it ended up getting a positive response."

Palmer has the support of town government, including Tom McNulty, chairman of the Board of Selectmen, and Town Administrator Tony Sasso.

"I believe the chief acted responsibly as relating to insuring the safety of Miss Woodward and the concerns of the town of Marblehead," Sasso said.

This article sums up the Marblehead Animal Shelter and the Louise Woodward episode:

It seems longer ago, but it was 1998 when Louise Woodward—the British au pair convicted in the death of a child in her care—was the talk of the town, state, nation and at least one overseas nation.

There were "Louise sightings" at restaurants, at the JCC, at the Phoenix Fitness Center, at Eastern Yacht Club. At one point, it seemed almost everyone who had seen Louise was interviewed by radio, TV and the Queen's own BBC.

Wooward was originally convicted of first-degree murder and sentenced to life imprisonment for the February death of 8-month-old Matthew Eappen, but her legal team, which included Marblehead attorney Elaine Whitfield Sharp, appealed her sentence.

Woodward stayed in Marblehead, living with Sharp and volunteering to work in the Marblehead Animal Control Office, taking care of cats and dogs. But Police Chief John Palmer turned down the volunteer, saying the town would not be able to keep hungry media sharks away from Woodward.

The story took a bizarre twist in March when Sharp was arrested for alleged drunken driving and subsequently dismissed from Woodward's defense team. Woodward moved into the Marblehead home of Tim and Mary Hunt, where she stayed until a June ruling in the Supreme Judicial Court.

Justice Hiller Zobel reduced Woodward's conviction to "involuntary manslaughter" and reduced her sentence to 279 days—the time she had already spent in jail. Middlesex District Attorney Tom Reilly said he wanted Woodward "out of this country."

She went.

You must admit I am not exaggerating when I say there is never a dull moment at the shelter. We never lack for excitement. Almost everyone in town was prattling about this incident and there was an array of opinions. My belief whether Louise Woodward was guilty or not is immaterial, even though I had a strong opinion on the matter. I will tell you whether I agreed with Chief Palmer's decision not to let Ms. Woodward volunteer at the shelter…I thought he was absolutely right!

Blackie and Whitie

Who are Blackie and Whitie? They were two cats brought into the shelter quite unexpectedly by a Russian woman. She was in a great hurry. She had to go back to Russia because of an emergency. There was nobody to care of her cats and she begged me to take them. What could I say; I took the cats. She gave me a brief history, a donation, and left crying. Blackie was a delightful all black cat and the mother of Whitie. Whitie was an all white adult female that was stone deaf. It was my first experience with a deaf cat and I learned quickly not to approach her from behind because it was unexpected and startled her.

The Russian woman requested we try to place them together. It was difficult because Blackie was so nice and adoptable. Whitie had horrible cage behavior because she was frightened. So many people wanted Blackie and nobody wanted Whitie. It was not fair to Blackie not to have a new wonderful home, so after a fairly long stay at the shelter, I decided to place her. She went to live with a lovely woman. It was sad for Whitie, but it didn't mean we were going to stop looking for a home for her.

This part of the story is so vivid in my mind. A woman whom I knew casually came into the shelter. We talked and she asked me lots of questions about the animals. When she came to Whitie's cage, the woman wanted to know her story; and so I told her. She was touched about the fact that Whitie was deaf and difficult to place. Out of nowhere she blurted out, "Why don't you put a notice up at The New England Home for the Deaf about the cat?" My eyes and ears opened up wide to the suggestion. I wanted to give it some thought. Why didn't I think of that? It didn't take me long to think about it and I decided to give it a try. It was a reach, but what the heck! The New England Home for the Deaf was not too far from the shelter. Candi was going out that way and offered to post it on their bulletin board. Now we only had to wait and see what would happen.

Life is full of surprises. You learn so much just by being at the shelter. A week or two later I received a call from one of the staff at the home. She was deaf also. It was my first experience talking to a deaf person on the phone, and it didn't take long for me to catch on. What an enlightening learning experience. The staff person told me a little lonely deaf man living at the home was interested in adopting Whitie. The home was willing to give their consent. Arrangements were made to meet at the shelter. I was bursting with excitement. There was a chance for Whitie to have a life out of her cage, plus someone to love her. On the other side of the coin Whitie would bring joy and comfort to a lonely deaf man.

The staff person, the man from the home and I met at the shelter. I must admit I was a little apprehensive about how I would do communicating with them. The staff woman read my lips and talked. She communicated with the little man through sign language. I knew they were anxious to see Whitie and brought them over to her cage. They saw a beautiful snow-white cat with one blue eye and one white eye. They were not disappointed. The little man was eager to have Whitie for a companion. I suggested they take the cat on trial. If things did not work out, they could bring her back. They agreed with me. I was bursting with joy. Whitie was going to get a second chance.

I did a pretty good job of communicating, if I do say so myself. I explained how to care for the cat in great length. They wanted to do the right thing and were receptive to what I had to say. The staff woman was taking notes. I put Whitie in the carrier, we said our good-byes, and off they went. I never saw Whitie again.

Do you realize the gratification I received from this adoption? Remember my sampler, "The Earth has Music for Those Who Listen." Believe me when I tell you the earth's music was especially loud that day.

Since Whitie, I have placed several deaf cats into super homes. This malady is not uncommon in all-white cats. Not all white cats are born deaf. The dalmatian breed of dog has the same malady, but not all are born deaf. An estimated ten to twelve percent of dalmatians are born deaf. Deafness is not always obvious, so it is important that hearing be checked by a veterinarian.

Tragic Surrenders

Throughout this book surrendering an animal to the shelter has been mentioned on numerous occasions. There are a million reasons and excuses why people give up their animals. There is never a good surrender, but some are extremely unpleasant. No matter how unpleasant it is for the owner to give up an animal; it is horrible for the animal. They simply don't know what is happening or what is going to happen. They are suddenly brought into a shelter with lots of other animals and put into a cage. There are lots of strange smells, which is threatening to them. People they have never seen before handle them. Would you be scared? They are very frightened and stressed.

I am going to tell you about three of the most memorable and unhappy surrenders that have occurred at the shelter during my tenure. Tragic is the word to describe them.

The first surrender was a long while ago, but I will never forget it. When I arrived at the shelter, I noticed we had a new lodger. She was a pretty tortoiseshell medium hair cat. I looked at the card that was attached to her cage, and noticed her name was Amelia. Her name was as pretty as she was. I took a closer look into her cage. She was sleeping on a t-shirt, which was peculiar. It was strange to me because we use clean linens in all the animal cages.

A volunteer whom I hadn't seen in a long while came in. It was so long since I had seen her, I didn't remember who she was. She refreshed my memory. I brought her over to Amelia's cage and showed her the t-shirt she was lying on. I was curious to know why it was there. The former volunteer was instrumental in getting Amelia into the shelter and knew the whole story, which she proceeded to tell me.

Amelia's owner went to a Chinese restaurant for dinner one evening. He did not realize there were nuts in one of the dishes he ordered. He was allergic to nuts. When he got home, he felt an allergic reaction coming on. He immediately called 911. When they got there, it was too late, the poor man, who was only in his late thirties, passed away with his two cats lying beside him. They loved their owner. The t-shirt Ameila was sleeping on was her owner's.

The unfortunate man's ex-wife flew up from Florida. She took the older of the two cats back with her. She felt Amelia had a better chance to be adopted. The former volunteer, who was a neighbor of the deceased man, contacted the shelter to take in Amelia. Every time I looked in Amelia's cage, I wanted to cry. The good thing was that life wasn't over for Amelia. She was placed in a loving home and is being treated like royalty.

~~

The second story about surrender is by far the worst. I was sitting at my desk in the shelter, when this elderly man came into the shelter with a cat in a carrier. He looked forlorn, distraught, and distant. He looked like he had the world on his shoulders. I told him to put the carrier on a table and invited him to sit down by my desk. He proceeded to tell me why he had to surrender the cat to the shelter. After hearing his story, I had to be excused and go into the bathroom to compose myself.

His story was about his daughter and the worst case of domestic violence. His daughter was separated from her husband and had a restraining order on him. He was never to come to the house. I don't even know these people and it is difficult for me to tell you this story. Well, her husband did not comply with the restraining order and went to the house. He rang the doorbell, the elderly man's daughter opened the door, and he shot her with a rifle. She died instantly. He then turned the rifle on himself and shot himself dead. No wonder this poor father was in that condition. He did have the world on his shoulders.

The deceased couple had two daughters. The older daughter was going to college and the younger daughter was in middle school. The family had two cats also. A close cousin of the deceased woman took the youngest daughter and one of the cats to live with her and her family. The oldest daughter was going to live at college in Europe. The parents of their deceased daughter took the other cat. They were going to Florida for the winter and needed to surrender the cat. A whole family was disjointed because of this horrid tragedy. I felt so sorry for everyone involved including the cats.

Mango was the name of the cat he was surrendering. The name was very appropriate. She was a beautiful diluted tortoiseshell with peach color in her fur. She was a nice cat that loved to be held. She was at the shelter for about three weeks, when the cousin of the deceased woman, who had taken her younger daughter and other cat into her care, came into the shelter. She wanted to bring Mango home to live with what was left of the family and the other cat, whose name was M&M. I was delighted! It made the younger daughter so happy to have her beloved family of cats with her again.

Three months had passed when we received a phone call from the deceased's cousin who had taken in her youngest daughter and two cats. She told us her son developed an allergy toward the cats, and would have to bring them both back to the shelter. What a sad state of affairs, especially for the poor cats. The younger daughter requested we please place the cats together. I took her request seriously and was going to try to do everything in my power to fulfill it.

Mango the cat was about four years old. M&M was a handsome eight-year-old brown tabby with big eyes. Time was passing and for some reason I was having difficulty placing these two cats. They had been there for months. It was getting to the point that I might have to separate them. I truly wanted to keep my promise to the young girl and place them together, but there were no takers. They were such good cats also. It was puzzling to me that nobody was interested in these two lovely cats individually or together.

Every few weeks a photographer from *The Salem Evening News* comes into our shelter to take a picture of an animal of my choice to be the pet of the week. I chose Mango and M&M to be the next pet of the week because they were in the shelter much too long and I wanted them to get a home. Their picture was in the paper and you would not believe who called for them.

This story is one big serial and endless. The older daughter of the deceased came back from Europe, saw the picture in the paper, and called us. She thought the cats were placed long ago. She asked her paternal grandmother to take care of the cats for her, and she agreed. Again, we were delighted the cats were getting out of the shelter and into a home with family. We were very attached to Mango and M&M by now and prayed for a forever home for them.

If you think this story is over, well, you guessed wrong. A month plus went by, when we received a phone call from the older daughter of the deceased. Her grandmother was moving and could not keep the cats. We were sick about it! Those poor cats! Back to the shelter they came. The family was told never to call us again.

Mango and M&M were up for adoption once again. It was so frustrating for me because I couldn't place these two wonderful cats. They had no luck, but the longer they were there, the more determined I was to find them a forever home.

During adoption hours on Saturday afternoon, a red-headed, tall, nice man came into the shelter looking for two cats. You know exactly what I was thinking. The red-headed man had a dog that passed away and missed him terribly. My friend, Candi, told me he was a wonderful pet owner because she used to take care of his dog. I talked to the man, but he couldn't make up his mind and left. He came back to the shelter looking at the cats several different times and still couldn't make up his mind. A couple of weeks later he came back into the shelter again. He really wanted to adopt. He needed some company. He also needed a little push, and I was just the one to give it to him. We talked and my little nudge worked. He decided to adopt Mango and M&M. It was a perfect situation for the tall, red-headed man and the cats. My body was tingling with joy. I started to get the adoption papers ready to be filled out when he told me he did not have time now. He had another commitment. We agreed to meet the next morning at ten o'clock. I was a little disappointed, but another day wouldn't matter. I wanted those poor cats to have a home so badly.

I had a restless night because I kept dreaming the tall, red-headed man wouldn't show up. It was wrong of me to think that, but those cats had been through so much; I didn't want anything to ruin the adoption. They had been thoughtlessly tossed around too many times. I went to the shelter a little earlier to get the cats ready. It was ten o'clock and the man showed up right on time with a big smile on his face. He was excited to adopt his two new friends. When all the formalities were over and the cats were put in their carriers ready to go to their new home, I couldn't help giving the nice, red-headed man a big kiss before he left.

Everybody at the shelter was exploding with joy knowing Mango and M&M were finally going to be placed! Those two babies paid their dues big time! That tall, red-headed, nice man was going to give them a loving, wonderful, forever home.

~~

The third story is a real show stopper! It was quite a story that the local media picked it up and went with it. The volunteers thought we had experienced and dealt with everything you could imagine that may happen in an animal shelter. Well, we were wrong and added one more event to the list.

When I arrived at the shelter one afternoon, there was a mess of activity going on. The animal control van, police cars, and trucks were parked all around the street with emergency lights flashing. I ran inside to see what was happening. Laura, the assistant animal control officer, grabbed me. She wanted me to quickly call the volunteers for an urgent call for help. Eighteen cats were confiscated from a family's home in town. The cats had to be temporarily housed in the cellar of the shelter. Most of the volunteers work during the day, but I called them anyway. Those who were available headed straight for the shelter to help, thank goodness. The job of cleaning those animals and setting them up in clean cages was daunting and time consuming.

The neighbors were complaining about a horrible odor in the neighborhood where all the cats lived, which led to their discovery. Those poor animals were living in squalor under the porch of the house. The cages they were living in were disgustingly filthy from urine and feces. As soon as the cages were taken out of the trucks the clean-up began and that same hideous smell where the cats came from enveloped the shelter. It was the build-up of the acidity from the urine and feces in their cages. Believe me when I tell you it was disgusting. Many of us were gagging and throwing up. It was so bad. One of the policeman on duty said, "As a policeman on the force for thirty years, I have experienced many unpleasant situations including dead bodies, but never experienced such a horrible case of animal abuse." He was also sick to his stomach and vomiting.

Laura took charge of the situation with the help of a small crew of volunteers. I was upstairs in the shelter looking after the animals, taking phone calls, and greeting the public. One by one each cat was cleaned up, put into whatever cages we had available with clean linens, fresh food, fresh water, and a clean litter box. It was a back-breaking, difficult job. I don't know how the volunteers tolerated the horrendous odor. They deserve so much praise for the fabulous job they did. The shelter cellar was not the best place for the cats, but compared to where they were it was paradise.

As you already know our shelter is small and we always seem to have twenty or more cats in there all the time. The question was—where were we going to put eighteen more? Each confiscated cat was taken to the animal hospital to get checked out, update their shots, get spayed or neutered, if needed, and take care of any other problems. Astonishingly, they were all in pretty good health! After their exam they were brought back to the shelter and put upstairs with the rest of the cats that were up for adoption. There were cages everywhere. Cages were stacked one on top of another. Some of the cages were not even cat cages; they were bird cages. We had to make do with whatever we had. Every available space in the room had a cage with a cat in it.

We did get some welcome help from two other no-kill shelters. We would only send them to no-kill shelters. Four of the cats went to a no-kill shelter in Gloucester, Massachusetts, which was very much appreciated. Four other cats went to a no-kill shelter on Martha's Vineyard, for which we were very grateful. I heard the cats who went to the Vineyard got seasick while being transported on the ferry, but were fine after their little sea voyage.

We thought the job was done until two more cats were found in the home, which made the number rise to twenty. There was another call to animal control that three more cats were in the garage, which upped the count to twenty-three. Would it ever end? Still another call came in. Two more kittens were confiscated from the attic of that house. There were no litter boxes and it was filthy dirty. Those poor babies lived in the worst conditions. The final tally of cats confiscated was a total of twenty-five. There was a mother, a father, eight children, a grandmother, two dogs, two geese, and twenty-five cats living together. It must have been real cozy.

News travels fast. There was so much publicity about the incident that people wanted to see the famous twenty-five cats that were confiscated and brought to our shelter. The shelter was mobbed with curiosity seekers. It was the trendy place to come visit at the time. Not all were curiosity seekers. Some were caring people who came to volunteer to help. We needed extra help badly and welcomed it. There was double the work cleaning and caring for so many more cats. Many people were sympathetic and were drawn to the shelter after reading the story in the newspapers or seeing it on TV. They were deeply touched and wanted to give a good home to one or two of those celebrity cats.

During this overcrowded period in the shelter, there was a boom of adoptions. Many of the shelter cats that were there prior to the influx were placed also, which was wonderful. My experience volunteering at the shelter has taught me many things. One of which is how many big-hearted, kind people are out there. Thank God we are there for the animals. I hate to think what would have happened if we weren't. We got through this crisis with the help and understanding of so many. Do you think the volunteers have experienced everything that could happen in an animal shelter? I think not. There will always be more surprises and challenges out there just waiting for us to tackle and deal with them we will.

Surprise Reunion

This inconceivable story started when a concerned sweet couple brought two adult male cats into the shelter. The cats were wandering around aimlessly in their neighborhood. The cats looked healthy enough to be somebody's pets. The couple combed the area asking their neighbors if they knew whose pets they were. Nobody had a clue and assumed they were dumped there. The couple did the right thing by bringing them to the shelter. They would not have survived without food, shelter, and the proper care.

Both cats went through the usual procedure. They were taken to a veterinarian for an examination, tested for FIV and FeLV, shots updated, and both cats were already neutered. Sadly one of the cats tested positive for FIV (feline immunodeficiency virus). Most shelters would have put that cat down immediately, but not ours. When cats are FIV positive, they are not easy to place. When both cats were comfortably back at the shelter, I started to monitor them, as I do with the all the cats. It is important to get to know about their behavior and personalities. They were both very nice, well-behaved animals. My next step was to take their pictures and put them in our website with their profile.

About two weeks into their stay at the shelter a serious outbreak of upper respiratory broke out. When one cat gets it—it spreads like wildfire to every animal in the shelter. It is quite a job medicating twenty-plus cats with antibiotics two or three times a day for two weeks at least. With the proper care the upper respiratory will eventually pass. The two cats the couple brought in came down with the upper respiratory, which was no surprise. Strangely enough the cat, which did not have FIV, could not seem to shake the upper respiratory. He got very sick. He was in and out of the vet's office. We continued to do everything in our power to help get him well.

Those two cats were in the shelter for at least six weeks when I received an extraordinarily unbelievable email from a man. This is the gist of his email:

He was a guy who got divorced and got word that we had two of his best friends, Abo and his brother Peaches, and he wanted his cats back. He was so happy they were alive. This made his day. He heard they were put in a shelter today and thought they were sick and were destroyed. He was planning to visit his son in New York and would pick up the cats later in the week, depending on his flight arrangements. He kept blessing our organization, and claimed it was donation time. *The cats are no longer orphans, so take them off the adoption list.* They were temporarily abused and misplaced and had been shell-shocked by all the changes. *Thank God they are okay!* We exchanged phone numbers. He just moved and told me it was tough to get a short lease for a condo in Florida with a five-year-old visitor and two cats. He said he almost died when he found what his drunken old friend did to his cats. His friend never called to tell him his cats were missing. He called his drunken friend several times to tell him he was on his way to get his two buddies, but he never called back. He asked him to please contact him to make arrangements to pick up his cats. *Thanks again and God Bless!*

Surprise! Surprise! Surprise! At first I was speechless and sat there staring at the computer and questioned whether or not I read the email correctly. Then I began to read the email over and over to digest the content. To tell you the truth I was flabbergasted to say the least! It took another minute to get to the phone to call the man on his cell phone. He could have been in Massachusetts, New York, or Florida. It really didn't matter where he was; I couldn't wait to speak to him. I called, he answered, and we both introduced ourselves. He was so excited to hear from me and wanted to know how the cats were. I had to tell him Abo was sick and trying to recover from upper respiratory. The other cat, Peaches, was just fine. He couldn't stop thanking me for taking care of his two best friends. He was so grateful.

He also told me when he went to pick up his cats from his untrustworthy friend and found they were gone, he called every animal shelter in the vicinity. They knew nothing about his cats. I explained to him that our shelter is in the Marblehead animal control office, which is town controlled. We are not listed under animal shelters. He would not give up trying to find his beloved cats and went online to see if he could come across his two buddies. Miraculously, he found his cats pictured on our website. It was unbelievable!

It turned out he was in Florida and wanted to fly to Massachusetts to pick up the cats. We arranged he would email me his itinerary and the approximate time he would arrive at the shelter. I exchanged my telephone numbers just in case he had to contact me, if there was a change of plans. He was going to pick up his cats and return on the next flight to Florida.

The big day arrived for the reunion. It was exciting! I couldn't wait to meet him. The percent of people claiming their lost animals sadly is rather low. Here was a man flying all the way from Florida to claim his buddies. It was rare and special and the music was already in the air. Sadly, there was one hitch. Abo was still very ill and could not breathe well. A plane trip could be extremely harmful in his condition; however, it was the owner's decision whether to take the sick cat or not.

While waiting impatiently for the owner to arrive, I started to prepare the cats for the trip. The shelter door opened and I knew immediately it was the owner. He was good looking, well over six feet tall, solidly built, and extroverted. Yes, it was definitely him right on time. Naturally, he wanted to see his cats and there they were. They were equally happy to see him. We talked about the sick cat. He wanted to take Abo to the nearest veterinary hospital. It was almost closing time at the animal hospital, but I took a chance and called. The owner got on the phone and explained the whole situation and was willing to leave the cat until he was well enough to travel, whatever the cost. He was a very forceful character and would not take no for an answer. He only wanted his cat to get well and would come back to get him. They told him to come immediately. I gave him directions to the hospital. It wasn't very far. We didn't have much time to talk because of all the rush. He thanked me hundreds of times, gave me a check for four hundred dollars, and rushed out with his buddies. This man loved his cats.

I was truly interested on how the sick cat, Abo, was doing and emailed the owner a couple of times. He never responded to my emails. It was disappointing for me and all the volunteers. They worked diligently caring and nursing those two animals. There really was no closure to this story. It was in limbo and as time passes, you move on to the next topic, which is exactly what happened.

That incident happened in the year 2001. While writing this segment in my book, I got very curious about the outcome of the story. Did the sick cat recover? Were both cats living in Florida? My curiosity got the best of me. It was now 2004 and I decided to look in my files and sure enough there was the owner's email and email address, so I emailed him. He did not respond. It would be nice to have closure to this story. His telephone numbers were on the email he sent me. My husband encouraged me to call him and get it off my mind. When he had come into the shelter for that brief period, we had a pleasant meeting. Of course it was a happy occasion. On one hand I was resisting calling him and did not know why. On the other hand my positive side supposed he would be glad to hear from me; after all, we saved his two best friends.

I decided to call. The owner answered the phone. What a mistake! I should have left things as they were. I never expected the response I got. I will never listen to my positive side again. He lambasted me for killing his cat. Yes, it was the sick cat, Abo. He dominated the whole conversation and wouldn't let me get a word in edgewise and suddenly hung up. He wasn't very nice and so unfair.

He told me he picked up his cat at the animal hospital in Marblehead one month after he left him. Apparently, the veterinarian he dealt with told him we were a bunch of crazy volunteers at the shelter. We don't have an isolation room and we bring in sick animals. This was why his cat got sick and died one year after bringing him back home to Florida. It cost him $4000 from the time he picked up the cat at the hospital and over the next year.

I was sad to hear his cat died. Every other cat in the shelter that contracted the upper respiratory completely recovered after the breakout. His cat must have had some underlying problem, which was never diagnosed. It was strange because it was the cat that did not test positive for FIV. It was not very nice of that veterinarian to say those nasty things about our shelter. There are two animal hospitals in town, and we do almost all of our business with that particular hospital, which is why I sent the owner there. Through the years there has been a turnover of doctors there. The doctor who owns the hospital has been very supportive of our shelter. He has attended meetings with the volunteers and town officials. He highly recommended an isolation room be built in the shelter. It was the town's decision to build an office for the animal control officer and not an isolation room.

If I only had a chance to respond to the owner's accusations, I would have explained to him that his cats were lucky to be alive. We are one of three animal shelters in the area. If those kind neighbors brought those cats to any of the other two shelters, they would have been rejected because of their age. They do not accept animals over five years old. The cat that tested positive for FIV would have been put down immediately. One of the shelters would have taken them in then would have had them destroyed. Those kind neighbors knew what they were doing bringing them to our no-kill shelter. I also wanted to tell this owner that despite not having an isolation room, we are saving the lives of hundreds upon hundreds of animals. I have one last word for him. He should look in the mirror and ask himself, "Why did I bring those two innocent helpless cats to a drunken, irresponsible person I called a friend in the first place?" My well-intended call to this illogical, thoughtless, ungrateful guy was not wasted. I got the information I needed to bring closure to this story.

Libby

Libby, Libby, Libby, a very sweet liver and white pedigree pointer. She gave the volunteers quite a fright. Not only did she give the volunteers a fright; almost the whole town of Marblehead got involved in her escapade.

Libby was a stray in Marblehead. She was very elusive. It took animal control many attempts to capture her. They finally did and brought her to the shelter. Libby was high strung and intensely shy. She feared almost everything. If you lifted your hand to scratch your head, she would cower. She was afraid to go outside, feared noises, and cars. We all agreed poor Libby was a victim of a clear case of abuse. Somehow she got away from her abuser and just kept running.

Libby received an abundance of love and kindness from the volunteers; still she was very skittish and frightened. Who knew if she would ever be able to trust again? The volunteers knew just how to care for her with love and understanding. Every time a stranger walked into the shelter she became tense. She needed a quiet, loving home with a person who has the patience to understand her issues.

Laura, the assistant animal control officer, developed a deep attachment towards Libby. She also places most of the dogs in the shelter. I knew for sure, when the right person came in for Libby, Laura would have a hard time parting with her. Libby was going to be a hard dog to place because of her issues. One thing was for sure, if and when she was placed, that person would be screened thoroughly.

A single gentleman who lived alone right here in Marblehead was interested in Libby. Laura explained all the dog's issues to him. He understood and still wanted to adopt the dog. He was sure he could handle Libby. Laura felt it was worth a try for the dog's sake, so she let Libby go on trial with the single gentleman. There was no question this dog was going to be a challenge to his new master. We all kept our fingers crossed and prayed it would work out.

Less than a week went by since Libby was taken on trial, when Laura received an urgent call from the single gentleman. He was frantic. He tied the dog outside and left her alone. That was a mistake. The dog must have been terrified and managed to squeeze her head out of her collar and took off. It was a horrible state of affairs. It was the dead of winter. It was going to take a miracle to capture this dog again because she was so damn scared. The single gentleman felt so guilty. He felt terrible.

Laura called the police immediately to keep a lookout for the dog. She asked me to put an SOS in the local newspaper with a picture of the dog as soon as possible. We didn't have an actual picture of Libby, but I found a picture of a pointer in my dog book that looked just like her. We wanted the public to be on alert for her. The newspaper was kind enough to put the picture of Libby and her story on the front page, so the community had a good description of the dog. Laura also notified practically every animal control officer and shelter in the state and some out of state. Posters were put everywhere in town. Animal hospitals were also alerted. Everything that could be done was done, but no sign of Libby

The word was out about Libby. Calls to the shelter and police station claiming Libby sightings were coming in constantly. When animal control or the police got to the area where Libby was last reported—the dog seemed to vanish. There were calls sighting Libby at different ends of town at the same time. Laura called me one evening to rush to the beach near my house because somebody saw Libby there. I rushed to the beach and there wasn't a living soul there when I arrived. Time was passing and still no Libby. It was winter and it was cold. She had no food or shelter. As if things weren't bad enough, a serious snowstorm was on the way. There were still no signs of Libby. We were still getting Libby sighting calls. That predicted snowstorm came and went and left mounds of snow. Could Libby survive? Shortly afterwards there were two more snowstorms, a rainstorm, and an unbelievable cold snap, which is typical New England weather. How could this dog survive? Some of us thought the worst; however, we were still getting calls from people spotting the dog. Most of the sightings were narrowed down to the old railroad bed in town. We decided to focus our search in that area.

The weather finally cleared up, so the volunteers devised a plan to walk the whole railroad bed in search of Libby. The department of public works was kind enough to plow the area for us. The volunteers split up. Half of us started from one end of the railroad bed and the other half started at the other end and we would meet in the middle. It was all for naught. There was no sign of Libby and every reason to worry.

While at home, I couldn't get Libby out of my head. It was so sad and so frustrating. What more could we do? I suddenly got a thought. It was a long shot, but anything was worth a try. My daughter, Tami, had a friend whose house backed up to the railroad bed. She was my friend as well and her name was Karen. I knew Karen was the type of person who would be vigilant and keep a watchful eye out for the dog. I called her, told her the story, and asked her to be alert. She was more than happy to help. I told her to call animal control, the police, or me, if she spotted the dog.

My long shot paid off and came quickly! I was home with my husband preparing lunch when I received a call from Karen. She and her five-year-old daughter, Hannah, were driving home, when suddenly Hannah saw a dog drinking out of a water puddle in her next door neighbor's yard. She thought it was Libby. Fortunately, the yard was fenced. Karen quietly got out of her car and slowly closed the gate. The dog was so busy drinking, she didn't even notice she was confined in the yard. There was no way for her to escape.

I told Karen I was on my way, stopped what I was doing, and told my husband to call a dispatcher at the police station to page Laura to meet me at Karen's address; Libby was there. It took me less than ten minutes to drive to my destination. Karen and Hannah were waiting in the car. I looked in the yard and there was Libby, thank God! By now Libby realized she had no place to run and was in a corner of the yard quivering. I grabbed the lead that was in my car in case of an emergency. Slowly I opened the gate, so she couldn't make a break to escape. She just stood there quivering. I think I was quivering too. All I had was the lead and none of the proper animal control equipment to capture a dog. I was going to try to get her on the lead. It was worth a try. Laura would be arriving directly. The dog was about twenty feet away from me; I walked so slowly toward her. She didn't move from that spot. When I was about five feet away from her, I got on all fours. I did that to be on her level because it was less intimidating. Little by little I got closer and closer and in a high, friendly voice I called her name. Boy, it was tense! Next thing you know I was right next to her. She didn't move from that spot. I gently, but hastily, put the lead around her neck and started petting her. The fact she just stood there and didn't try to run was peculiar. Maybe she remembered me from the shelter.

A big sigh of relief was in order. Don't ask me how, but the dog seemed to be in good health. We will never know how she managed to survive the elements without food and shelter for three or so weeks. She was a little thinner, but we could take care of that. My chest was sticking out a mile filled with pride. I put Libby in my car, thanked Karen and Hannah, and took off to the shelter. Laura passed me on the way. I signaled her that I had Libby and was on the way to the shelter. When I arrived at the shelter, Laura pulled up behind me and rushed to the car to see the dog. She hugged and hugged Libby with tears running down her face. She truly loved that dog. Libby never went back into the shelter. She went to live happily ever after with Laura. What could be better than that?

The whole Marblehead community participated in the search for Libby. It was really something and heart-warming to see how so many people sincerely cared about a little dog they never met. The volunteers, Laura, and Libby want to thank you for all your help. The shelter sent a beautiful flower arrangement to Karen and Hannah to show our appreciation for their significant participation in the capture of Libby.

Mystic

My youngest daughter Terri married for a second time to a terrific guy named Jeff. Terri's new brother-in-law and sister-in-law had just bought a home in Marblehead. While they were preparing to move into the house, their new next door neighbor came over to welcome them. The neighbor also wanted to tell them about the expected guest that comes to their home at approximately five o'clock every night for dinner. The expected guest is an all black abandoned cat. The man, who lived in their house before, fed the cat every night. He also left cases of cat food and a check for one hundred dollars to go toward the care of the cat.

This was quite a revelation to my daughter's brother-in-law and sister-in-law. The family knowing how much I love animals and volunteer at the shelter, gave me a call from my daughter's new mother-in-law. She requested the cat to be taken to the shelter. I told her I would speak to animal control to pick up the cat around the time he showed up for dinner. He would be brought to the shelter for safe keeping and put up for adoption.

Animal control captured the cat and brought him to the shelter. He was named Mystic after the name of the street where he was picked up. The cat was a very nice male all black cat with a little white tuft on his chest. The volunteers thought he had an encounter with another animal because the tops of both of his ears and a portion of his tail were missing. The poor thing must have had some tough times out there in the wild. He was safe now and going to be well taken care of.

Per usual Mystic was taken to the animal hospital for the works (shots, tests, and neutering). When he was brought back to the shelter, the volunteers were told some hideous news. Mystic's ears and tail were not missing because of an encounter with another animal. Mystic was mutilated when he was a kitten. The veterinarian explained the areas on the tops of his ears and tail that were missing were too smooth and even. If he had an encounter with an animal, the area would be uneven or jagged. Can you imagine the pain this poor cat must have endured? No wonder he must have run away. Who knows what other disgusting things were done to him? How could anyone be so cruel? Yet, with all he has been through he is still so loveable and trusting toward humans.

Police Chief Carney and his lovely wife Sandy have two cats and a dog. One of their beloved cats passed away. They love animals and when one of their cats passes on, they come into the shelter to adopt another. I have placed three cats with them. I placed two cats to the chief's mother-in-law. I placed a cat to his daughter's significant other at the time, and a cat to his daughter. The chief's wife Sandy would check our website and pop into the shelter to have a look-see at what cats were in the shelter. She is a compassionate person and was drawn to Mystic every time she would visit. One day she brought her daughter in to meet Mystic. The next time she brought her husband, the chief, in to meet Mystic. I took Mystic out of his cage and put him in the office with the chief and his wife. They needed some private time with the cat. I wanted them to see what a wonderful cat he is. They petted and played with him. The cat loved all the attention. The chief couldn't get over how trusting the cat was after what some mean, cruel, and deranged person did to this sweet helpless cat. It got to the chief. He stood up and in a moment of anger he said, "If I ever find out who did this to the cat, I will break both their legs!" The chief is a good man. He is a man of peace. Yet, you can't help being angry when you witness a useless brutal act on an innocent, helpless animal. He reacted like any normal, decent person would. Anyone with a shred of decency would have reacted in the same manner. If his wife weren't there, I think I would have kissed him. The chief and his wife adopted Mystic. What a wonderful ending to a sad beginning. Believe me when I tell you, Mystic hit Mega Bucks!

It's been two and half years since the chief and his wife adopted Mystic (now Nubbins) from our shelter. Through a friend, they learned that Nubbins was the "model" for an oil painting to be entered in a silent auction at an MSPCA fund-raiser. Needless to say, the chief and his wife traveled to Boston to attend the fund-raiser and bid on the painting. Upon entering the auction, the chief's wife relayed to the chief that she was willing to go up to $1,000 for the painting…he hoped she was kidding. They did have the highest bid and the oil painting of Nubbins now hangs proudly in their family room. How lucky Nubbins is to have the chief and his wife for a forever family. Here is a picture of the painting.

9-11

Who could ever forget that horrible day, or should we ever forget it? I remember waking up that morning to an absolutely gorgeous day. My husband went to play golf. It was my house cleaning day. I decided to listen to classical music while cleaning. Not long into the morning the phone rang. It was my middle daughter, Toby. She sounded troubled and kept asking me if I was watching TV. I told her I wasn't. She could hardly talk and blurted out, "Put Fox News on quickly!" I knew something was very wrong, so I ran to put on the TV and could not believe what I was witnessing. It wasn't believable; it was horrible, and shocking. It looked like a movie, but it was real! I told Toby I would get back to her because I had to speak to her sisters. At that moment it was vital for me to hear the voices of my whole family. My sons-in-law traveled occasionally. It was important for me to know everybody was safe, and they were. It was impossible for me to get in touch with my husband on the golf course. He probably had no idea what was happening. I thanked God my family was safe. This horrific event stunned the world. If you were lucky not to lose a loved one, a family member, or a friend in the 9-11 tragedy, without a doubt you still had to be affected emotionally. Our country was attacked. We must never, ever forget that horrible, tragic day!

What does 9-11 have to do with the shelter? Think of the pets of the people who perished in the buildings and planes that went down. Many other buildings, some apartment buildings near the Twin Towers were severely damaged. The people in those apartment buildings had no home to go back to—they were displaced. Many of those residents had pets that needed to be rescued immediately. The pet owners were not allowed to go back in the buildings to save their beloved pets. It was too dangerous. I can't imagine how helpless they must have felt. All was not lost. I was riveted to the television at that time and watched a news report on how the New York City Animal Control had risked their lives rescuing the animals left behind in those dangerous damaged buildings. They also were true heroes. Those very special people saving the animals deserve much kudos.

As a result of so many people left without a home animals were homeless too. Many had to be brought to animal shelters for safe keeping. This was a desperate time in New York City and there weren't enough animal shelters or space to house all the animals. They were bursting at the seams. Enter animal shelters from all over the country offering their help. Volunteers drove great distances to New York to pick up animals, drive back to their shelter, and care for them. Some of the pets were never claimed. Sadly, many of the pets were surrendered by their owners because they had no choice. It must have been so hard to give up their pets, but many had no homes to go back to and no place to put their pets. It was because they loved them so much and thought it was for the best. What people had to go through because of this travesty.

You guessed it! Our shelter was one of those who reached out to help. A person networking with a New York contact called and invited us to participate in the program. We were willing to do anything to help out. Over a period of time about ten dogs were delivered to our shelter. They were all to be put up for adoption. Frankly, we were asked to do so little; however, the volunteers felt really good contributing whatever we could during this time of need.

The dogs' pictures and profiles were put in the website and newspapers. You wouldn't believe the response we received for those animals. Each day we received several fabulous applications. It became a competition between potential adopters to adopt one of those dogs. All the applicants were interviewed and practically all of them were worthy of a placement. The hardest job we had was determining who would get what. We never experienced anything like this in the shelter before. The public only wanted the 9-11 dogs. There were other wonderful dogs in the shelter that were not linked to the 9-11 calamity; the adopters only wanted the 9-11 dogs. They didn't even want a glimpse of the others. Human nature is funny. Strange things occur in this business all the time, so you just go along with the flow. The good news is every dog from the 9-11 tragedy was saved and placed in fabulous homes. The other dogs in the shelter were eventually placed in good homes also.

Our shelter was connected to another 9-11 tragedy. When we were at the old shelter an extra large orange and white long-haired cat named Allen came into the shelter. This magnificent cat tested positive for FIV. These cats are always difficult to place even though they can live as long as any other cat, if they are kept indoors. If you recall I spoke about Katie in this book before. She was the first volunteer at the shelter. Katie used to work in an office with a gentle, kindly gentleman who loved animals. She got a notion and called her friend to see if he would adopt Allen. Without hesitation he agreed, so Allen went to live with this nice man. A few months later another cat named Dylan came into the shelter. He tested positive for FIV also. Katie got another notion that maybe her kind friend would adopt Dylan for a friend for Allen. They both were FIV positive and could live together nicely. Katie's friend did not hesitate and gave both these homeless cats a loving home. For almost ten years the kindly gentleman and his two cats had been a happy little family.

On September 11, 2001 the kindly gentleman was on Flight 11 when it crashed into the north tower of the World Trade Center. When you hear something like this, there are no words to describe the sick, sad, angry feelings you have all at the same time.

The family of the kindly gentleman contacted Katie to pick up the cats. Once again they were homeless. Katie was grief stricken by the fate of her friend. She picked up the cats, but did not have the heart to bring them into the shelter. She decided to take them home with her until she could find them a new home. Shortly after she brought Allen and Dylan to her home, Dylan became very ill and had to be put down. Allen was a twenty-pound-plus, healthy cat.

Katie found a new home for Allen. He lived happily with his new owner and friend (a golden retriever) for well over a year. When his new owner's mother moved in with the family; it turned out she was allergic to Allen. Poor Allen had to go.

Allen's original owner, that kindly gentleman, would be so happy to know what a lovely new family Allen has now with lots of animal friends. Don't feel bad for Allen. He is living with Laura, the assistant animal control officer. Remember, I described her as being a descendant of Dr. Doolittle.

This was a difficult time in the history of America. The American people are strong, resourceful, and pull together in difficult times, which is exactly what happened.

ANNIE

Sadly, my sweet, adorable, loveable, gentle, and kindly red bloodhound, Annie, passed away. She came from Missouri, so I named her Annie Missouri. She and my Bernese mountain dog, Moses, were the best of friends. When Moses passed away, I thought Annie would be lonely without him, but quite the contrary. Annie loved being an only child because she got all the attention. Annie was my constant companion and a great comfort to me.

I will miss looking at that unique bloodhound face and long ears. I will miss her howl when she greeted her favorite friends. I will miss seeing her run along the beach. Most of all I will miss her sweet personality. She will be missed, but will live in my heart forever and ever.

This quote by Roger Caras simply and perfectly defines the meaning of having a great dog like Annie. "Dogs are not our whole life, but they make our lives whole." I was so very fortunate to have Annie for eleven wonderful years. It is so very hard to say good-bye.

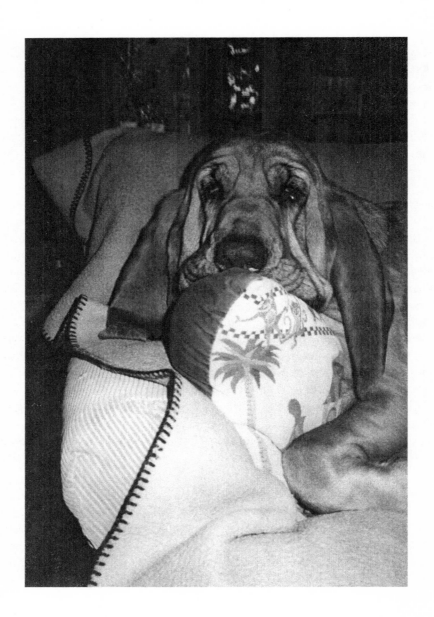

KIND HEROES
Chapter 9

My book would not be complete if I did not recognize my fellow volunteers. They are the most dedicated, devoted, kind, nurturing, caring human beings on the face of this earth. There aren't enough high words to describe these wonderful people. They are servants of God. I would like to characterize each and every volunteer who has given his/her all volunteering at the shelter, but that would require writing another book.

Come a blizzard, a hurricane, rain, snow, or an ice storm, somehow the volunteers will find a way to get to the shelter to care for the animals. They provide daily care and nourishment, clean cages, clean litter boxes, walk dogs, wash linens, groom, medicate, perform endless veterinary visits, and provide much-needed love to all the homeless, abandoned animals. We also help the community when there is an emergency. For example, a water pipe burst in a senior citizen home. The residents were evacuated and were found temporary places to live until they could return. Many of them couldn't take their beloved animals. Enter the Marblehead Animal Shelter to bring in their precious animals and care for them until they could be reunited with their owners. The tasks are numerous and endless.

Beyond caring for animals we have endless meetings brainstorming on how to raise funds to continually provide food, supplies, and pay for expensive veterinary care. Here is a sample of some of the fund-raisers we have organized: numerous yard sales, 50/50 raffles, open houses in the shelter, dog shows, auctions, a calendar, pictures with your pets, Halloween Hike for homeless animals, and pet pictures with Santa during the Christmas holidays. I was especially proud of my husband because he volunteered to be Santa. Everyone got a kick out of him because he was a Jewish Santa. He turned out to be a great Santa. Not only did he have pets pictured on his lap; he allowed children to sit on his lap and give him their Christmas lists. This is a picture of my husband Harv as Santa and Kate was the elf. Kate was a vet tech and helped out at the shelter. She has since become a veterinarian. I was behind Santa holding the kittens.

To become a volunteer you have to be eighteen years of age. If a younger person wants to volunteer, his parent or a close adult will have to volunteer with him. Some of the animals could be difficult, and we try to avoid any liability. Children who love animals often volunteer with parents. Husband and wife couples come to volunteer. Senior citizens love to help out. Teenagers volunteer at the shelter to do community service. It is a requirement to do community service to get on the high school honor society. They must work with our adult volunteers. They learn a lot while working there.

As I have mentioned many times before, the work is not easy. There is a constant turnover of animals, which never stops. The work is hard and burnout does occur. Many volunteers have to take a sabbatical. Other volunteers burnout and leave. Every volunteer, past or present, whether they volunteered for an hour a week or ten hours a week, were profoundly important to the welfare of the animals. No amount of money could apply to the priceless contribution they have given to the shelter. They can't be thanked enough for their service.

It really is amazing how a group of people can get together with different backgrounds, from different areas, who have never met and become part of a hard-working team. Seven days a week a team of volunteers go into the shelter to do their work and get the job done week after week. This is how I characterize it. Each volunteer is like a piece of a puzzle. They each have a particular job to do on a specific day and time. Starting at the beginning of the week the puzzle will start to form and take shape. Midway through the week the puzzle is half way solved. By the end of the week the puzzle is completed and all the pieces are put in place. At the beginning of a new week, we are ready to start a new puzzle. It really is extraordinary how it works and what is more extraordinary is the job gets done.

Who are these crazy, remarkable, diverse groups of people? They are everyday exceptional people, who come together because we all have one thing in common—our mission is to help animals. They are teachers, lawyers, nurses, electrical engineers, secretaries, homemakers, salesmen and women, vet techs, flight attendants, artisans, nannies, real estate agents, bankers, mothers, fathers, husbands, sisters, wives, daughters, sons, etc. I am proud to work with these heroes and be a part of this unique organization.

I have just another word about these exceptional volunteers. They don't volunteer expecting a banquet in their honor, nor are they looking for recognition or publicity for their good deeds. Certainly, fame and glory is not their motivation. Their rewards are very simple and meaningful. They give their heart and soul to the animals during their temporary stay in the shelter. Every time there is an adoption there is instant gratification and that is their greatest reward.

When we receive updates about our adopted animals, it is a bonus because we love to hear how our babies are doing. Through the years, I have compiled letters, notes, cards, and email updates about our adopted pets. It is a pleasurable read, so enjoy. We are a little shelter, but we do big things.

~~

Hi Linda

Tyrone has been with us for 7 days and he is one of the nicest cats that we ever owned. He was accidentally introduced to my 80 pound yellow lab who hopped on my bed and layed down next to Ty and he just snuggled right up to him. He now has free rein of the house and he is getting along great with my 2 dogs and my other cat Dixie. They both will sleep side by side. When people come into the house they are amazed at how Ty is so friendly. He acts like he has lived with us since he was a kitten.

Thanks!

~~

Dear Linda and all my wonderful "family" at the shelter,

I am getting adjusted to my new home and family; better and better every day. I am still a bit weary at times, and only come out when I feel it is safe and secure. When I do venture out to say hello and investigate, I play with my toy mice, animated spider and of course my new mom and dad. I am eating and drinking and using my litter box like a good boy, and do not need to hide in the cage anymore. So, my Mom and Dad will be bringing it back to the shelter on Thursday afternoon. I would like to come for the ride and visit, but I am not comfortable being held yet, so I don't think I'm ready to be lifted into that carrying case.

In about a week or so I am going for my first appointment at the veterinarian, so I guess I'd better practice being held. My Mom and I are working on that...!

Love you all, and thank you so much for taking good care of me before my new folks chose to take me home with them. I had a pretty rough start, but you helped me trust again so that now that I've to live with Joan and Lenny the transition has not been so traumatic. When I get more used to traveling in my carrying case, I will come to visit you all...won't that be a party!

It's going to be a good New Year 2006...happy! happy! happy!

I do believe there truly is a God, and he is so fortunate to have you all helping him in his work.

Love,
Thunder

~~

Linda

It's been eight weeks since Boo-Boo joined our family and I wanted to give you an update.

Since Boo-Boo started a new chapter in his life, we felt it was appropriate that he have a new name. Boo-Boo is now known as Rocky the Cat.

Rocky is doing marvelous. The progress he is making is outstanding. Initially he was somewhat shy and found it necessary to spend a lot of time under the bed. This has changed for the better. He has become a very social cat and very much enjoys attention we all lavish upon him. He eagerly meets visitors at the door, insistent on a personal greeting as a rite of passage into our home.

Rocky is extremely playful and delights in all his cat toys. Rocky is very young at heart and has a gentle spirit. Rocky also enjoys spending time at the screen door that overlooks Carlton Park at the rear of our home. He sits and watches the comings and goings (people, dogs, squirrels, birds) in the park with great fascination.

Rocky has been to South Bay Veterinary Clinic and has met Dr. Costantino. While Rocky was not too happy about the trip it was necessary one. Rocky got his teeth (and ears) cleaned and was given a clean bill of health.

Thank you and God bless everyone at the Marblehead Shelter for all the good work you are doing.

I still owe you a photo.

Sincerely

~~

Friends at FOMAA:

Happy Thanksgiving! It's been about 7 months since we adopted Hansel and Gretl, and they are doing great! We have attached a few photos from our first Thanksgiving together; they spent most of it in front of the fire place!

They both weigh about 12 pounds now, have nice healthy coats and are both big cuddle bugs: a far cry from being found in a dumpster in Salem. Their first vet visits were very informative; Gretl's front paws were x-rayed and we discovered that she is missing a radius in one of her forearms and her joints formed so that her leg is in a "L" shape. We also found out quickly that Hansel is blind in the one eye that he has, as he was bumping into walls, stranding himself on the couch, and falling down the stairs when he first arrived. We put up baby gates on the stairs so he wouldn't fall down them, but he is inquisitive and so brave that he learned how to climb the baby gate in two weeks, so he has evening lessons on how to climb up and down the stairs. He's a pro now that he knows the layout of the house and runs up and down the stairs, hardly missing a beat. He occasionally still bumps into things, but that's mostly when mom and dad move things on him! They both are remarkable animals, and we love them dearly! Thank you for saving them for us!

~~

Dear Linda, aka Bubbe,

You'll be pleased to know that Angel, now know as Koska, has thoroughly taken over the house. She follows me around the house purring, trill, and is a hog for everyone's attention.

Bao-bao and Kicka are thoroughly flummoxed by her and are in hiding, as predicted. She is also the smartest cat I've ever owned, responding to her name by the time we arrived home.

Saturday night she decided that the mat in front of our kitchen sink was her territory and swatted at everyone who walked by. Then, during dinner she alternated, twining around my legs, running down under the middle of the table to my daughter (who was sitting at the opposite end), twining around her legs, running back to me, and so on.

Koshka has become our computer cat, sitting on the desk next to the keyboard, batting playfully at whoever is typing or snoozing in the sunny spot next to the screen. As I'm typing this note, she's staring intently at the cardinal and chickadees that perch on the tree about 4' from where we sit. Surprisingly, she's chosen my husband as her favorite person, sleeping next to him while he's reading. She's willing to be held for about 60 seconds before she jumps away, but clearly thrilled to be out of that cage and living with us. I'm a big believer in healing with hugs and she's clearly responding. I feel she's got great potential, and obviously has an engaging personality. My son said, "Geez Mom! You sure know how to pick 'em!"

It's a good fit. I know that within the month she'll be sharing the same couch with the other cats and, in time, she'll be a great snuggler. Please read this note to your colleagues and let them know that this adoption has resulted in one happy cat.

Thanks so much,

~~

To Everyone,

Thank you for taking such good care of me during my stay with you.

My new family is taking good care of me (I am already spoiled). I have two floors in my new house to run through. And I do!!

I can be picked up and know I don't have to go back in a cage. I have also decided to sit on a lap, when it suits me.

Best to all,

Gusto

~~

Dear Linda,

Well it is that time of year again, and just wanted to let you know it is my third anniversary adopting Kayla. She is such a little character. She continues to blossom; she loves to be loved. I silently thank you every day for saving Kayla and letting me adopt her. Kayla still and may always have this issue with expecting to get hit. It is almost like the recent movie that came out, entitled *50 First Dates*. Kayla forgets that I will never hit her, that she is a good girl, and that she is loved. Kayla will never have to fear a day in her life as long as she resides in my home. Kayla greets me every day with her head down and ears back expecting me to hurt her. It took almost three years for her to sit on my husband and slowly beg for some petting. I believe she was hurt by a man. Well that is all behind her. I will continue to reassure her that she is safe and that she can trust us. I will have to send you an update picture of her soon. I just wanted to thank you from the bottom of my heart for your overseeing that Kayla went to the perfect home. It became perfect when I adopted her.

Your Friend

~~

Dear Mrs. Greenberg:

The 4th grade class of the Glover School recently held a bake sale to earn money for local charities. Each classroom then voted on where they would like the money to go. Our class voted to send the money to the Marblehead Animal Shelter. Several of us have gotten our cats from the shelter, and we

know there are other cats (and other animals) that could use our help. Thank you for caring about our lost and abandoned animals. We hope our donation helps.
Sincerely,
Mrs. Purdin and Students.

~~

Dear Friends at the Marblehead Shelter,

Last year I adopted Sissy, the Persian kitty, from your shelter. I hope you remember her. She was shaved and rather thin, but a beauty within! Her fur grew in and she is now a natural silver point Persian. I never imagined how I could love a cat that I hadn't raised from a kitten. We nicknamed her "piece of work" because she has totally taken over our hearts with her quirky personality. She demands combing every morning by letting out a huge meow and then rolling on her side to wait for me to comb her. She'll lift her legs so I can comb the pantaloon tufts on the back of her legs and even her belly. Then, she'll get up, chirp and bark, then roll onto her other side. She has a scratch post in the bedroom that she will scratch and stretch, then wait for me to begin playing with her string that she will chase around the scratch post. She loves foam balls that she will chase but then look at me when it stops like, "hey, what happened, is the thing broke? Throw another!" For her birthday, my husband and I bought her an activity blanket which I have taken a photo of her playing with it. As soon as it comes out, I'll email you her new picture. She is now 10 pounds in comparison to the 8.5 at the time of adoption. Her favorite meal is fancy feast ocean filets but I mix it with special px food that helps her and her furry sister, Benita, digest due to their miles of fur. I hope all is well. Sissy Olivia Noel would like to send you a donation to commemorate her new life. God bless our little furry friends.

Hello, I am pleased to say that my friends do not think Olivia (Sissy) is the same cat I adopted 6 months ago. She has grown, and I'll send you a new picture. We live on Cape Cod in the summer. Although the integration with the other cats has not gone well, Olivia loves to spend time on her harness outdoors with me, eating grass. She enjoys cool afternoons watching birds through her six foot slider in her penthouse. Her favorite new snack is "cool claws" ice cream for cats. Olivia must have her belly rubbed several times a day and LOVES being combed. I would love to know how she got all her great manners. You are angels!

~~

Dear Linda,

How are you? I miss you, the volunteers, and all the other cats and dogs! However, I want you to know, I'm very happy in my new home—and with my new name.

Her are some pictures for your scrapbook. I enjoy looking out at the birds and goings on outside. Sometimes JL (my owner) and I box on the staircase. In the mornings I take a sun bath upstairs on "my" bed. In the evening JL and I do yoga together. We really have a good time.

I'm trying to be a good little cat. This week I found a mouse in the laundry room. JL just closed the door and let nature take its course. I did the deed! I was exceedingly proud of myself. JL was pretty impressed too.

Linda, I want to thank you, and Candy, for giving me shelter when I needed it.

Love from,

Daisy (the cat formerly known as Jane)

~~

Dear Old Feline Friends,

I miss you all very much, but I am enjoying life with my new family. We are getting ready to celebrate my first Christmas. They put a big green tree from outside in the middle of the living room and I'm having a great time taking the bottom ornaments off every day!! By magic they keep getting put back on the tree and I take them off again. There is a stocking that has a cat on it—I think it is going to be mine! There is also a nice fireplace that I like to stretch out in front of and I like to sleep on the bed in the guest room—well, I think of it as my room now!

I wanted you all to have a nice Christmas too, so we put some surprises together for you all to have. There is something special for Chewy and Sterling—hope this makes you both feel special again. Don't get discouraged, I know that you all will find wonderful homes in the New Year. In the meantime, you are safe and warm with some people that will take good care of you until your lucky day comes.

Love,
formerly known as (fka) "Fuzzy Face"

~~

Dear Linda,

Thanks for letting me join such a nice family. First I thank you and all the animal helpers, that took such good care of me, while I was lucky enough to be kept at the Marblehead Animal Shelter. My first day in my new home, I was a little overwhelmed with all the comfortable chairs, and two couches to choose my spot…Well after I let them pet me, someone rang our doorbell and I hid under the couch and did not come out until it was just my family & I. I was told my new name would be JAKE, a nickname my mother had when she was young…It sounds like me don't you think?? We all three of us got cozy and went to bed…I stayed downstairs in my big chair with a soft blanket. The next morning, my father said, "I can't find Jake." Well down came my mother and she found me. I was hiding in the bathtub behind the shower curtain. They sure did think I was funny. Out I jumped and had breakfast. Then I performed for them; they seemed really awesome…I jumped up on the table and looked out the window and then on the floor and saw myself in the window of our dishwasher…that was cool. Next day we had an appointment with the vet. He checked me out to be fine and then my family wanted me all groomed up, so the girl upstairs did that & I must say I feel and look pretty good. While I was getting beautiful, my mom & dad went shopping at the pet store for ME. Boy, I got toys, dishes, scratching board, ball, new blanket and most of all LOVE they give me and I give back. I now sleep on a twin bed upstairs, where they are near me. In the daytime I sleep in the sun and we play a lot. When my extended family visits me they love me too. At night we all sit together on the couch and I cuddle up, while we watch TV. LIFE IS GREAT ISN'T IT??
LOVE FROM,
JAKE (formerly Romeo)

~~

Dear Marblehead Shelter Staff,

I am so happy with my new home. There are lots of rooms and long hallways I can run down. They even have some great toys. Look guys, I am growing up; I can now walk on two legs. I miss all the other cats there and hope they find great homes like mine.

Love,
Catalina (AKA Franny) the Cat

~~

Dear Linda,

Seven years later after we first met you, we are still smitten with the two cats—and a later addition from FOMAA—as ever. When we dejectedly walked in to the shelter that winter day in 2000 after losing our seventeen-year-old cat, you took us through the adoption process that resulted in our picking Abigall and, at your suggestion, Uno (now Bruno) to make a twosome. Our home immediately brightened with the new occupants and they continue to be a constant source of fun, amusement and love for us. Four years later we were having a "playtime" at the shelter with Sterling, a big bear of a gray cat who was feeling low in his cage, and we decided to bring him home, too. He was soon diagnosed with a serious heart ailment and not given much time, but he continues to thrive three years later on a daily regiment of pills and the companionship of his two older "siblings." Sterling was a favorite of Jean's while in the shelter and, as she did, we kiss his head every day for her. He is such a good boy, like Tiny Tim (except he's twenty-one pounds) and he loves being around us as much as we adore him. Bruno and Abby are likely to sleep next to us be we can count on Sterling to be on our bed with us every night. We can't imagine life without these guys, and we owe so much to you and FOMAA for introducing us.

Thanks forever

~~

Hi,

Just want to say thanks for allowing us to adopt Alexander. I'm not sure who is having more fun—Alexander or us. He has immediately taken over the house and staked claim to a few favorite spots. He loves to sit at the bay window and watch everything that is going on (in between a couple of naps of course)! He is a very giving cat, loving to get attention and has quite a friendly personality. He loves to play with his toys and loves for us to play with him. He definitely is curious as he is always exploring. If he wakes up before us he will come up to visit us and after he gives us a couple of soft taps on our heads with his paw it is now his time for attention and of course who can resist!

A few thoughts on the shelter. Our entire process of adoption was an extreme pleasure. This was our first adoption and first cat and we had concerns and a lot of questions. With the help of Linda and the others we were well prepared and educated for Alexander. There were no surprises or disappointments. We also left a support network in place in the event we needed help. All the people at the shelter are very giving and dedicated and should be commended for the tremendous job they do every day. Thanks for everything and keep up the great work that you all do.

~~

Hi Linda,

Sammy is a total nut in the snow. He goes out into the cat pen and digs down deeper than his own little body to use the snow as a litter box! Now I scoop three litter boxes and the cat pen. Sammy comes in soaking wet and jumps on us.

Sammy's new obsession is drinking straws. I drink about a ½ gallon of water a day, out of a 24-oz glass with a straw sticking out of it. Sammy gallops into the kitchen whenever he hears water running or a glass on the counter. He snatches the straw out of whatever glass he finds, even if I'm drinking from it at the time! Then he runs around the house with the straw in his mouth and plays with it like it's a catnip mouse. Sometimes the other cats join in, but mostly they think he's nuts. We have to agree.

I hope all is well with you and all the lovely furry beings in your charge.

~~

Hi Linda,

I've been meaning to write again for a while now but work has been very busy and I haven't had a chance. I hope you got the pictures of Evie and Elli that I sent. Every time they do something cute, I think of writing you to let you know how funny and sweet they are.

Every day brings a new surprise with these cats. The best thing is coming home from work at night and seeing their little faces waiting in the lighted window for me and then the sound of their little feet scrambling down the stairs to meet me at the door. They both are clever and talented, each in her own way. Genie (Elli) is a retriever, if you throw her toy mouse for her, she will fetch it and drop it at your feet so you'll throw it again. We do this about five or six hundred times a day and it's still never enough for her. She is the most playful of the two cats and is always in motion.

Pepper (Evie) likes to play sometimes, too, but you could throw toys all day long and she would just look at you like you were nuts. She much prefers to cuddle and be petted although she also enjoys running through the apartment and having the occasional wrestling match with her sister. And that always ends in both cats grooming and licking each other, which is a great thing to see. Pepper does have other talents; today she discovered that if she stood on her hind legs and batted the door knob, the door would open. I don't know who was more surprised: her or me.

So Pepper, Genie, and I are becoming quite a family. I'm very glad I adopted them and I think they're pretty happy about that too. I hope all is going well at the shelter, and I'll send more pictures the next time I can catch the girls doing something especially cute.

Take care.

~~

Linda,

I have 2 huskies who need a new home! You were recommended.

Pander and Gina are brother and sister, 10-year-old Siberian Huskies who are strikingly beautiful, gentle, smart and tremendously loving (their mom just passed away at the age of 16). They are losing their current master who must go overseas for the coming year at the end of June, and they need a loving home with a yard where they can settle for the long term future. They love to romp with other dogs, like children, and happen to have figured out how to pick and eat blueberries. Thanks.

God bless you for your incredible help and concern and energy and efforts. I believe it is thanks to your putting Pander and Gina on Petfinder that I was contacted by a woman in Nashua (among several) with whom we visited and with whom Pander and Gina have been for 2 weeks now and to whom they seem to be making a brilliant adjustment. Gina did escape and get to the border of Massachusetts in the first days. But I did go back for another visit after that, and she seems to have begun to really appreciate the new people in her life and make herself at home on the bed etc. I am so relieved and incredibly grateful to you for your HUGE Mitzvah!

I have been here in Israel for a week. After a little visit in Jerusalem and Safed I am setting into Haifa where my Hebrew course is very good and I will make great progress (soon as I get to that homework). All my best to you.

~~

I just wanted to touch base and say "hi." Tony's doing just great—he's quite a character and has a wonderful disposition and personality. His favorite pastimes are eating, watching birds and constantly "kissing" whoever he's with—especially when we're trying to use the computer. He eats like a "horse" but gets plenty of exercise when he and Roxy are chasing around the house. He's perfectly content being an inside cat, which is a great thing. At least he has the enclosed screen porch he can enjoy when the weather gets better.

Hope everything is fine with you all—I think of all you do and maybe someday I'll be able to help out in some way. Between work and helping my elderly mother out (she's still in her own home which keeps us pretty busy) I don't have too much time.

I've been telling people about your organization and hopefully when they are in the market for a "new companion"—they'll be over. I'd like to have another one but Tony and Roxy are like having 5 when they start playing and finally are "bonded" to each other.

Stay warm and say "hi" to everyone.

~~

These are just a small sample of the hundreds of updates we receive from our adopters. Reading these updates and knowing our animals are safe, happy, well taken care of, and loved is what our work at the shelter is all about.

SANCTUARY

Chapter 10

I have told you how deeply I got involved in the animal shelter. I have given you a candid look at what happens behind the scenes in the shelter, including exposing our many struggles to get to where we are today. I have shared with you our shelter policies, protocols, and how well we advocate for our animals. I have given you some insight into the care and special attention we give to all our animals. I have written a variety of authentic animal stories throughout the book for you to enjoy. I couldn't say enough about our devoted volunteers. I hope I conveyed to you the inspirational happenings that take place regularly in this obscure modest special little building. Now, I am going to explain how monumental the shelter has been for me and what it has personally meant to Linda Greenberg.

The shelter means a lot to me. Not only is it a place where I enjoy dealing with the animals, work with my fellow volunteers, meet so many wonderful people; receive tremendous pleasure and gratification—it is my second home. The shelter means more to me than you will ever know. I am going to take you into my confidence and reveal something I never told anyone including my family.

For a period of about five years the shelter was a source of much needed therapy for me. Nobody goes through life unscathed. They were serious years and not my happiest. To give you a clear perspective of why the shelter was my retreat; I will have to go back and give you some of my personal history.

My story starts during the summer of 1957. I had just graduated from high school. My dream, since I was a little girl, was to become a ballerina. I took serious ballet for thirteen years. As I got a little older, I came to realize that a quality ballet company would never take on a five foot ballerina with big boobs. Most ballerinas are tall and thin in stature, and are flat chested. It was important for me to further my education, so come September I enrolled in a secretarial school in Boston.

During that summer I worked part time in a clothing store and hung out at a very popular ice cream parlor in the evening. It was called Roland's. Young people from all over used to congregate there to meet other young people. It was the in place to be at that time.

Like so many glorious summer evenings I drove my girlfriends to Roland's in my parents' brand new green and white spiffy Super 88 Oldsmobile to hang out. When I got to the entrance of the parking lot, I would step on the gas and speed in to make a grand entrance. This one particular evening I was wearing a tennis outfit that my mother bought me. I don't know why she bought me a tennis outfit because I didn't play tennis. After I raced into the parking lot there were several boys hanging out there. I got out of the car in my tennis outfit and proceeded to go into the ice cream parlor with my friends. Unbeknownst to me I must have gotten the attention of this one guy. He followed me into the ice cream parlor and sat down on the stool beside me. He introduced himself and tried to make some small talk. He was a perfect gentleman, but I didn't want anything to do with him. The style of clothing at that time was collegiate. The look was three-button shirts and buckles on the back of pants. This guy wasn't bad looking, but was dressed all wrong and did not look good to me. It's silly when you're young how much importance you put on trendy things of the times. This guy was wearing a silver shirt with black pants. It did not appeal to me. He kept trying to talk to me, and I kept ignoring him. It was getting annoying, so I told him to get lost. He walked away in shock. Yes, I could have been polite and more ladylike and given him a chance, but who knew that guy, whose name was Harvey, was going to be the man I would marry.

Summer ended much too quickly. I started secretarial school and commuted to and from Boston by bus and subway every day. During the fall, winter, and spring of that year, I could not escape that guy from the ice cream parlor. We were at the same house parties and socialized at the same hangouts. He would never miss an opportunity to antagonize me. I really couldn't blame him after the way I treated him. We both knew he wasn't being mean or malicious; he was really flirting.

Finally, he got to me, and I wanted to know more about him, so I started to ask around. I learned he was from the city of Malden. I also learned he enlisted in the Army right out of high school and served our country for three years. He was stationed in Germany during the Korean War. He got an honorable discharge from the military and immediately enrolled at Suffolk University Business School on the GI Bill. He was going to college full time nights and worked during the day, which was a grind. He wasn't like most of the boys I knew, especially a Jewish boy. The boys I knew went straight into college after high school or went into their fathers' businesses.

The others girls found him to be very attractive, but he was so different from most of the other boys. I decided to rethink my first impression of him and take another look. I noticed he was a fabulous dancer, always had a joke or a trick up his sleeve and was the life of the party. When there were serious discussions, he more so than the other boys was so much better informed about world affairs. He was extremely opinionated. After taking another look I discovered this guy was really good looking, well built with a super personality. He also looked great in his new wardrobe of collegiate clothing. No wonder all the girls liked him. He looked so much better to me, but I was not entirely convinced about him. I like to take things slowly. He never called me or asked me out on a date. We just continued to provoke each other.

The year passed and before we knew it, glorious summer was here again. All the young people would congregate on Fisherman's Beach in Swampscott. The beach was so crowded on weekends; it was hard to find a spot on the sand to put your blanket down. Now Harvey and I were on the beach continuing to give each other the business. The beach was a lot of fun with all the young people. We would play in the water and on the beach. That was when I noticed Harvey was an excellent athlete. He was a natural and that really caught my interest.

One quiet day at the beach a bunch of us were sitting on a blanket talking. The subject of tennis came up. I innocently said, "I have never played tennis." Harv perceived my comment to be a hint to play tennis. He immediately piped up and asked me to play tennis with him that evening. He caught me completely off guard. Everyone on the blanket was waiting with bated breath for my answer. They all knew we had a contrary relationship. I paused a moment, then said, "Yes." Everybody was surprised, including Harv and myself.

That evening we played tennis and afterwards went out for a bite to eat. We had a fun time. Harv and I continued to see each other every day for the next three weeks. We liked each other a lot. He was always a gentleman and treated me like something fragile and very expensive. At the end of the third week, Harv admitted the first time he saw me at the ice cream parlor he pointed me out to his friends and said, "That girl is for me." I appealed to him because I was petite, cute, and well built. These are his exact words, I was his "Marilyn Monroe, and it was love at first sight." He was very serious, sincerely loved me, and proposed. Well, he swept me off my toe shoes! I never expected this and was taken aback. Was it possible for an eighteen-year-old girl and a twenty-two-year-old guy to fall in love in three weeks and want to get married? Yes, it was most definitely possible, because I accepted his proposal of marriage. I knew he couldn't afford to give me an engagement ring and didn't care. We just wanted to be together. Suddenly, I was engaged to be married.

Overnight our lives changed dramatically. Yesterday we were two carefree kids and today we were planning our future together. The big question was how were two kids, who were very much in love and had absolutely nothing, going to do it. Our parents weren't of means and couldn't help, nor did we expect it. Our main objective was for Harv to graduate from college. We came up with a plan. I would leave secretarial school, get a full-time job, and start saving some money. Harv would start going to school full time days and work nights. This way he would graduate in two years. We knew it was going to be a struggle, but we were gutsy, determined, and a little crazy. They say love can move mountains—we sure enough were going to try.

Just like in the movies Harv went to my parents and asked them for my hand in marriage. They liked Harv a lot and were very happy. He went to tell his parents without me and they were vehemently opposed. Our plan was taking shape and nothing was going to stop us. The wedding date was set for June 6, 1959. We had eleven months to prepare. I got a job in the bursar's office at MIT (Massachusetts Institute of Technology). Harv started college full time days.

During the eleven months of our engagement, I had so much fun planning for the wedding. Harv bought me a lovely hope chest. My parents made me a fabulous bridal shower. We found the perfect place for us to live. It was a furnished attic apartment in a two-family house in Allston, a suburb of Boston. The subway was just a block away. There was a little bedroom, a small living room, a tiny pantry kitchen, and a mini bathroom. The apartment was perfect for us and within our budget. It was our little love nest.

Most importantly, during our engagement, I got to know the man I was going to marry. Aside from my physical attraction to this five-foot-ten, athletically built, blonde, handsome guy; I learned my future husband had excellent qualities. He was a hard-working man with strong character. A man you could depend on. Sometimes he was a little too outspoken. He was a man of integrity, principles, honesty, and you always knew where you stood with Harvey. What I liked best about him was he played by the rules. People who do not play by the rules irk me. He also had an uncanny innate wisdom. The more I got to know him; the more I loved, respected, and admired him. Together I knew we were going to make it.

On May 5, 1959 I turned nineteen. Harv would turn twenty-three on July 19, 1959. On June 6, 1959 we were married. My parents made us a grand wedding. It was a festive occasion and a great send off. Sadly, Harv's parents parting words to him were, "This marriage won't last six months." It was most discouraging because he did so want their blessing. It was unfortunate they felt that way; however, it was not the time for unpleasantness, so we ignored the whole thing. Here we were, two gutsy kids with chutzpah, on our way to make a life for ourselves.

The truth was our start was not easy and there were hard times. Money was tight and occasionally we ran out. Sometimes we didn't have food and would go through our pockets to muster up enough change to buy a sub sandwich to share. When we were totally out of pocket change and very hungry; it was time to make a visitation to my parents' house. We knew we were in for a good meal, and my mother always prepared a large doggie bag for us to take back with all kinds of goodies.

Still very much in love and just about hanging in there we ran into a snag. It was a snag we never planned for. It turned out our apartment was quite the love nest. We discovered I was pregnant and due in September. It was the same time Harv was going to start his last year of college. Our future depended on him graduating. The company he was currently working for part time loved him and offered him a good-paying position after graduation. How were we going to do it? We had to rethink our original plan and come up with a new one.

We decided I would work as long as possible. Harv would continue to work full time during the summer and part time when school started again. We needed all the money for the baby now. When I no longer could work, we would give up the apartment and move in with my parents temporarily. My parents were delighted, but it really was not the best situation. We had no choice.

September 17, 1960 our beautiful, wonderful daughter was born. She was a miracle and the love of our life. We named her Tami. Harv started his last year of college. It was paramount he finish! We stayed on with my parents for a couple of months, until we discovered I could collect unemployment. It was like finding a pot of gold. It enabled us to move into a three-room apartment that wasn't the nicest place, but it had to do for now. The important thing was the three of us were together. We gave the baby the bedroom, and we slept on a sofa bed. We were just managing and determined to get by, when all of a sudden I found out I was pregnant again. What is it about these small, three-room love nests? The baby wasn't due until October. By that time Harv would have graduated from college and working full time at the position that was promised to him.

Don't ask me how, but for the grace of God the day of my husband's graduation from Suffolk University finally arrived. It was a monumental goal for us, and we will never forget it. I was very much pregnant and went to the Statler Hotel in Boston to watch the ceremony. Senator Wayne Morse from Oregon was the commencement speaker. When my husband's name was called to receive his college diploma, I was so proud. Inside I was saying, *We did it! We accomplished the impossible!* It was a time to celebrate with our precious daughter, Tami.

Our family was growing, and we needed a bigger place to live. My husband's innate wisdom went into action. For years he saw his and my parents pay rent and only receive rent receipts and no equity. He wanted us to buy our own place. Our thought was to buy a two-family home and have a tenant help pay the mortgage. It was the most logical idea for our situation. We knew we wanted to stay near the ocean because we loved the area so much. On the very first day with a real estate agent, we went through a couple of two-family houses in Swampscott that needed lots of work we could not afford at that time. The agent told us about a single-family home, which was just around the corner. It had been up for sale for a very long time. She wanted us to see it. We knew there was no way we could afford a single-family home, but we went to see it anyway.

We pulled up in front of a little cape home that was set up high from the street. The grass was overgrown because nobody had lived there for a year. The street the house was on was a cul-de-sac and at the end of the street was the main park in Swampscott. It was also located a block away from the beach. The location was fabulous and a perfect place to bring up children. We went inside and there were only four rooms—a kitchen, living room, and two bedrooms. The attic was unfinished and there was no cellar. Harv and I looked at each other and knew what we were both thinking. We both thought the house was absolutely charming and saw so much potential that could be done to improve the house in the future. It was a dream house in our eyes. We asked the agent the asking price. She told us and it was out of our reach.

That evening and the next day we couldn't stop thinking about that little cape house. It was perfect for us. Harv kept figuring and figuring how we could afford it, but nothing worked. It was out of the question. We were really stuck on that house and wanted it badly. It was on the market for such a long time, so we decided to take a shot and make a ridiculous offer. The owners by this time must have wanted to get it off their hands and to our amazement they accepted our offer. Who would have believed it? Harv started figuring all over again. Even with the GI Bill and the new offer, we were still two thousand dollars short. How frustrating it was for us. We needed help. We could have gone to my parents for help. Believe me, if they had to borrow the money, they would have come through for us. We couldn't ask them; after all, they made us a lovely wedding and opened their home to us. It wouldn't have been right to burden them.

Harv had a thought. Across the street from our apartment lived Harv's fraternal grandparents with his bachelor uncle and bachelorette aunt. They were very close to us and very supportive. That evening we invited his aunt and uncle up to the apartment to talk to them and told them about the house and what we needed to purchase it. We asked them each to loan us a thousand dollars. We promised to pay them back a portion of the loan every year until it was paid in full. I can remember it just like it was yesterday. They went into the kitchen to talk privately. Harv and I were holding our breath and praying they would say yes. After a few minutes they came back into the living room to tell us we could have the money. I can't tell you how relieved we were. Auntie Raye and Uncle Jack truly preformed a benevolent act that evening. We will be forever grateful for their support, generosity, and with their help a new beginning for our little family. Incidentally, we kept our promise and paid them back every penny. As of today, we have lived in the house forty-six years. We really don't want to live anyplace else because it is perfect for us and we love it.

No time was wasted that summer. We bought the house and moved in. We owned a tiny piece of the earth. What a glorious thought that is. On October 13, 1961 another miracle occurred. Our second child was born. A blessed, beautiful, wonderful, healthy daughter we named Toby. Since the day we got engaged, it has been an exciting journey with so much more to look forward to.

Early in our marriage Harv and I made a conscious decision that we would live on his income alone. It was important I be a stay-at-home mom. Frankly, I loved being a mother and a homemaker. We felt we both had to be there for the girls to instill the proper values. Harv was a great dad. He wasn't one of those fathers who wouldn't dirty their hands changing baby diapers, or disliked caring for the babies if his wife wanted to go out. I don't consider those kind of fathers very manly. Harv had a much younger brother he took care of and he taught me plenty about caring for the babies. The girls adored their father because he played with them all the time. We were all so blessed.

Since that evening Harv and I played tennis, we have experienced one momentous event after another. Hold on to your hats because another momentous event is about to happen. A few months after Toby was born I discovered I was pregnant again. Nine months later at the young age of twenty-two we had another miracle. A beautiful, wonderful, blonde, healthy daughter was born on January 11, 1963. We named her Terri. Everyone told us we had to give her a name starting with T, because her sister's names started with T, which was not done on purpose. My three daughters were each approximately a year apart.

I was pretty tired and needed some quiet time to get back on my feet. We couldn't afford a nurse, so Harv took some time off from work to help me. At the time we didn't have many of the conveniences there are today. There were no disposable diapers. We had cloth diapers and with three babies there was lots and lots of wash. Ready-made formula never existed. We made formula from scratch. Every day we had to boil the bottles to sterilize them. A dishwasher was a luxury we could not afford. Believe it or not we never heard of car seats. I used to hold the children in the back seat of the car while Harv drove. We didn't know any different, and we did what we had to do without all those conveniences and did it well.

That was our start in life together and still there was so much to look forward to. The girls were growing up beautifully. Our little house expanded. We had a dormer built onto the attic to enlarge the rooms so the ceilings weren't pitched. My vision of the attic became a reality. In one of the rooms I had three beds and all their bureau drawers built in. The other room was a playroom for them and a fun place to bring their friends. Life was good, and we were a loving, happy family.

Harv made a few beneficial job changes to better both himself and financially. He became a corrugated box salesman. A friend of his told Harv he was working for the wrong company and set up an interview with one of the best corrugated companies in the field at that time. It was called Allied Container owned by the Schwartz family. Eventually Union Camp, a huge national paper company, bought out Allied Container. The Schwartzes continued operating the company. Harv went on the interview. They wanted a sales representative to start canvassing in the state of Maine. During his interview they asked Harv if a Jew could sell boxes in Maine. They also asked him if he would consider putting Harvey Green on his business cards instead of Harvey Greenberg. My husband refused to change his name. He said his grandfather's name was Greenberg and his father's name was Greenberg and his name was going to stay Greenberg. Many other aspects of the position were discussed. They came to a mutual agreement, and Harv was hired on the spot.

With only a map of the state of Maine and a Maine directory, every Tuesday Harv would drive up to Maine canvassing for new business for the company and come home on Thursdays. It was all virgin territory and it wasn't easy. On Mondays and Fridays he would make local calls in Massachusetts. The question, "Can a Jew sell boxes in Maine?" was finally answered. Traveling to Maine for four years, getting to know the purchasing agents, and convincing them to buy corrugated boxes from his company; Harv proved a Jew could sell boxes in Maine. The company made a decision to build a new corrugated box plant in Auburn, Maine. Not only did they build a new plant, my Jewish husband became the top salesman in the company.

The fact of the matter is religion, color, or gender has nothing to do with being a good salesman. It is most definitely personality and ability. Harv related well with the men and women he did business with in Maine because most of them were good, honest and loyal people who were from the old school, when a handshake meant something. My husband is an old school type of guy; that is why his customers trusted him.

The next eighteen years were glorious. Our girls were growing up. They were all so different, and it surely made life interesting. They were our whole life, and we adored them. Our little cape house was transformed into a Maine post and beam home. It dramatically changed from a four-room home into a seven-room home. We wanted our little home to be informal, comfortable, and invitingly warm. That was exactly how it was decorated. My oldest granddaughter, Haley, out of the blue used the word "timeless" to describe our home. For her to describe our home that way gave us a warm feeling all over.

Let's not forget all the beloved pets we had through the years. Our family would not have been complete without them. Our first dog was Tabetha, a beagle mix. There was a little sandwich shop three short blocks from where we lived. Every day before there was a leash law Tabetha walked up to the sandwich shop to beg for snacks. She was on the chubby side, but did not miss a day trekking up to the sandwich shop until she passed on. My brother and sister-in-law's pedigree golden retriever had a litter of puppies and they gave us the runt of the litter. It was a gift of love, and I will be forever thankful. I named her Elsa because she looked like the little lion cub from the movie *Born Free*. When she passed on, we got another golden retriever from a breeder in Vermont. My daughter Toby was in college at the time in Amherst, Massachusetts, which wasn't far from where the breeder was located. She and her friend were kind enough to pick up the puppy, and keep it in her dorm room, until she was able to bring her home. This adorable golden puppy was reddish in color and we named her Cecily. A year later we decided Cecily needed a sister and purchased another golden puppy from the same breeder in Vermont. She was lovely, light in color, and we called her Sophie. Cecily and Sophie were wonderful playmates. They loved each other. When Cecily passed on Sophie was very lonely and needed a friend. I had never seen a Bernese mountain dog close up; when I did I knew I wanted one to be my next dog. Sophie got a friend. It was a Bernese mountain dog puppy we named Mighty Moses. He was something! When little Sophie passed on, my children presented me with Annie, a red bloodhound puppy. She was so cute with ears bigger than she was. Along with the dogs we always had cats. There was Zorro, Cheswick, Flossy, Stinky, Spooky, Prissy, Grayson, and Tchaikovsky, our cross-eyed Siamese cat. We loved them all, and they could never be replaced, but we did start new relationships. They will always have a special place in our hearts.

We traveled with the girls to all the important places: Disneyland, New York City, Washington D.C. and more. Harv and I took some major trips without the children. My husband was chosen to participate at the Macabia Games in Israel for the volleyball team. The trip was for three weeks. Our next trip we drove and toured California from Yosemite National Park all the way down to Palm Springs and San Diego. We did a bed and breakfast trip through the countryside of Scotland and England and ended up in London for five days. The greatest of all trips was to Kenya on a safari, including a hot air balloon safari.

Our family loves to celebrate occasions. If we didn't have an excuse to celebrate; we would make one up. When each of our girls reached thirteen, we celebrated their bat mitzvahs. You can bet there was a celebration when the girls graduated high school. They all went to the University of Massachusetts in Amherst, MA. There was cause to have a huge celebration, when Tami, who majored in economics, graduated college with honors. I think I invited everybody I knew to that party. The next year Toby got her degree in education and graduated with honors as well. She always wanted to be a physical education teacher and fulfill her dream. I think I invited everyone I knew plus some I didn't know to her graduation party. Last but not least my baby, Terri, graduated with a degree in education also. I invited the world to that party. It was a wild one!

Our celebrations were hardly over. There was plenty more to come. Shortly after Tami graduated college she met a terrific guy named Richie. He was handsome, well educated, intelligent, responsible, reliable, a successful business man, and a good golfer. Richie was from a wonderful family and the kind of young man you would want your daughter to marry. They started to date and after three weeks they were engaged. The apple doesn't fall far from the tree. Richie was from Swampscott also and the announcement of their engagement was the talk of the town. Next thing we knew we were planning a wedding. It was a super happy fabulous occasion!

Four years later Toby met the love of her life, Jeff. He is a sweetheart of a guy. Very good looking, reliable, a great sense of humor, warm, and a super athlete. He was also from a good family and the type of young man you would want your daughter marry. Toby and Jeff have so much in common and are a match made in heaven.

Yes, we were planning another wedding. Toby and Jeff were getting married at the Temple, which was not far from our home. The day of the wedding was approaching quickly, and I was running back and forth to Temple making sure everything was going to be perfect. One day as I rode by the front of the Temple something caught the corner of my eye. At first I thought I was seeing things. I parked the car and walked slowly to the front of the Temple. I was not seeing things. There were three adorable kittens frolicking behind some bushes. They were about ten weeks old. One was all black, a little blue cream, and a calico. It was obvious they were a homeless family living behind the grill work in front of the Temple. Their mother was probably away searching for food.

Why do these things happen to me! I had so much to do preparing for the wedding. Out-of-town guests were coming into town that needed attention. I couldn't sleep thinking about those kittens. I had to help. The next day I started putting food out for them, went to a pet store, and rented a have-a-heart trap. The trap was set with a can of food in it near where the kittens were playing. There was only two weeks left for the wedding to take place. Every day I would go to the temple and check to see if any of the kittens took the bait. It didn't happen so fast. I guess the little blue cream was hungry and was the first to appear in the trap. I took her home and put her in the upstairs bathroom. I brought the trap back, set it up, and waited. You would think I had nothing else to do but rescue kittens. A couple of days later the little black kitten was in the trap. I brought him home and reunited him with his sister in the bathroom. Again I brought the trap back to the temple and set it up with fresh food every day. Nothing was happening. The third kitten was not taking the bait. The wedding was a few days away and I continued checking the trap. The trap was always empty. I even checked the day of the wedding, but nothing. The wedding turned out to be a jubilant, fun and joyous celebration!

The wedding was over and my guests left for home. I continued to put fresh food out and check to see if the little calico kitten was in there, but with little success. I was disappointed and was not going to give up. Then one day when I went to check the trap, to my surprise I saw an animal in the trap that I did not expect to see. It was the mother cat! Now what was I going to do? She was feral and difficult to handle. Now that I had captured her; I had to get her spayed, so she wouldn't reproduce more litters of homeless kittens. I called a vet and explained, "I trapped a feral cat and she needed to be spayed quickly because I can't keep her in the trap indefinitely." I brought the cat to the hospital and she was spayed. When she recovered, I would release her back in the wild, but where was she going to recover? The light bulb came on! While Toby and Jeff were on their honeymoon, the cat could recover downstairs in their condo. I went over to feed the cat every day and she was recovering nicely. The day before Toby and Jeff came home the mother cat was released back into the wild. Meanwhile I still had the have-a-heart trap set up at the temple for the third kitten. I kept it there for four more weeks, but the little calico kitten eluded me. Calico cats are always females. I especially wanted to rescue her, so one day she won't reproduce litters of homeless kittens also.

The two kittens that were at my house were checked out by the veterinarian, had their shots, and were in perfect health. I presented them to Toby and Jeff as a wedding present even though Jeff was allergic. Over the years he became immune to them. Remember these kittens were rescued at the Temple, so they were given Jewish names. The blue cream was a female and named Cital. The black kitten was a male and named Schlomo.

Our beautiful youngest daughter was seeing a fellow off and on for a while. He was an interesting guy, but not the type of man we envisioned Terri to marry. She loved him and decided to get married. We made them a small tasteful wedding for the immediate family. He was our daughter's husband and we accepted him as part of our family.

Our family was growing; three daughters and now three sons-in-law. The best part was all the girls settled not more than three miles from the house where they were brought up. It was an added plus having them close to the nest.

We hardly had a chance to catch our breath, when the best of our blessings was about to happen. We became grandparents and started changing diapers again. My hubby and I were overjoyed. We were blessed with six magnificent grandchildren. We had three grandsons and three granddaughters. Each of my daughters had a boy and a girl. We love those grandchildren and couldn't get enough of them and still can't. It was truly a bonus living so close by because we shared so much with them. We were living the American dream and every day thanked our lucky stars for all our good fortune.

Just when you think you are on top of the world life comes back to snap you.

During Harv's eighteenth year with his company, new management came in and things started to change drastically. The changes were becoming disastrous. Without wasting a minute the new management immediately fired the old management. Throughout the next year and half, one by one the loyal salesmen who helped build the company were systematically terminated. Both Harv and I knew it was a matter of time before they would get to him. Harv was now in his twentieth year with the company, when the hatchet men started to work their dirty deed on my husband. They were making unreasonable demands on him alone and not on any of the newer salesmen. One day he was called in to sign a document that had a list of unrealistic demands that were impossible to live up to. He was doomed if he signed it and doomed if he didn't. No other remaining salesmen were asked to sign a similar document. He was going to be replaced by a younger man in his early twenties for substantially less of a salary. Harv knew this man because he used to be in customer service and knew he had absolutely no sales experience. This is not a new scenario, but it is a cruel way of doing business and treating good people. It was clear that years of hard work building up a customer base, constantly working toward acquiring new customers, loyalty to the company, and being the number one salesman, building a new plant in Auburn, ME, mainly off his sales, did not matter.

To put it bluntly, my husband was getting screwed! Nobody likes to be treated poorly, and we are no different. We have always been fighters, so we decided to speak to an attorney for guidance. As a matter of fact we spoke to attorneys at two different law firms. Without getting into legalities both law firms validated what we already knew—we had a solid age discrimination case against his company. We were warned these cases could be difficult because one little guy was going against a multi-million dollar corporation. It was a David and Goliath story. They also told us law cases take on a life of their own. Harv and I strongly believed in the justice system and had powerful faith that truth would win out. We went ahead and sued the bastards! I only wish we knew then what we know now.

At the beginning of every lawsuit lawyers prepare what is known as a summary judgment for the judge to confirm if we have a prima-facie case before going forth with the suit. The judge confirmed we had a prima-facie case, and we won the decision. The corporation appealed the summary judgment, so our lawyers prepared another one and submitted it to the judge again. Again the judge's decision came down in our favor. The judge obviously felt we had a solid legal age discrimination case to pursue. It took four years for the case to finally get to court for trial. Four very long years of emotional exhaustion and the cost financially was exorbitant. Four years of the highest of highs and lowest of lows. It was like being on a roller coaster. Our only desire was a trial by a jury of our peers.

Finally, the day of the trial arrived. A jury was selected, and listened to our case for two straight days. On the third day the judge decided to take the law into his own hands and become judge and jury. He issued a directed verdict. If you know anything about the law, a directed verdict is very, very rare. He dismissed the jury and that was the end of it; just like that! Our lawyers didn't even have a chance to finish pleading our case. We went through four years of hell for that!

We risked everything pursing this lawsuit because of faith in the law of the land, truth, honesty, and believing in the justice system. Boy, were we naïve! Everything we believed in and the principles we lived by were defeated and trashed by this outrageous judge. Is this how the justice system treats a good man who worked hard since he was thirteen years of age, served his country in the military for three years, a decent, honest citizen, a fantastic family man who achieved the American dream? Is this justice?

So ended our dreams of economic ease, and Harv's cherished job. The irony is the company no longer exits.

During the course of our lawsuit we were faced with some alarming news about our oldest grandson Harrison Ross Bane. To my delight he was named after my father, Harry Ross. Most people call him Harry. When he was an infant, I carried him on my back while walking the dogs in the park. He was a grandmother's dream come true. As soon as he could hold a ball his grandfather, Harvey started teaching him what to do with it. Harry walked at nine months old and couldn't get enough playing ball with his grandfather. Harv bought him his first baseball glove and bat. They would go to the park at the end of our street and practice constantly. Harry wanted to learn the fine points of baseball and was very receptive to his grandfather's instruction. He was also a grandfather's dream come true.

Harry's sister, Haley, was born almost to the day a year after. A boy and a girl was the perfect family. As grandparents, we were very close to our grandchildren and couldn't get enough of them. We loved babysitting for the kids, but didn't like to babysit at their house. The grandkids came to our home and slept over. There were cribs, toys, and we provided them with all their needs. It was a fabulous arrangement because their parents could stay out as late as they wanted and sleep as late as they wanted the next morning. It was like a mini vacation. On the other hand we had the privilege of enjoying more time with our grandchildren. Our relationship with those six beautiful children was warm and close. It went on until the grandchildren were old enough to babysit themselves.

The alarming news we received about Harry was the worst. No grandparent wants to hear it. It was a tremendous blow to the whole family. Our four-year-old grandson was diagnosed with a rare form of bone cancer located on his lower right leg. The name of the cancer is called adamamtinoma. The doctors told us there were between two hundred and two hundred and fifty cases in the world.

This kind of news gives you pause. You think about the mammoth task ahead for our daughter and son-in-law. You also think about the pain and suffering that precious baby boy is going to have to endure. You can feel the fear of the unknown. Maybe you don't say it out loud, but you think it and ask yourself, "Why! Why does Harry have to go through this unpleasantness? Why should any child or adult have to suffer?" As his grandparents we wished, if it was going to happen, why it didn't happen to one of us. There are no answers. You have to face it and fight it.

Harry's mom and dad searched for the very best physicians, who were knowledgeable about this type of rare bone cancer. Fortunately, in our own back yard at the Massachusetts General Hospital there was an orthopedic oncologist who was very familiar with this hideous disease. Harry was put in his care. The doctors examined and checked little Harry hundreds of times over and every which way. They concluded the tumor was too close to his growth plates, and it was slow growing, so surgery would be put off until the proper time. The logic was, while Harry was growing, the tumor would shift away from his growth plate and they would operate then.

The doctors were not happy about Harry playing sports. Tami and Richie wanted him to live a normal life and allowed him to play. They set a wonderful tone to follow for the whole family, close friends, and acquaintances. Harry was treated like any kid on the block; besides, there was no way you could stop Harry from playing sports. It was in his blood and he was born with natural ability. He excelled in every sport he participated in— soccer, baseball, basketball, and golf.

I know I sound like a prejudiced grandmother and admit I am prejudiced. His coaches, assistant coaches, and teammates wanted Harry to be on their team because not only did he play well; he had respect, followed directions, and was a team player. Everybody wants to team up with a winner. Watching Harry play sports was a joyous experience. We were proud grandparents and wouldn't miss any of his games. His grandfather went to all of his practices also.

At seven years old his tumor shifted away from his growth plate. It was time for Harry to have an operation. At ten years old he had two more surgeries three months apart. At thirteen years old he went through another surgery. Without getting into medical technicalities none of his surgeries were routine. On the contrary they were all quite complicated. Harry was an amazing young man and handled things like a brave soldier. Despite his doctor's objections, after completely recovering from all his operations, he returned to playing team sports. His Zayde (grandfather) describes Harry as being a stallion, and you cannot put a stallion out to pasture.

When he was fourteen, while playing basketball, he landed at an odd angle on his bad leg, which resulted in a nasty break. Back he went into the hospital for emergency surgery. The leg healed, but it healed bowed at a fifty-eight-degree angle. There was a specialist in the state of Maryland who could straighten out his leg. The procedure was called the Illzarov Technique. A fixator was inserted into the leg, which had to be adjusted daily. Harry and his mother traveled back and forth to Maryland for two years until the fixator was removed and his leg was perfectly straight.

To say the least Harry's ordeal was worrisome for the whole family. Harry's future depended on major decisions his parents had to make for him. They had the ultimate burden. They also had to balance and bring normalcy into his sister Haley's life during this horrific period. Tami and Richie are to be commended on how they handled their son and daughter. They did not panic; they listened to all their options, and made wise decisions. Tami and Richie are a dynamite couple. They are community leaders, charitable, and devoted to their family and extended family.

My husband and I observed our daughter during this trying time. We love her so and hated to see her go through this. Tami was like a rock through it all. She was strong, kept a clear head, took it day by day, and never felt sorry for herself. Tami has been the woman's golf champion at her club for fourteen years—she is also a champion mom, daughter, sister, and person. Our daughter has TRUE GRIT!

While we were still in the middle of our lawsuit and coming to grips with the knowledge of Harry's cancer, my pregnant middle daughter, Toby, was rushed to the Woman and Brigham Hospital in Boston with labor pains. She delivered a son six weeks premature. He weighed five pounds, had red hair, and looked like an adorable little chicken in his incubator. He was named Jacob, but everybody calls him Jake.

Jake was too small to go home with his mother so he had to remain in an incubator. Toby and my son-in-law, Jeff, lived in Salem, MA, so the doctors decided to transfer Jake by ambulance to Salem Hospital. It was more convenient for Toby and Jeff to be with their son. It was also more convenient for us to visit our new grandson.

Moving Jake from the Boston hospital to the Salem hospital turned out to be very timely. Salem Hospital instituted a brand new therapeutic program for preemies, which included occupational therapy and physical therapy. The professionals felt that early intervention was crucial for the future of preemies. Generally preemies are at risk for having special needs. Jake's therapy continued after he left the hospital and at six months old they included speech therapy for him.

Naturally, Toby and Jeff were concerned about their son's future and were determined to do whatever it took to provide him with everything he needed to become a productive citizen.

As I mentioned before, Toby received her college degree in education. While teaching, she taught special needs children. She also experienced how the educational system dealt with special needs children. Toby was not going to be in denial about her son's problems and decided to educate herself on the subject, which included ADHD (Attention Deficit Hyper Disorder). She read books, went to seminars and support groups, talked with professional advocates, and was trained by therapists. She even educated herself on the law concerning special needs children in the educational system. She became extremely knowledgeable on the subject of her son's problems and was going to make it her full-time job. Jeff was a sweet, loving, patient dad, who was getting educated through Toby. Little Jake didn't know how lucky he was to have a mother and father who were going to be right by his side to help him along the way.

It was an anxious time in our life with so many worrisome things going on all at the same time. Some good news was certainly welcome, when Toby and Jeff told us they were going to have another child. Harv and I were excited to have our fourth grandchild. Eleven months after Jake was born, he had a gorgeous little sister. We were thrilled it was a little girl. Unlike Jake she was a full-term baby and she was named Rachel. Rachel was a colicky baby and cried constantly. Toby had her hands full. Jake was still like a baby himself and now the new baby. I tried to help her as much as I could. When I took care of Rachel and she would cry, I would sing to her. Don't ask me why, but she would instantly stop crying. Believe me it wasn't my singing because I can't keep a tune. She just loved people to sing to her. Eventually, her colic passed and she became the most lovable, sweetest child.

When it was time for Jake to enter preschool, he was diagnosed globally delayed. It meant he was delayed in occupational, physical, and speech therapy. Fortunately for Jake, Salem had a special integrated kindergarten program that provided all the special services he needed. When it was time for him to move up to kindergarten midway through (Jake was diagnosed with ADHD), his teacher recommended he stay behind and go into a special class. It was the last thing his parents wanted to hear. Toby sincerely believed from the bottom of her heart that with her help he could be mainstreamed into a regular educational kindergarten classroom. Both Toby and Jeff knew it was going to be the fight of their life to get Jake mainstreamed into a regular classroom. Should I say it was a fight for Jake's life? There were numerous important reasons why they wanted Jake mainstreamed. One of the reasons was it would have been devastating for Jake's self-esteem to end up in the same year with his younger sister.

Well, after endless emotional meetings and discussions Toby and Jeff won their battle for their son. He would be mainstreamed into a regular classroom. They knew it was not going to be easy; however, they were prepared to take full responsibility for their decision. Jake was going to need constant direction and guidance. Jake's mom and dad are wonderful parents, who love their son so much and will make sure it is going to work out. Little Rachel loves her big brother and looks after him as well.

There is no question that Toby's dedication directed towards her son's success in school went beyond the call of duty. She became involved in the school community and volunteered her services. She volunteered on the school council hiring committee. For the entire Salem school system she was the president of the School Council Round Table. She was also the chairman of the Parents Advisory Council, for parents of children with special needs. Toby met with the superintendent of schools on a monthly basis to give her input on various things going on in the system. She never went for her license to become a professional advocate for families with special-needs children. She could have easily gotten her license, if she wanted to, but she knew many families in Salem who needed help could not afford a professional advocate. Toby unselfishly helped many families and never expected anything in return. Her reputation for assisting families in need became well known and led to calls for help, not only in Salem, but in other communities as well. I am not through with Toby, yet. Physical education was Toby's background, so when her children were old enough to participate in sports, she volunteered her services again. She coached her son's and daughter's basketball teams. She assisted Rachel's softball team. Toby was the pied piper of Salem and the kids loved her.

Dull will never be the word to describe my life, especially during this pressure-packed period of our law case, Harry's health problem, and Jake's future. To our delight our youngest daughter, Terri, announced she was going to have a baby. It would be our fifth grandchild. Rachel and the new baby would only be six months apart. There was so much unbelievable excitement for us to consume at that time.

Terri delivered a beautiful, healthy baby girl and named her Fredi. We hardly had a chance to take a deep breath, when three months later Terri announced she was pregnant again. This would be our sixth grandchild. A little boy who was named Jared was born a year later, four days before his big sister, Fredi's, birth date. He was a handsome little guy. Harv and I had three absolutely wonderful gorgeous grandsons and three absolutely beautiful granddaughters. Each of our daughters had a boy and a girl and had them close. I believe when siblings are that close they are called Irish twins. Our joyous family has grown dramatically, and our dreams have come true.

Shortly after our law case so abruptly came to an end and while adjusting to the shock of it all, we learned our daughter Terri's marriage was in trouble. It was disturbing to hear such news, but not a surprise. Next we heard she was getting a divorce. Harv and I were very worried because going through a divorce is no fun to say the least and especially when there are children involved.

Terri's whole life turned around. She and the children moved out of their magnificent home. She had to work two jobs because the children's father was not doing his part providing for them. The worst of it was the courts did nothing to help. There are names for fathers like that; however, out of love and respect for my grandchildren, I will restrain myself from going into details about my ex-son-in-law. Terri had the world on her shoulders and did not have an easy task ahead of her. She had to be mother and father to those children and make all the decisions. It was also an enormous struggle financially because she was the sole provider. Believe me the children loved their mother very much and felt her pain. She was lucky her family was there for support. As her parents, we will always be there for her and do what we can. I will tell you this; Terri is a gutsy kid and the most forgiving person I know. She is a survivor and will come out of this with her head held high.

Between taking care of the children, working, and all her other responsibilities, she was unable to care for the dog properly, so she asked us to take him. Of course we said we would. Wellington was a beautiful, well-behaved golden retriever. He was over our house all the time playing with our Bernese mountain dog and bloodhound. He loved living with us. I used to take all three dogs for walks at the same time. All three were pretty good-size dogs. People who didn't know me thought I was a professional dog walker. They walked like Westminster champions, and I was proud to be with them.

Why have I given you a history of some of my life experiences, most of which were wonderful and some of which were most unpleasant? Nobody goes through life unscathed, and I am no different. The point is, in that five-year period in my life there was one aggravation after another. The court case was so stressful. My grandson's problem with his leg was the worst. My other grandson's learning disabilities problem was a big worry. My daughter's divorce and struggle weighed heavy on my mind. Everything seemed to happen all at once. They were serious years even though there were some bright spots.

Why have I told you all this? I will tell you why. During that period I felt down, so low, so unhappy. I was depressed and feeling sorry for myself. All I wanted to do was stay home. I definitely didn't want to socialize and be in crowds. I didn't tell anyone and kept a happy face on, so nobody would guess how I really felt. I never felt like that before, and hated myself for it. It was completely out of character. This could n't happen to Linda Greenberg. It wasn't healthy, and I had to work myself out of it. I thought of going for professional help, but went that route once before on another matter and it did not work for me, and I concluded the professional needed counseling more than I did.

Enter the animal shelter. The animal shelter became my retreat, my sanctuary, my much-needed source of therapy. It was my second home. The animal shelter was not only therapeutic; besides, rescuing animals it rescued me. It put things in the right perspective. Socializing with the volunteers and the public was helpful too. Slowly but surely I was coming out of my doldrums. I will be forever indebted to this most unusual refuge.

As soon as you walk into the shelter and see all the homeless animals, you immediately forget about your own problems and start thinking about those poor, helpless creatures. Your mind and body immediately go to work caring for them. You witness first hand the horrors and struggles the animals go through to survive. Yet, through it all they are still so loving and forgiving. The animals by example inspired me to move on and realize what I should have known all along—I have so much to be grateful for.

There have been many times when I am the only human in the shelter with all the animals. The animals were fed, their cages were cleaned, and they were quiet and content. The atmosphere at this time is so very peaceful. I look around at the animals, they look back at me, and with their body language I swear they are saying "Thank you." It is hard to explain, but it feels spiritual. There is great solace in knowing you are saving their lives. Not only is the shelter a sanctuary for animals; it is a sanctuary for people too. It was for me.

I have shared with you personal stories about me and my family. You must have heard this truism at one time, "Time is a great healer." Well, it is true. Some years have passed, and I would like to follow up on the outcome of some of those personal stories.

As far as our court case, it was over and nothing will ever change that. I will always be angry, disappointed, and cynical about the justice system. I have completely lost trust.

This is the latest on my grandson, Harry, who is a very special young man. While going through his ordeal with his leg, he never ever complained and had an unbelievably positive attitude. The best news is that Harry has his leg; it is as straight as an arrow, and best of all he is cancer free. He is handsome, six feet four inches tall, a gentleman, and going to Middlebury College in Vermont. He is following in his mother's footsteps and won the club's 2005 men's golf championship at nineteen years old. He was the youngest ever to do so. Harry is the most courageous person I know.

Let's not forget about our granddaughter, Haley; after all, she was an intricate part of her brother's ordeal. Harry was our first born grandson and Haley was our first born granddaughter. We were ecstatic when we found out that Tami and Richie had a little girl. Haley was in a tough position because of her brother's fourteen-year battle with cancer. Most of the attention was directed toward him because of that. Not to our surprise our granddaughter emerged into quite a star. The immediate family nicknamed her Bell Star. She is beautiful, blonde, intelligent, independent, athletic, talented, and quite an achiever. This girl has got her head together. When she danced, she danced well enough to earn the lead role of Clara from the ballet *The Nutcracker Suite*. When she played sports, she played hard and was a winner. While in high school, she became captain of the softball and golf teams. She also worked hard in school and graduated high school with distinction. All her hard work paid off and was greatly rewarded, when she was accepted early admission to Cornell University in New York. Haley is quite a gal to say the least. Her grandparents are bursting with love and pride for her.

Now let's see what is happening with my red-headed grandson, Jake. Toby and Jeff's decision to mainstream Jake into a regular kindergarten classroom and take full responsibility for him paid off. He went off to elementary school, middle school, and is now entering high school. He has never fallen behind and managed to stay right in the middle of the bell curve. He has quite a personality and is very popular with the boys and the girls. Thanks to his parents going to endless team meetings throughout his school years, making sure proper support systems were put in place for him to learn properly, which included some modifications and accommodations in the classroom. His parents had to be on top of it continuously because they were not going to give up on their son. Harv and I have faith and believe Jake is going to succeed in life because of all the love and dedication his parents give him. We love that cool little guy.

Every day is an adventure living with Jake. His sister, Rachel, our fourth grandchild and second gorgeous granddaughter understands her big brother and doesn't mind his antics. Rachel has a kind heart and is the type of child who only wants to please. She is a conscientious student in school and makes the honor roll consistently. Her peers voted her senator of their class, which means they trust Rachel to represent them. When she participated in the school play, the musical version of *Little Women,* the director awarded Rachel the citizenship award. These kinds of things are important and tell you exactly what kind of a sweet child Rachel is. For many years she took dancing lessons and was good at it. She went with her company to perform at Disney World in Florida. It was a fabulous experience for her. Rachel's real passion is basketball. She loves it, plays well, and it is a joy to watch her play. Softball is her second passion. She is a comer at field hockey with the help of her mother's coaching. Not only is Rachel a good student, dancer, athlete; she is a great person and has given her family a lot to be proud of.

Do dreams come true? Yes, they do. Eight years have passed since my daughter Terri's divorce. She and her children are once again about to take a complete turn around. Quoting Terri, she found her "perfect soul mate!" His name is Jeff and he is a real nice guy. They lived in the same community and have known each other for a long time. It wasn't until they found each other alone together one night after a party that Cupid struck. They fell in love and after a brief courtship Jeff proposed and Terri accepted. Not only was Jeff going to marry Terri; he was going to have an instant family with my two sensational grandchildren Fredi and Jared. His life is also going to change dramatically.

It won't take long before Jeff falls in love with Fredi. She is very creative and loves arts and crafts. She is also conscientious and works hard at getting good marks in school. Fredi took dancing lessons, gymnastics, played softball, basketball, and was on the track team in school. All my grandchildren love animals; however, I think Fredi inherited my passion for animals. Most of all she loves her mother and looks after her like a mother goose.

Jared and Jeff will become real pals. Jared is a real boy, who loves sports and plays baseball, basketball, and soccer. He is a good kid with a gorgeous smile. He is also very adept at video games. Whenever Jared gets together with his Zayde Harvey they have a lot of fun wrestling with each other. Jared will always be the baby in the family.

The news of their up and coming nuptials spread through the community like wildfire. Everyone was genuinely happy for this perfect pair. Harv and I were ecstatic for Terri and the children. Jeff will be a wonderful role model for the children, and Terri's struggle will come to an end. She will have a partner to share her life. The only problem was Jeff is allergic to cats. Once again Terri asked us if we would take her cat, Tigger. The children loved their cat and were disappointed. They also knew Tigger was going to have a wonderful life with us, and they could come over to visit with him anytime. Of course we said yes, and Tigger joined our family of animals. The wedding took place outside in the garden at Tami and Rich's house. It was a perfect August evening. Fredi was the maid of honor and Jared was the best man.

They are a real family. They ski together, Jared and Jeff take drum lessons together, and Fredi takes guitar lessons. Jeff helps the children with their homework. The children are real campers and go to camp all summer long and love it. Terri has never been so happy. She also has become quite a business woman. It does our heart good to see how happy they all are. Time is a great healer and with hope your wishes will come true too.

I consider myself the luckiest person in the world. I have been truly blessed with an extraordinary family. My greatest accomplishment is my beautiful family. We are a close family, share the good, the bad, and we are always there for each other. I was also blessed with a devoted husband. He has kept me laughing for forty-seven years. I admire his principles, courage, and good sportsmanship. He is a great dad, a super grandfather, and my one and only hubby.

Harv always liked animals, but does not have the same passion for them that I have. He has put up with so much from me, and my animal antics. For example, cats walking on his head while he is asleep. He didn't like it, but cleaned up throw-ups and other kinds of accidents from our pets. Richie, our number one son-in-law developed allergies to cats, so Tami asked us to take her two cats, Sheckie and Seymour. Of course we took them. Harv never in his life dreamed of living with six cats and three large dogs at one time. Frankly, I didn't either. He put up with me bringing home litters of kittens or cats from the shelter to foster care until they were placed. They used to run all over the house and sometimes the odor from the litter box did not smell like perfume. When one of our pets was sick or had to be put down, Harv was always at my side for support. He understood those were difficult times for me emotionally. On so many occasions he patiently put up with me running out of the house at the spur of the moment on an animal emergency and the endless animal-related phone calls. Why does he put up with it—he loves me!

I was never, ever, as scared in my whole life as I was in September of 2004. My husband became very ill and thought I was going to lose him. After a series of tests, the doctors discovered a growth in his pancreas blocking a bile duct. The situation was very serious. The doctors were very somber about the diagnosis because there are an extremely high percentage of pancreas tumors that are malignant. Tami and Richie went into action and instantly got us an appointment with the chief of surgery at the Mass General Hospital in Boston. He does all kinds of surgery; however, his specialty is with pancreatic problems. Our children wanted their father to have the very best. I did too.

I don't know how they did it, but the day after we received the results of the tests, Tami, Richie, Harv and myself were sitting in the doctor's office. We were praying Harv was a candidate for a highly complicated operation known as the Whipple. It was the only procedure left to save my hubby. I was sitting there watching the doctor looking through his x-rays, ultrasounds and CAT scans that were taken prior to this visit. I was so frightened, you could hear my heart beating and my knees were shaking. All I wanted to hear the doctor say that Harv was a candidate for this complex operation. The wait was getting unbearable. My fingernails were already bitten down to my knuckles. Finally, while holding my breath, the doctor said he would take him on as a patient and perform the operation. A huge weight was taken off our shoulders. They were tense moments and I felt I was having a bad dream.

The doctor explained what the operation entailed. Part of his pancreas and stomach were going to be removed. They would remove his gallbladder and rearrange some of his organs, which is why the operation is called a Whipple. We wanted the operation done yesterday. The sooner it was done the better. The doctor arranged to perform the operation quickly because of the threat of cancer. We were all so grateful. As we were leaving his office, I told Harv and the kids, "We were just in God's office." It was the way I felt at that moment.

On the day of the operation I brought Harv to the hospital at seven o'clock in the morning. We stayed together until it was time for him to be wheeled out. It was a horrible moment. We kissed and I told him to think happy thoughts. We had so much to be thankful for. While they were wheeling him out on the gurney, I felt so empty and completely helpless. I did everything in power to hold back the tears.

Slowly I walked down to the gray waiting room, where relatives and friends would wait to hear the results of their loved ones' operations. I was the first person in the room and sat down and prayed for my husband, companion, best friend, buddy, lover, and my strength. One by one my daughters arrived. They were a great comfort to me. Periodically, a liaison came down to update us on how the operation was progressing. The doctor told us it would take between six to eight hours, so we knew it was going to be a long day. Toby went to the gift shop and bought a deck of cards. The four of us passed the time playing whist. One by one my sons-in-law started to arrive. I was surrounded by my wonderful children. Their support was awesome. The boys started to participate in the card game also. Six hours passed and no word. Seven hours passed and still no word. The doctor did say it would take six to eight hours. Eight hours passed, and we thought for sure we would hear from him soon. Nine hours passed, and I started to get anxious. Believe me I didn't want to think something was wrong, I knew in my heart something was not right. The kids were trying to calm me with all kinds of excuses. Ten hours passed and still no word. Big time worry was starting to take over my body. I couldn't stand it any longer and went up to the two women sitting at the desk and told them there was going to be another emergency in this hospital because I was going to have a heart attack, if I didn't find out what was happening with my husband. They contacted the operating room for me. Two minutes later the phone range. It was one of the operating room nurses. I was so emotional at that time. I couldn't grasp what she was saying, so I gave the phone to Tami. The nurse explained that some of Harv's blood vessels were going in the wrong direction and presented a small complication. She reassured us everything was all right, not to worry, and the operation would be over soon. We sat there and waited and ended up being the last people in the waiting room.

It was almost midnight when the doctor came down. He was tired and sat down. We surrounded him. He started saying there was good news and bad news. I held my breath. He started off with the good news. The growth was benign. That was big! That was grand, wonderful, and fabulous! Now Harv wouldn't have to have chemo-therapy. The doctor appeared to be surprised and happy it was benign because it is so rare in these cases. He told us there is only a one percent chance this happens. It was a miracle! We were all elated.

Now for the bad news; during the operation the main artery to his intestine was severed. The doctors tried and tried to mend it with no luck. A team of vascular surgeons were rushed in to correct the problem. Finally, to correct the problem the vascular surgeons created a gortex bridge to hold the artery together. The doctor assured us there was no reason why he couldn't live a normal life with that gortex bridge. That was the reason why the operation took so much longer than expected. My poor husband was under anesthesia for twelve hours.

When the doctor finished with his report, the kids and I bombarded him with a host of questions. He was tired, but patient and answered them all. He also allayed all our fears. My only thought was to see my husband. The doctor suggested I wait until the morning. I really wanted to see my husband. He promised to meet me at eight o'clock the next morning in his office and he would personally escort me into the recovery room to see Harv. Emotionally drained we all went home. I simply couldn't sleep knowing what my husband went through. I had to see him.

Early that morning Toby promptly picked me up, drove me to the hospital, and we were in the doctor's office at eight A.M. I couldn't wait to see my husband. The doctor was on time and escorted Toby and I through a maze of back doors to the recovery room. There he was fast asleep attached to all kinds of machines with a tube down his throat and unable to talk. His whole body was swollen from being under anesthesia for twelve hours during surgery. It was not a pleasant sight. He was alive and that was all that mattered to me. I grabbed his hand and kissed him. Toby and I started talking to him even though we knew he was out of it. We couldn't wait to tell him the miracles of miracles—the growth was benign! We kept talking to him and got no response. When it was time for us to leave, we told him we would be back in the afternoon and kissed him goodbye. As we were leaving, we heard all kinds of bells and whistles go off. We turned around and saw Harv trying to get up out of bed and disconnected all the machines he was attached to. All the nurses, Toby, and myself rushed back to him. He was moving his mouth trying to talk to us, but couldn't. It was a ghoulish scene out of a horror movie. The nurses calmed him down and reattached him to all those life-saving machines. Where did he get the strength after what he'd been through? Apparently, he heard everything we were saying and didn't want us to leave. To this day he does not recall the incident. Toby and I will never forget it.

My husband was in the hospital for a total of ten days. He was treated like royalty. Many of the nurses requested to have him for a patient. They used to say there was good karma in his room. His roommates thought they were sharing a room with a rock star. Harv always took care of me like I was one of his little girls. Now that he was coming home it was my turn to care for him.

It was going to be a six- to eight-month recovery period. After a Whipple procedure there were definite dietary guidelines to follow. He had to have six small meals a day. He was recovering nicely but slowly. Every day he was feeling a teeny bit stronger and making progress. Suddenly, he started getting these excruciating pain attacks. The pain was so bad, we had to rush him into the emergency room at Mass General Hospital by ambulance. He was given all kinds of tests, but the doctors couldn't find the cause. They sent him home after the pain subsided. Those attacks occurred several times and we rushed him to the hospital. My husband was suffering. At last they discovered the cause of his attacks—it was adhesions from his previous operation. My poor hubby had to be operated on again to get rid of the adhesions. It was a tremendous setback because he was already in a weakened condition. He lost sixty pounds and did not look like the man I married, but he was alive and getting stronger every day. We were thankful we were going to share many more years together. Our life together would continue to be an adventure.

Again the shelter played a huge part in my life during this trying time. I took a three-month leave of absence from the shelter to nurse my sick husband back to health. Liz, Jean and Jane covered for me in my absence. I will be forever grateful. They did a great job! Every night when I came home from the hospital, I worked on the computer to keep the shelter website updated and reply to the emails. Working on the website was an excellent diversion for me. It was a superb escape from my worries. It also relaxed me, and I was able to get a few hours of sleep. While home nursing my husband, keeping the website updated was good for me. It kept me in the loop. I missed being at the shelter with all the animals. When I did go back, it was like I never left.

There is no question in my mind a higher authority had a plan for me. Since I was born, I had an innate passion for animals. When I was young, I used to bring home the strays in our neighborhood. It used to drive my parents crazy. We always had pets in our home. My whole life I dreamed of going to Africa on a safari. My husband made that dream come true on our thirtieth anniversary. It was the ultimate experience for me. My husband and family made me a sensational fiftieth birthday party. Instead of bringing me gifts, they knew I would be so pleased if my guests donated to the World Wild Life Fund. My guests were very generous. My fiftieth birthday was before I started volunteering at the shelter; otherwise, the shelter would have been my first choice for donations.

On other occasions I went to great lengths to defend animals and improve the quality of life for them. For example, my town of Swampscott had very strict leash laws and dog owners had nowhere in town to exercise their dogs. I decided to help do something about it. I ran for town-meeting and got elected. We live in an area where there was a perfectly safe place for dog owners to exercise their dogs that wouldn't interfere with anything. Our beaches were desolate from October to May. Dogs were not allowed on the beaches at any time. I put an article in the town warrant to allow dogs on the beaches from October 1st to May 26. It would be brought up at town-meeting and voted on. I went before all the town-meeting members in the auditorium, stood behind the podium, and stated all the reasons why I believed dogs should be allowed to exercise on the beach between October and May. Well, it would be an understatement to say it was not well received. One by one town-meeting members got up and spoke against my article. This was a new experience for me, and I was baffled at the response I received. To me it was a fair and reasonable request. My article lost big time, and I went home disappointed crying.

Apparently, there were people who agreed with me and went before town-meeting with a similar article and received the same response. Year after year town-meeting vehemently turned down any article allowing dogs to exercise on the beach. You might think that would discourage me from going before that unreasonable crowd of town-meeting members. You don't know me because I am determined to get this article passed and not giving up. Anyway, what harm was going to come from owners with their dogs exercising on an empty beach? Yes, I am a glutton for punishment and went before town-meeting once again and gave them my spiel. There was some opposition. When it came down to the vote, it passed! The vote was close and barely passed, but it passed. This time I went home numb, shocked, and so very happy.

During the months of October to May, I take my dogs to the beach almost every day. I only wish you could see how wonderful the beach is for the dogs and their owners. The dogs frolic, run, swim, and play with each other. It is a joy to watch. A whole new culture has emerged since dogs were allowed on the beaches. The dog owners have gotten acquainted with each other and it's become a social meeting place. When I think of what it took to get here—it was worth it. The beach is a paradise for dogs. Nothing makes me happier than seeing the animals having so much fun.

On another occasion I organized the Pooper-Scooper Brigade. Many of the town residents were complaining about dog-owners not picking up after their dogs. You should pick up after your dog. That is a no-brainer. The Fourth of July Parade was coming up, so I contacted several of the resident dog owners to march in the parade. I got a great response. The Pooper Scooper Brigade marched with their dogs holding signs saying "PICK UP AFTER YOUR DOG," "OBEY THE POOPER-SCOOPER LAW." I remember it was the hottest day of the summer and the animal control truck followed us with water for the dogs. It was a lot of fun and the children on the parade route loved seeing all the different dogs.

A group of dog owners called on me to help them with an impending dog issue. It seemed an official somewhere inadvertently omitted one of the dog laws from the bylaw book. I knew about the omission for a long time because the animal control officer at the time told me. The law was about dogs being in the park. It meant, if you were in the park with your dog, you could be cited. Because the law was omitted you could bring your dog to the park anytime and couldn't be cited. It was that way for a couple of years. Most people had no idea the law was omitted and still went into the park with their dogs. So many families bring their family dogs to the park while watching their children participate in sports and as long as you pick up after your dog, why not?

The group of dog owners who contacted me got wind that the recreation committee was going to put an article in the warrant and reinstate the law, which would be voted on at town-meeting. I joined the group and went with them to the recreation committee meeting to discuss it. The article they were putting in the warrant was restrictive and unreasonable. After much discussion it was decided the dog owners could rewrite the article and bring it back to the committee for approval. That was exactly what we did. The new article was less restrictive and by far more reasonable, but within the law. The recreation committee approved it. Now it had to be voted on at town-meeting.

Town-meeting was approaching and the group of dog owners had to plan how we were going to handle town-meeting, and who was going to represent our group. Some were not town-meeting members, some were not going to be around that evening, and some were too frightened to speak. I couldn't blame them because when it comes to dog issues, the town-meeting members turn from Dr. Jekylls to Mr. Hydes without exaggeration! You guessed it, I was the only one left to represent the group. Believe me I didn't want to. I am not that courageous, but we started something I truly believed in and couldn't let my four-legged friends down.

The night the article came up I went up to the podium below the stage to speak. Inside I was so scared, but kept a stiff upper lip and a strong front on the outside. Well, what I expected happened, only worse. The room turned ugly and I mean ugly. The town meeting members were booing, hissing, and yelling at me. It was terrible. They wouldn't let me speak. Every time I tried to speak they would interrupt by booing, hissing, and yelling. These were adults carrying on. I told them how rude they were. Where was the moderator? Why wasn't he bringing order to the meeting? He was behind the podium on the stage doing absolutely nothing about the chaotic atmosphere in the auditorium. Finally, I turned, looked up, and asked him to bring the meeting to order. I had to ask him to bring the meeting to order! His lack of control of the meeting did not surprise me. This person had been the moderator in the town for at least a hundred years and should have know enough to bring order to a meeting that turned into mayhem. He finally got around to bringing the meeting to order. By that time I lost my train of thought and couldn't remember what I wanted to say. There were some members who felt terrible for me and came up to me to ask if I was okay. The whole experience was humiliating for those town-meeting members who behaved so vulgar.

What is town-meeting? Town-meeting is the purest and oldest form of democracy. Elected town-meeting members come together with their opinions, suggestions, and ideas. You politely listen to whomever is speaking and show respect. If you have an open mind, you just may learn something. If you do not agree with the speaker, you are free to vote anyway you choose.

When it was time to vote on my article, it was no surprise they voted against it. However, that meant because town-meeting voted against me it was going to revert back to the original law, which was inadvertently omitted in the town bylaws. This was exactly what the town-meeting members were against. By not giving me a chance to speak and explain the situation, they assumed there was an existing law in the books not allowing dogs in the park. Well, they assumed wrong and got what they deserved! There would be no law against dogs being in the park in Swampscott. I and the dogs got the last laugh! Town-meeting actions were uncalled for. Shame on them all! It was the last of my town-meeting days.

Swampscott has been my home for over forty-seven years. I am saddened to see the direction it has gone toward. Swampscott is a very dense community with too little green wooded areas left to enjoy tranquility and nature. To me these green wooded areas are God's natural gardens and it is a sin to destroy what's left. Environmentally trees play an important, intricate role in our lives. They are too precious to destroy and replace with concrete. We are also encroaching on the wild life habitant, which breaks my heart.

I and many others have fought hard against the establishment to preserve and conserve to keep the character of the town of Swampscott. We managed to save one side of town, but unfortunately, the demographics in town changed dramatically. Over the years the last of the green wooded areas have been destroyed, so the establishment can reinvent Swampscott. It is a pity our little town was not appreciated for its own unique beauty. With fewer career politicians, some fresh new thinking, wiser management, and intelligent planning, we could have had everything. We may have lost our fight to save the rest of the town from the bulldozer; however, the biggest loser is my poor little New England town of Swampscott.

Not only am I disappointed in the direction the town is going; I am also so very annoyed with the inhumane attitude the town has towards the animal community. For many years there was a part-time animal control officer to take care of hurt and abandoned animals. Some time later a full-time animal control officer was hired because there was a need. I was very pleased about that, and it lasted for several years.

Swampscott is a bedroom community comprised of mostly single homes, small businesses, and no industry, which means there is a limited amount of revenue coming into the town each year. Some of the town politicians thought it was a good idea to hire professional help to run the town. For example: a town manager. That was fine until gradually professional help was hired to almost every department in town at pretty substantial salaries. The town has so many more layers of government at high salaries including other out-of-control, outrageous spending that we could ill afford; the budget has to be cut. Guess who was first to be cut? Yes, you guessed right—the animal control officer.

When the animal community got wind of this, we got together and prepared a petition for the residents in town to sign. We received an enthusiastic response from the community. Hundreds of residents signed the petition because they truly felt it was humane to have an animal control officer. The petition was given to the selectmen to be presented at town meeting. Our efforts were for naught. We might as well have thrown those petitions in the garbage. Town-meeting didn't waste any time voting out the animal control officer. Since I was not a town-meeting member any longer, I am not even sure the petitions were even presented.

The town had to cover the law in Massachusetts to have some kind of animal control, so some nincompoop in town came up with a brilliant idea. The nincompoop's recommendation was to give a $10,000 stipend to a policeman to play animal control officer. So, they gave a $10,000 stipend to a full-time policeman, who had no previous experience in animal control. A policeman who cannot leave his job while on duty. If that is the case, who is going to be there when there is an emergency or when help is needed immediately? Will he take the time to network with different rescues and save animals' lives? When I heard about this maneuver, I was justifiably worried. My passions are with the animals and this maneuver was not in their best interests. You don't have to be a brain surgeon to know it is not a good situation. It is absolutely astonishing to me that just over the border from Swampscott to Marblehead what a remarkable difference in attitude about the humane treatment of animals. I will have to hope for the best because there isn't a damn thing I can do to change the situation.

When you live in a small town for as long as I have, everybody knows everybody. Most everyone in town knew my affiliation with the animal shelter. They also knew I was not afraid to voice my opinion on a number of issues in town. While home minding my own business, I started receiving calls from frantic residents about animal-related issues. They wanted me to help them. For example: many residents were under the impression Swampscott no longer had animal control. I set them straight and told them whom to call with their problems. The calls to me did not stop. Residents called animal control, left their messages, and waited for a call back that never came. Whatever the problems were, they were not getting resolved. I was not surprised about what was happening with animal control. I was furious because there were animals out there in distress and not getting help. My advice to my neighbors was to continually call the police until they got action. It was important my neighbors knew I was not an experienced animal control officer; I was an adoption coordinator at the shelter. The fact is I wished I could help, but it was out of my control.

One day, while I was out, I received at least three calls on my answering machine. It was so frustrating.

When I receive complaint calls about our ACO, I suggest to my friends that they do not complain to me. Call and complain to our five selectmen or the town manager. Those are the so called people in charge. The problem is most people are afraid to complain and voice their opinions, especially against a policeman. They don't want to make waves because of fear of repercussions. If that is the case, the residents in town get what they deserve—incompetence! The animals deserve better. Would you believe I am still getting calls? The older I get the smarter I get. Ever since that horrible experience I had at town-meeting, I was not going to be duped into being the only outspoken voice. When the time was right, I would voice my opinion.

It was just a matter of time when I personally was going to have to deal with the policeman/animal control. The time had arrived and I had no choice but to call him. I called animal control. As a matter of fact, I called a number of times before I received a response. I explained to him how a poor lost elderly dog came to my door. This dog was in my care for over a week hoping to find her owner. The dog's owner also called animal control that week several times looking for her dog. Animal control made no connection. It was only by chance the owner of the dog was found without the help of animal control. I was very upset at how little effort was put into reuniting the dog with her owner. I have lived in this town long enough not to waste my breath complaining to our town fathers. There had to be another way to get my lack of animal control story out and at the same time make the animal community cognizant of what is going on. What if someone else's dog gets lost and won't be as lucky to find it? Something had to be done. Instead of using my mouth, I would use my pen and write a letter to the editor and submit it in all the local papers. Here is my letter to the editor, which will tell the whole story:

SWAMPSCOTT LACKS ANIMAL CONTROL
Guest Commentary
Linda Greenberg

During the bad thunder and lightning storm on Saturday June 28, a woman was at my door ringing the bell.

She was in a great hurry, but very concerned. She had picked up a small terrier dog in the middle of Puritan Road. It was in her car. She came to me because she knew I was affiliated with the Marblehead Animal Shelter.

She did not know what to do with the dog and asked me to take it. I followed her down to the car to look at the dog. I recognized the breed right away. It was a Pedigree Cairn terrier. It looked just like Toto in the movie *The Wizard of Oz.*

I did not want anything bad to happen to the dog, so I took it into my home and immediately called the police. I reported I had the dog and described her. I was told they would call animal control to contact me. I waited and waited, but no call. The owners of the dog must be frantic. I know how I would feel.

My good friend, who is animal control officer in Hamilton, told me to call the police again when the shift changed, and I did. The lieutenant on duty was very nice and assured me she would contact animal control.

Not long afterwards animal control called. I told him my story. He told me he had no place to put the dog. I told him I would be happy to foster the dog until the owner is found. If nobody claims the dog in 10 days, I will be happy to try to adopt it out of my shelter with his permission.

I did not hear from animal control and could not understand why nobody claimed this darling dog. Five days had passed and still no word. I called animal control and left a message and heard nothing.

It was July 4th and exactly one week had passed and still no word about the dog.

My alert neighbor, knowing the story about the dog, called the house to tell us that the police log in the weekly paper logged two reports of missing dogs in the area where the terrier was found.

I immediately called the police to find out who filed the reports. They told me they would contact animal control. Animal control did contact me.

I told him about the missing dog reports in the newspaper. He claimed he was never told about missing animals. I asked him to look back in the police log for the names of the people. I wanted this pet to get back to its rightful owner. They must have been out of their minds. He said he would call back.

Three hours passed, and I was getting impatient. I went to the police station myself to get those telephone numbers.

I told Officer Caruso my story and it took him two minutes to look up the numbers. He made a call and lo and behold we found the owner on the first try. Arrangements were to pick the dog up at my home. I could not thank Officer Caruso enough. He was so helpful and nice.

Shortly after I arrived home from the police station, the owner arrived. The reunion was wonderful for her and the dog. She was out of her mind looking for the dog. She called the police and reported it, but nobody ever contacted her. She almost lost hope of getting her beloved dog back.

The owner had moved here from another state and did not license the dog, which was a big mistake. I suggested she do so immediately in case she got away again. With a license an animal can be identified immediately. The owner appreciated what we did for the dog and off they went. My husband and I were happy too.

I have spent a good part of my life helping animals, and my life has been enriched because of it. I volunteer at the Marblehead Animal Shelter, which is located in the animal control office.

Marblehead has a full-time animal control officer and two assistants. I see first hand what animal control entails. I have taken all kinds of calls for the Marblehead office, ranging from removing a mouse in a resident's bureau draw to capturing a rabid animal.

Swampscott no longer has a full-time animal control officer. We have a policeman doing part-time animal control. It is virtually impossible for a part-time animal control person to focus on numerous animal-related issues in any community and do a proper job.

The current system in Swampscott failed that little helpless dog and me. Luckily my alert neighbor made the discovery. To say the least, there was a total lack of communication between the police and animal control or animal control and the police. I do not know which.

I called about the missing dog on June 27 and the owner called about the dog on the 28th. A whole week went by without a word.

Our community has lost a very important service of an experienced full-time animal control officer. It is vital to have a trained, qualified person with compassion who knows animals, how to handle them, and how to be available in case of an emergency.

If I did not foster the dog, it would go to the pound in Lynn for 10 days. Two things may have happened. The dog might be brought to another rescue or shelter to be placed for adoption. I really do not want to talk about the other option.

This dog was 12 years old, did not see or hear well. What do you think was going to happen to the dog?

I am writing this letter not only to be critical of the way things were handled, but with hope improvements will be made in the system.

I want to prevent this happening to others. It was sheer luck this little dog was reunited with her family.

How many other animals were not so lucky?

Whenever we get calls for missing animals in the animal control shelter/office, we have these special sheets to post the description of the missing animal, and owner information.

I intend to bring a sheet into the police station to copy, so the police and animal control can cross reference. This is not the end-all answer to recovering missing animals, but it will help and be useful, if implemented.

When a call comes into the station for a missing animal, the sheet will be right there for the dispatcher to take all the information, and ready for animal control to be vigilant.

I wanted to make the animal community in Swampscott aware of my experience in case their precious pet accidentally wanders off. Animals are a very important part of people's lives for a number of reasons.

The impact of losing one's pet can be emotionally devastating. Our pets are devoted members of our family and our best friends. We adore

our pets and want quality protection for them as well.
Linda Greenberg is a resident of Swampscott.

Please don't think I was under the delusion things were going to improve because of my letter. On three different occasions three different neighbors called for my help about stray animals. I advised them to call animal control. Animal control never responded back to two of my neighbors. Animal control did respond to the other neighbor, and from what she told me the situation was handled poorly. Would you believe I still receive calls for help from the residents in town?

If I sound angry, you are absolutely right. The winter of 2005 was a hard one. There was lots of snow, high drifts, and it was bitter cold. Not only was it hard on humans; it was especially hard on animals. Animals become disorientated, lose their scents and can't find their way back home, and could develop hypothermia because of all the snow and severe cold weather. That winter our shelter was filled to the brim with strays, lost, and abandoned animals. Many of those animals were rescued from Swampscott. So many Swampscott residents called our shelter seeking our help. They were frantically pleading for our help because they weren't getting it in their own town. How can we not help an animal in distress and suffering? I am very proud of our organization for many reasons. The biggest and most important reason is we do the right thing because it is right! Our poor little shelter rescued those animals, kept them alive, absorbed their medical bills, and placed them in forever homes. I hope Swampscott is proud of their nincompoop ideas. Shame, Shame, on them!

Animals have been my whole life. When my girlfriends were playing dress-up with dolls, I played dress-up with my dogs and cats. Growing up I loved going to the zoo to see the exotic animals close up. I believe there hasn't been a documentary about nature that I have missed. It is so fascinating for me to see how all the different animals from all over the world evolved and adapted to their individual environments. I have read and watched amazing animal stories. When I volunteered at the zoo, my experience was incredibly educational. My own domestic animals have shown me devotion, loyalty, endless affection, friendship, gentleness, kindness, protection, and most of all unconditional love. Now you can understand why it breaks my heart when animal issues are placed on the back burner. More often than not animal issues are ignored, put in the bottom of the pile, or thrown in the garbage. I have the utmost respect for animals. They can't speak, but I can. I am currently sixty-six years young and hope I continue to have the strength and health to advocate for animals in an intelligent, reasonable fashion for many more years to come.

My family is my greatest accomplishment. My second greatest accomplishment is my volunteer work at the shelter. For approximately sixteen years the shelter has been my second family. I was destined to help animals and the shelter has fulfilled my needs and my dreams. Just knowing I have helped save hundreds upon hundreds of animals gives me a great sense of achievement. How many people wake up every day loving what they do? I also take pride in knowing I have made a difference. There is always more work to be done because in this business it never stops. It couldn't be done without the help of my dedicated colleagues.

There are those who say to me, "It is a shame you didn't get paid for all the years you have devoted to the shelter." Those people have absolutely no understanding how important my work is and what it means to me. Those same people cannot comprehend that there are other ways of getting paid besides monetarily. I get paid when I see an excited child pick out his first pet. I get paid when a lonely senior citizen brings home a new friend and companion. I get paid when a woman with a huge heart comes into the shelter to adopt a pair of cats she saw on the website. Those particular cats were found in a dumpster and were abused. One of the cats was blind and the other crippled. How much is that worth? I get paid every time one of our animals leaves the shelter with its new, loving forever family. I get paid when our service men and women have to surrender their pets to the shelter because they had nobody else to care for them during their duty to fight for our country in Iraq. It was a privilege to help these brave young people. I get paid when two senior cats age fourteen and sixteen were placed with a woman who couldn't bear to see them spend the rest of their days in a shelter. I get paid whenever I encounter one of my adopters and he goes on and on about how much he loves the pet I placed with him. I am like the godmother to all the pets I've placed. I get paid with the warm notes, cards, pictures, letters, and emails I receive. I get paid working side by side with the most wonderful people in the world. Finally, I get paid for the gift the shelter gave me in helping me out with my personal situation. There aren't enough adjectives to describe how handsomely I have been paid. The beauty about this kind of payment is it will never be spent—I can savor it the rest of my life. I consider myself very rich!

The Marblehead Animal Shelter is a very unique special place. Miracles happen in that modest little structure. I take great comfort in the knowledge that every animal that passes through our wonderful shelter will be safe from any harm. My very own original expression describing the shelter is: "**WE ARE A SMALL SHELTER, BUT WE DO BIG THINGS!**" I have expressed it many times throughout the book and truer words have never been spoken.

I consider myself a very fortunate person. It took me some time to complete this book because I am one busy lady. I was determined to finish it, and worked on it every spare minute I had. I methodically wrote every word on a legal pad and after each completed chapter I typed it in the computer. It was an act of love. If this book is ever published, many animal lovers from all over will read it. My hope, my desire, and my dream are that after reading this book, animal lovers will be inspired to become pioneers like the volunteers at our shelter. That they get together with their animal control, and organize a no-kill animal shelter like the Marblehead Animal Shelter. You start by rescuing just one animal, caring for it, and eventually placing it in a good home. Only then will you get the thrill of it all and stop a lot of needless suffering. You will be doing God's precious work, and you will be blessed.

LOUIE

We have a new addition to our family. He is a French bull dog we named Louie. When he was only four months old my three wonderful daughters and their families surprised my husband and me with this little, adorable, intelligent package.

We never had a small dog before, but this guy thinks he is a big fellow. He runs and plays on the beach with all the dogs, big and small. Everyone knows Louie. This personality plus pup sleeps with us, and we have already spoiled him.

Louie can never replace our other dogs, but we have started a new relationship with this irresistible little guy. All you have to do is look at that face. What a comfort and joy he is. Louie has captured our hearts.

Louie and Louie's mom are on the back cover of the book.

LaVergne, TN USA
13 February 2011
216359LV00002B/29/P